Newsworkers Unite

*To Arnold—
with my thanks
Catherine
Sept. 29, 2002*

CRITICAL MEDIA STUDIES
INSTITUTIONS, POLITICS, AND CULTURE

Series Editor
Andrew Calabrese, University of Colorado

Advisory Board

Patricia Aufderheide, American University
Jean-Claude Burgelman, Free University of Brussels
Simone Chambers, University of Colorado
Nicholas Garnham, University of Westminster
Hanno Hardt, University of Iowa
Gay Hawkins, The University of New South Wales
Maria Heller, Eötvös Loránd University
Robert Horwitz, University of California at San Diego
Douglas Kellner, University of California at Los Angeles
Gary Marx, Massachusetts Institute of Technology
Toby Miller, New York University
Vincent Mosco, Carleton University
Janice Peck, University of Colorado
Manjunath Pendakur, Southern Illinois University
Arvind Rajagopal, New York University
Kevin Robins, Goldsmiths College
Saskia Sassen, University of Chicago
Colin Sparks, University of Westminster
Slavko Splichal, University of Ljubljana
Thomas Streeter, University of Vermont
Liesbet van Zoonen, University of Amsterdam
Janet Wasko, University of Oregon

Recent Titles in the Series

Deregulating Telecommunications: U.S. and Canadian Telecommunications, 1840–1997,
    Kevin G. Wilson
Floating Lives: The Media and Asian Diasporas,
    edited by Stuart Cunningham and John Sinclair
Continental Order? Integrating North America for Cybercapitalism,
    edited by Vincent Mosco and Dan Schiller
Social Theories of the Press: Constituents of Communication Research, 1840s to 1920s, second edition,
    Hanno Hardt
Privacy and the Information Age,
    Serge Gutwirth
Global Media Governance: A Beginner's Guide,
    Seán O. Siochrú and Bruce Girard
The Global and the National: Media and Communications in Post-Communist Russia,
    Terhi Rantanen
Newsworkers Unite: Labor, Convergence, and North American Newspapers,
    Catherine McKercher

Forthcoming in the Series

Principles of Publicity and Press Freedom,
    Slavko Splichal
Critical Communication Theory,
    Sue Curry Jansen
Internet Governance in Transition,
    Daniel J. Paré
Digital Disability: The Social Construction of Disability in New Media,
    Gerard Goggin and Christopher Newell
Herbert Schiller,
    Richard Maxwell
The Party System and Public Service Broadcasting in Italy,
    Cinzia Padovani
Elusive Autonomy: Brazilian Communications Policy in an Age of Globalization and Technical Change,
    Sergio Euclides de Souza
Recovering a Public Vision for Public Television,
    Glenda R. Balas
Contesting Media Power: Alternative Media in a Networked World,
    edited by Nick Couldry and James Curran

Newsworkers Unite

Labor, Convergence, and North American Newspapers

Catherine McKercher

ROWMAN & LITTLEFIELD PUBLISHERS, INC.
Lanham • Boulder • New York • Oxford

ROWMAN & LITTLEFIELD PUBLISHERS, INC.

Published in the United States of America
by Rowman & Littlefield Publishers, Inc.
An Imprint of the Rowman & Littlefield Publishing Group
4720 Boston Way, Lanham, Maryland 20706
www.rowmanlittlefield.com

12 Hid's Copse Road, Cumnor Hill, Oxford OX2 9JJ, England

Copyright © 2002 by Rowman & Littlefield Publishers, Inc.

All rights reserved. No part of this publication may be reproduced, stored in a retrieval system, or transmitted in any form or by any means, electronic mechanical, photocopying, recording, or otherwise, without the prior permission of the publisher.

British Library Cataloguing in Publication Information Available

Library of Congress Cataloging-in-Publication Data

McKercher, Catherine, 1952–
    Newsworkers unite : labor, convergence, and North American newspapers / Catherine McKercher.
    p. cm. — (Critical media studies)
Includes bibliographical references and index.
    ISBN 0-7425-1596-6 (alk. paper) — ISBN 0-7425-1597-4 (pbk. : alk. paper)
    1. Journalists—Labor unions—United States. 2. Journalists—Labor unions—Canada. 3. American newspapers—Ownership. 4. Canadian newspapers—Ownership. I. Title. II. Series.
PN4827 .M35 2002
331.88′110713—dc21   2002017895

Printed in the United States of America

∞ ™ The paper used in this publication meets the minimum requirements of American National Standard for Information Sciences—Permanence of Paper for Printed Library Materials, ANSI/NISO Z39.48-1992.

Contents

Preface and Acknowledgments vii

1 Convergence Considered 1

2 Convergence and Corporate Control 17

3 Convergence, Technology, and Labor 37

4 Mergers and More Mergers 57

5 A Partner for the Guild 85

6 Answering the Canadian Question 107

7 Convergence on Command 147

8 Convergence and Beyond 185

Bibliography 201

Index 215

About the Author 223

Preface and Acknowledgments

My first job in journalism came in 1970, when I spent a summer as a copy girl at the *Ottawa Journal*, a conservative-leaning daily founded in 1885. This newspaper was one of two English-language broadsheets in Ottawa, both of them housed in aging downtown office buildings near Parliament Hill. As a copy girl, I fetched, carried, and delivered things to every part of the newspaper plant, and got an in-depth education in how newspapers were made. I began to think of the *Journal* as "the daily miracle." Given how many people, how much heavy machinery, how many bits of paper, and how much hot lead it took to put together a newspaper, the fact the presses began running at precisely the same moment each day struck me as magical. When the rival *Ottawa Citizen* moved to the suburbs a few years later—and invested in video display terminals and cold type instead of typewriters and hot lead—some of my *Journal* colleagues predicted smugly that this would be the end of the *Citizen*. How wrong they were. The *Journal* was the paper that shut down, in 1980, the victim in part of bad management and labor strife, but also of a newspaper economy favoring local monopolies.

My career as a full-time journalist, which stretched from the early 1970s to the late 1980s, coincided with an era of unprecedented change in the newspaper business, a time of corporate concentration and technological upheaval that affected every part of the newspaper. Both the pace and extent of the changes were stunning—all the more so given that the presses continued to roll out the papers, day after day and almost always on time, while newsworkers scrambled to adapt to new computer systems, and their unions struggled to cope with what the changes would mean to their members. I worked in unionized and nonunionized newsrooms over those years, and was, at various times, a member of The Newspaper Guild and the International Typographical Union. I preferred, on the whole, to work in a unionized newsroom. Certainly the wages were better, and so were the working conditions. Indeed, for a brief time in the 1970s I was secretary of my Guild local, a post I saw as a way of helping make my workplace better.

When I took a teaching job in the late 1980s, my early research focused on how technology affected news, and the workers who made the news. I knew that the lives of unionized workers, including some of my friends, had been turned upside down by technological change, and I wanted to explore what this meant. I soon realized that while lots of people were studying the linked phenomena of technological convergence and corporate convergence, labor's role was largely unexplored. The event that set me on the path toward this book, though, was a 1995 Guild–Communication Workers of America conference I attended in Washington, D.C., where the idea of labor convergence took center stage.

This book would not have been possible without the help of a number of people. These include Bill Buxton, Mary Vipond, and Enn Raudsepp of Montreal's Concordia University, who kindly and generously helped me help myself over six years of work on my Ph.D. Several people at Carleton University have earned my thanks for their support. They include Barbara Freeman, Chris Dornan, Dan Pottier, Roger Bird, Carman Cumming, Lois Sweet, Mary McGuire, Janice Neil, Peter Johansen, and Klaus Pohle. Pat Bell, now at the University of Regina, offered helpful suggestions on Guild contacts. I'd like to thank Allan Maslove, who provided some much-appreciated research funds from his budget as dean, and Bob Rupert, who read the entire manuscript and offered many helpful comments. I owe special thanks to Vincent Mosco; I feel blessed to have him as my partner and my colleague. I'd also like to thank my father, Doug McKercher, my daughters, Rosemary and Madeline Mosco, my family and friends for their patience through my long years of study and writing.

But the largest group of people I'd like to thank includes the staff, members, and leaders of the unions under study here. They were consistently kind, generous, open, and enthusiastic about this research, and some of them offered eagle-eyed editing of various drafts. It is to the good people at the unions that I dedicate this work. Any errors in this text are of course my own responsibility, but I hope the readers of this volume find it a useful exploration of the evolution of media unions in the computer age.

1

Convergence Considered

This is a study of a labor convergence that is still very much a work in progress. It looks at how and why the main North American trade union for journalists, The Newspaper Guild, wound up as part of the Communications Workers of America (CWA), the major player in what its leaders call the TIME businesses—telecommunications, information, media, and entertainment. It also tells the story of how some breakaway Canadian segments of the Guild wound up in the Communications, Energy and Paperworkers Union of Canada (CEP), an all-Canadian union whose profile is strikingly similar to the CWA's. Both unions started out as telecommunications workers' unions—indeed, the "communications" component of CEP was at one time the Canadian branch of CWA—but through a series of mergers have incorporated broadcast technicians and newspaper printers, in addition to reporters, editors and other white-collar newsworkers.

For The Newspaper Guild, convergence was a critical idea driving the decision to merge with CWA in the mid-1990s. The union felt that in an age of corporate convergence and technological convergence—a time when its members were increasingly working for the same bosses, and using the same tools—labor convergence made sense. It was seen not just as a way of protecting what the Guild had, but also as offering new opportunities for organizing beyond the traditional confines of the daily newspaper. In Canada convergence was also a factor, though for some Guild locals nationalism was even more critical. Those locals that joined CEP saw it as a union that would offer the same kind of protection and promise as the CWA, but in a distinctly (and comfortably) Canadian context.

Regardless of whether they chose CWA or CEP, though, the members of The Newspaper Guild knew they would be breaking new ground as they transformed their union from what Guild historian Daniel Leab called "a union of individuals" (1970) to a sector of a much larger union representing a much wider range of communications workers.

But if labor convergence is new territory for media workers' unions, it is a variation on a theme that has captured the attention of scholars, media corporations, and consumers in recent years. Dennis and Pavlik (1993, 2) define convergence as the integration of or interface between and among different media systems and organizations, made possible by the development of new technologies. These technologies affect not only the production of information, but its distribution, display, and storage (Pavlik 1996, 2). The key innovation that allows for convergence is the computer, which converts messages into patterns of electric pulses based on the digits 1 and 0 (or "on" and "off"). With digitization, a host of previously separate communication forms—newspapers, television, radio, video, still photography, and telecommunications—now share a common digital language. Previously, a photograph and a paragraph of text were distinctly different ways of communicating information. It took different sets of skills to create them; different types of machinery to make them; different skills, techniques, and technologies to edit, reproduce, or distribute them; and different skills on the part of the audience to "read" or understand them. Rendered digitally, however, a photograph is no different from a paragraph of text. Both are composed in the "language" of ones and zeros. Both can be edited using the same tool—the computer terminal and mouse—and stored in the same format, on computer disk or compact disk. With the additional convergence of telecommunications and computers, digital images and text (along with voice and video) can be transmitted across town, to the other end of the country, or around the world.

Much of the writing about convergence, in the popular and trade press and in some scholarly works as well, focuses on gadgetry, on the new and amazing things people do with digital technology, or on reveries about what we might think of, paraphrasing Leo Marx (1964), as the digital sublime. Convergence, we are told, fuels the engines of the new economy. Convergence, we are told, promises instant information for all. Convergence, we are told, will even obliterate time and space. (See, for example, Patten 1985, Negroponte 1995, Fulton 2000.)[1] According to Mosco,

> Supporters of this view typically maintain that we are going through a period that rivals in significance the development of agriculture, which, about ten thou-

sand years ago, took us out of a nomadic hunting and gathering way of life, and the development of industry, which, starting three hundred years ago, made manufacturing products more central than farming for modern economic and social life. This view maintains that today computer communication is bringing about an Information Revolution which links people and places around the world in instantaneous communication and makes the production of information and entertainment a central economic and political force. (1996, 1)

The gadgetry of convergence is, indeed, excitingly new and endlessly engaging. But understanding convergence means going beyond the gadgets. New technologies simply offer "new platforms on which old groups confront one another" (Marvin 1988, 5). In the North American newspaper business, the main employer of the unionized labor under study here, convergence is linked to the social, cultural, political, and economic factors that weave the fabric of capitalist social relations. In other words, it is not just the computer that lets people dial up a World Wide Web version of the *Washington Post*, it is the social relations that underlie the technology, including the corporate structure and regulatory climate in which *Washingtonpost.com* operates. In the North American context, therefore, convergence is best understood as part of the strategy of capitalist accumulation, in which owners and managers use computers as new means for achieving old ends: acquiring profits; deepening and extending control over the relations of production, reproduction, and consumption; and deskilling workers.

In recent years, the convergence of technologies has proceeded hand in hand with the convergence of the corporations that promote, own, develop, disseminate, buy, sell, and above all seek to profit from technological innovations. Dennis and Pavlik write that in the 1980s media companies acted as though "convergence was an idea whose time had ... come" (1993, 3). Companies like Capital Cities or Disney or Time Warner began to buy up newspapers, magazines, radio stations, TV networks, book publishing firms—any form of the communication business they could acquire. They also relied increasingly on market research to develop their plans and more effectively sell their products to consumers and advertisers.[2] Concentration of media ownership in the 1980s was by no means a new thing in the United States, Canada, or elsewhere. What was new, however, was the intensity, depth, and pace of this concentration. This became even stronger in the 1990s, a time when Wall Street firms and communications corporations alike seemed to share the mantra of "grow or die." Companies chose growth, and the result was a series of mergers of unprecedented size and scope. In the United States, CBS and Viacom agreed to a $50 billion merger in 1999, which Viacom described as the largest media transaction ever.³ A few months later, America Online Inc. raised that claim by a factor of three, announcing plans to acquire Time Warner Inc. for roughly $182 billion in stock and debt (Johnson 2000). In Canada, Bell Canada Enterprises bought the CTV network in 2000 and wrapped it into Bell Globemedia, along with *The Globe and Mail* national daily newspaper and the Sympatico Internet portal. Shortly thereafter CanWest Global Communications, a private television network, emerged as Canada's largest media conglomerate, buying up many of the Canadian properties of the Hollinger newspaper empire, including daily newspapers in most of the country's major cities and the *National Post* daily newspaper.⁴

Converged corporations are not simply large companies with a set of similar properties, like old-fashioned newspaper chains or traditional broadcasting networks. The holdings of the new media conglomerates cross the lines between media forms (newspapers, television stations) and media products (news, advertising, and entertainment). This raises the prospect of integrating previously distinct media forms not just horizontally or vertically but diagonally as well, and on the Internet. At this point, the precise parameters of the new converged media are still unclear. Some of the results of convergence have been remarkably banal, like cross-promotion of the products of various divisions. Other experiments have been much more inventive. The Canadian Broadcasting Corporation's Web site includes not just audio and video but text versions of stories, as well as links to the broadcaster's enormous archive of previously broadcast material. So far, though, most online news sites have been remarkably weak at signing up paid subscribers (Ledbetter 2000, 26).

Nonetheless, convergence is apparent in the newsrooms of newspapers and television stations across the continent. An estimated 93 percent of U.S. print publications had Web sites in 1999 (McNamara 2000, 25). Many contained what is known as "shovelware"—material already published in print form and dumped onto the Web site—but others contained original content or featured constant updates. In some areas, convergence has altered longstanding relations in the newsroom. In Tampa, Florida, for example, WFLA-TV, the *Tampa Tribune* newspaper and the TBO.com Web site have begun sharing space and news resources, including a joint "superdesk" that coordinates crews, provides news research, and tracks developments. Reporters are, increasingly, interchangeable among all three (Tompkins and Colón 2000). According to a report posted on the Poynter Institute's Web site, dozens of other newspapers and TV stations across the United States have teamed up on projects "resulting in cross-promotion, close co-operation and even—can this be?—mutual admiration of each other's journalism" (Mitchell 2000). The Chicago-based Tribune company, which owns newspapers, television stations, and a range of Internet properties, has emerged as a leading proponent of multimedia work: "In most Tribune newsrooms and in its Washington bureau, reporters and editors from print, television and the Internet sit at special multimedia desks to share their stories" (Hickey 2000, 19).

In Canada, where concentration of media ownership is more extreme than in the United States, the two major private television networks recently claimed victory in a fight with the federal broadcast regulator over the idea of convergence between broadcast and print newsrooms. In renewing the seven-year broadcasting licenses for CTV Inc. and Global Television (part of the CanWest Global conglomerate), the Canadian Radio-television and Telecommunications Commission (CRTC) called for separate management structures in the newsrooms of the newspaper and broadcast holdings of the two companies. The requirement for separation does not, however, extend down to the level of working journalists (Fulford 2001); in other words, a company would be able to share reporters, information, and research among its broadcast and print newsrooms as long as the newsrooms had separate managements. The idea of combining forces in the newsroom has raised concerns about diversity of coverage, even among some CRTC commissioners.[5] Additional concerns about the impact of convergence on content rose in late 2001 when CanWest Global announced it would begin producing national editorials for its Southam newspapers. The newspapers were required to run the editorials, and the ideas in them in effect became the editorial position of the individual newspapers. The policy drew protests from journalists, especially at the company's *Montreal Gazette*, where a number of reporters removed their names from stories in a two-day protest (*Guild Reporter*, 7 March 2002).

Part of the appeal of the converged or cross-media newsroom arrangements being tried in the United States and Canada is that they allow media companies to "reach more people and therefore charge more for advertising without raising news-gathering costs" (Cole 2000). Hickey offers a similar explanation: "Multimedia means not only getting your news out around the clock through a variety of avenues, but offering advertisers a richer menu of choices for how to spend their money with a single company" (2000, 19).

Babe (1996) writes that understanding convergence requires an understanding of how a diverged media structure emerged in the first place. Traditionally, he notes, the information industry has been seen as embracing three sectors: publishing, broadcasting, and telecommunications. Though they have been considered distinct for decades, these sectors were initially conjoined, and their segregation came about through conscious acts by corporate players and the state. The daily press and the telegraph emerged at the same time in Canada, he notes, and from the 1850s until 1910, when three newspapers complained to a government regulator about telegraph rates, the main news correspondents in the country were telegraph operators (285). Similarly, broadcasting and telephony were separated as a result of an agreement made in 1926 to settle a patent dispute. "Not only were facilities thereafter segregated and deployed for distinct services, in 1932, a unique legal/policy/regulatory framework for broadcasting was created as well" (289). In recent years, however, deregulation has opened the doors to reconvergence among cable television, telephony, and broadcasting. Indeed, Babe argues that convergence, or reconvergence, is by and large a code word for the deregulation of capital flows in media industries, part of a trend toward "the aggrandizement of transnational corporate power and the concomitant lessening of national sovereignty, the weakening of labor, and the comparative diminution in the relative strength of domestic-only businesses" (301). In other words, convergence is mainly a function of transnational capital.

UNION DIVERGENCE

In some ways, the convergence of labor unions examined in this work also represents a reconvergence. Many of the printing trade unions got their start in the original North American printers' union, then broke away as their crafts became specialized and as newspaper production took on the characteristics of small-batch manufacturing (Kalleburg et al. 1987).

Printers, identified by Hobsbawm (1964) as among the aristocracy of labor,[6] founded craft-based organizations in London and New York in 1795 and in the Canadian city of York (now Toronto) in 1832 (Zerker 1982, 3–6). During the 1830s and 1840s—the time when the American factory system was taking root (Baker 1957, 49) and a new "penny press" was bringing newspapers to a large and previously neglected public of working-class readers (Emery and Emery 1978; Schudson 1978; D. Schiller 1981)—printers' locals began to organize in many major U.S.

cities. In 1850 they set up the first successful trade federation on a national scale in the United States, the National Typographical Union (Zerker 1982, 66). Following the addition of Canadian locals, the organization renamed itself the International Typographical Union (ITU) in 1869 (76).

In part, the early success of printers' unions had to do with literacy. Printers were able to read and write at a time when most people could do neither, and they were exposed to the world of ideas through their work. The craft of printing traditionally embraced all phases of putting type to paper. Printers composed type by hand; fed, inked, and operated the presses; and understood the craft of bindery (Baker 1957, 59). But in the first half of the nineteenth century, the fast-growing craft of printing began to become specialized. Book work became distinct from newspaper work, and newspaper work itself was broken down into a series of tasks requiring specialized skills and tools. This trend accelerated with the rise of the commercial newspaper, funded by advertising, produced on an industrial scale using innovations in printing and press technology, and distributed to a mass market (Rutherford 1982; D. Schiller 1981).

Various groups of printers began to chafe under the National (later International) Typographical Union almost from the moment of its founding. An early problem, Baker writes, was that the union was very decentralized, which meant that each local could more or less make its own laws. The result was "a maze of conflicting regulations" that bred discord (54). Some of the first locals included pressmen as well as typesetters; others did not. Indeed, in some cities and towns, pressmen who wanted to join the union "found themselves no more welcome than women" (61).[7] By the 1880s, the union had begun moving toward a more centralized structure, which brought more order to the craft. A second problem was mechanization, which began in different parts of the print shop at different times. Pressmen were among the first to operate power machines, in the 1830s, while typesetters of that time "would have made Gutenberg feel at home"; within the craft, though, "the typesetters ruled" (55). As Baker explains,

> The fact that the typesetters possessed the parent craft which had stood unchallenged for centuries and that they had a knowledge of words and some under standing of sentence structure and subject matter were conditions that quite naturally placed them in a position of power over the more recently arrived pressmen. (59)

The pressmen, however, viewed their own occupation as "quite as important as that of setting type" (60).

In terms of numbers and influence, one particular group of typesetters, those working for newspapers, dominated the union. This irritated compositors and pressmen who worked in the book trade, or as job printers. In 1853, New York book and job printers demanded their own charter, separate from New York Union No. 6, the local that would eventually become the biggest and most influential in the ITU. They were rebuffed by the parent union (Baker 1957, 60–61). Internal divisions in the union came to a head in the 1890s. A group of New York pressmen who refused to join Local No. 6 sent out an international call for a meeting of pressmen in 1889. Delegates from thirteen groups attended, and agreed to create their own union, the International Printing Pressmen's Union (75). The new union claimed continent-wide jurisdiction and began to work on a formula to allow other pressmen's units to secede from the ITU. The pressmen's secession was the first of several. In 1892, the bookbinders left the ITU to establish their own international union, in a move that was seen as an attempt to assert their own identity. By the mid-1890s, the ITU had agreed to allow other craft workers to separate and form their own unions (Brasch 1991, 46). The stereotypers and electrotypers, whose job was to produce plates for the printing press, did so in 1902, and the photoengravers, who began their withdrawal from the ITU in 1900, finalized it in 1904 (Baker 1957, 81). Brasch notes that there were significant jurisdictional battles, especially between the ITU and the pressmen's union. The creation of the Allied Printing Trades Association in 1911 was intended in part to resolve interunion problems.

The divergence of the printing trades into separate unions was the result of two interrelated factors. One was the increasing specialization of the craft of printing, brought about by the explosion of publishing and the growth of printing plants that looked more like factories than small businesses. The specialization created separate categories of printing workers within the ITU. The second factor was the ITU's inability to make these new crafts feel adequately represented in a union dominated by one element, the newspaper compositor. The creation of specialized crafts fed dissension within the union, and eventually prompted the exodus of several groups from the ITU.

Though this exodus caused strains, the parent union flourished in the final years of the nineteenth century. Much of this had to do with its success in adapting to—and claiming jurisdiction over—the linotype machine. Barnett (1926) sees the introduction of the linotype as a case where a thoughtful union managed to stay on top of its trade, and where technology created employment rather than displacing it. Unlike pressroom work, where mechanization resulted in a steady series of changes over fifty years, the transition from hand-set type to machine-set type occurred with stunning speed. Barnett estimates that less than 100 linotypes were in operation in North America in 1888 (9). A mere sixteen years later the number had grown to 7,500 (4). Because the machines could set type four to five times faster than a compositor working by hand, Barnett calculated that linotypes could have potentially displaced up to 36,000 workers (5). That didn't happen. One reason was technical: the machines, at first, didn't operate as quickly or as smoothly as their manufacturers predicted, and could not, as some newspaper managers hoped, be run by lower-paid women and children.[8] Other reasons were economic: linotypes and other mechanical innovations allowed for bigger newspapers that were sold to broader audiences, eventually requiring more printers. But one of the strongest reasons was the ITU's farsightedness in embracing the machines rather than fighting them. In 1888 the union adopted a resolution at its annual meeting, urging locals to recognize the linotype machines and work to "secure their operation by union men upon a scale of wages which shall secure compensation equal to that paid hand compositors" (quoted in Barnett 1926, 9). Some locals bought or rented machines so their members could practice (15). In 1891, the union recommended a change in payment for members, to a weekly scale rather than on a piece basis. It also recommended that the locals negotiate a shorter work day of eight hours. Both were seen as ways of protecting the wages and jobs of a maximum number of printers.

Barnett writes, "Of direct opposition to the introduction of the machine, there was practically none. Occasionally a small union refused for a time to make a scale for machines, but the international union steadily discountenanced such a policy" (17). Kealey (1986) concludes that printers entered the twentieth century with much of their power intact. They combined craft customs with vigorous trade unionism to assert control over their work. At the same time they gained jurisdiction over the new machines by "cleverly acceding to a process of reskilling" (93). Once the linotype was in place, the job of composing type was further subdivided into machine operators, machine tenders, operator-machinists, straight-matter compositors, ad compositors, proofreaders and makeup specialists, and so on. Sleigh notes that while the power of the ITU and other craft unions created obstacles for newspaper publishers, there were benefits for employers too: "The union-controlled apprentice system, which in some trades lasted up to seven years, ensured a high level of technical competence while placing the union in a position to supply labor" (1998, 79).

Until close to the turn of the twentieth century, unionization in the

North American newspaper business was limited to the blue-collar crafts. The ITU began organizing editorial workers in the 1890s, mainly to prevent reporters from working as scabs during printers' strikes (Jacobson 1960, 6).[9] Between 1891 and 1918, the union chartered thirty-eight journalists' locals. Most were short-lived; indeed, only three were still in operation at the end of the First World War (8). Another round of organizing began in 1919, but only one of the fifteen ITU editorial locals formed between then and 1923 survived. In 1923, the ITU voted to suspend organizing of journalists, surrendering jurisdiction over them to the American Federation of Labor.

Journalists formed their own national union in the United States in 1933. Leab (1970) traces the beginnings of the Guild to the Depression-era U.S. National Recovery Administration (NRA), which required industries to write codes that would enable them to promote widespread reemployment when the economy improved, and which guaranteed employees the right to organize. Newspaper publishers wanted to have journalists declared professionals, as they would then be exempt from some aspects of federal labor legislation (39). When New York columnist Heywood Broun scoffed at that idea and suggested in a 1933 column that reporters should form a union, he sparked an enormous response (Leab 1970, 45). By December of that year, a national organization had been launched as the American Newspaper Guild.

In its early days, the Guild saw itself largely as a professional body for reporters, not as a trade union. Over the next few years, however, it realized that neither the NRA nor a professional model of organization would improve working conditions for members. In 1935, it adopted a resolution to reconstitute itself as an industrial union in the newspaper industry, though it held off for a year on extending its jurisdiction to noneditorial workers in the business, clerical, circulation, and promotion departments. The most difficult question for early Guild members was whether to affiliate with the craft-based American Federation of Labor. It did so in 1936, then left the AFL for the Council of Industrial Organizations in 1937, joining as a full industrial union. Leab notes that within just three years, the organization transformed itself from a loose association of local groups of newsworkers into a centralized union with a "rudimentary but broad collective bargaining program" and a membership in organized labor (281). It became an international union in the 1940s, organizing Canadian workers in Toronto first, then in other parts of the country.

By the 1960s—the start of the period under study here—the unionization of North American newspaper workers was, in a word, piecemeal.

Almost every department of a newspaper had the potential to be represented by a different union: white-collar workers had the Guild, compositors had the ITU, and separate unions were available to represent photoengravers, stereotypers, pressmen, and distribution workers known as mailers. Other unions whose main membership was not in printing and publishing nonetheless represented some newspaper workers—truck drivers, for example, or machinists or electricians. And since under both Canadian and U.S. labor law each bargaining unit had to be organized and certified one by one, the number of unions operating at any individual newspaper ranged from none to seven or more. Inevitably, there were tensions between and among the various unions over things like jurisdiction, respecting each other's picket lines, organizing the unorganized, and so on. Nonetheless, the labor unions and the production process they engaged in at newspapers across North America were remarkably stable during much of the twentieth century, until the advent of the computer.

The divergence of the unions had been accompanied by a detailed and rigorous division of their turf or areas of jurisdiction. But the industry in which they worked, meanwhile, was heading in the opposite direction, toward consolidation. By the early 1960s, some in the ITU had concluded that the union made an enormous mistake when it allowed various groups to hive off into other unions. ITU President Elmer Brown, one of the leading proponents of a reconvergence of the printing trades unions, warned in 1960 that the growing power of the corporations threatened the very existence of the unions. He told the Guild's convention, "we are down to the alternative of amalgamation or annihilation" (*Guild Reporter*, 15 July 1960, 3).

DESKILLING AND CONVERGENCE

If corporate consolidation prompted the unions to think about reconvergence, it was not enough on its own to effect serious change in 1960. In fact, the unions were about to encounter a new phenomenon, computerization, that would change their world. The effect of a series of digital innovations was to hollow out the production process of newspapers, collapsing previously separate stages and eliminating previously separate crafts. To use Braverman's term, the craft workers were about to be deskilled.

Braverman's 1974 analysis of the capitalist system of manufacturing sees increasingly sophisticated machinery and administrative techniques as ways for capital to assert control over labor (45–58). The conception of a task becomes the job of management; the workers are left with the execution. In addition, management breaks up the execution stage into a number of component parts or motions, each requiring a minimum level of skill. Management asserts that the work must be done in a particular way, regardless of how the workers might see it. And once management has identified the individual component parts or motions to carrying out a task, it uses machinery to automate them. As a result worker skills fall, both in an absolute sense, through the loss of traditional craft skills, and in a relative sense, in terms of understanding how to control increasingly complex and sophisticated machinery. Citing Marx, Braverman describes machinery as embodying "dead labor," or the skills and knowledge of the workers who did the task before automation: "The ideal toward which capitalism strives is the domination of dead labor over living labor" (227).

Braverman's deskilling thesis has prompted a wide range of commentary, criticism, debate, and scholarly research on the nature of work under capitalism. (For a summary of the strands of this debate, see McLoughlin and Clark 1994.) Braverman sees deskilling as moving relentlessly and steadily in a single direction, from skilled work requiring a unity of head and hand to deskilled work in which the intellective component is stripped away and the physical component is routinized and, eventually, mechanized. Critics of the thesis question how it can account for instances where new technology leads to a reskilling, or even an upskilling, of work. Paul Thompson resolves the problem by contending that deskilling should be seen as the major *"tendential* force" (1989, 118; emphasis in the original). At the same time, he notes there are sources of variation and constraint on management's drive to deskill.

As the deskilling effects of computer technology began to be felt in North American newspapers, the fight to preserve skill became a key contest—not just between labor and management but sometimes between the unions themselves, in fights over jurisdiction. Though all the unions were affected, the pace of deskilling in newspapers has been uneven. Some unions, like the stereotypers and compositors, were hit early and hard. Others, like the pressmen, escaped relatively unscathed until the 1990s. Still others, like The Newspaper Guild, found that while some members—photo technicians, for example—were deskilled, others were reskilled and perhaps even upskilled. For example, Russial, studying how copy editors coped with computerized layout systems known in the industry as "pagination," found *both* a reskilling and a degradation or deprofessionalization of copy editing work (1989, 259–60). By contrast, Patten (1985) predicted the rise of the "technojournalist," skilled in information retrieval, analysis, and management as well as interviewing and writing.

Clearly, two broad tendencies in twentieth-century capitalism—the drive to control the labor process by using mechanical or bureaucratic tools that tend to deskill workers, and the drive toward convergence as a strategy for control and accumulation—have affected newspaper workers and their unions. Clearly, too, neither tendency operates in simple or absolute terms. Workers may respond with strategies of resistance or accommodation, or both; technology may result in an increase of skills for some workers at the same time that it decreases skills for others; corporate enterprises may compete with each other with deadly intensity even as they grow and prosper. But seen as tendential forces, deskilling and convergence offer ways of understanding the transformation of the workplace.

But how do these ideas connect in the digital age? Zuboff (1988) has attempted to wrestle with the question of what distinguishes computers and information-processing technology from other technological innovations. She concludes that automated technology essentially translates human agency into mechanical action. Information technology goes one step further: it not only automates but "informates." In other words, it not only translates information into action, but registers data about those actions, generating new streams of information. This provides "a deeper level of transparency to activities that had been either partially or completely opaque" (9). Zuboff argues that while blue-collar jobs have been gutted by mechanization, information technology has enriched white-collar work. Elements of management work that are most easily subjected to rationalization can be "carved out [of management], pushed downward, and used to create wholly new lower-level jobs" (98). This does not mean higher-level positions are eliminated. "On the contrary, they [come] to be seen more than ever as the depository of the organization's skills" (98). Zuboff offers a cozy vision of an "informated" workplace:

> a group of people gathered around a central core that is the electronic text. Individuals take up their relationship toward that text according to their responsibilities and information needs. In such a scenario, work is, in large measure, the creation of meaning, and the methods of work involve the application of intellective skills to data. (394)

Others see a less comforting picture. Menzies (1996) contends that the development of the microchip brought computer intelligence to every conceivable line of industrial and bureaucratic activity, setting the stage for a restructuring that has hollowed out clerical, administrative, and middle-management work, and integrated production work into almost cybernetic modules (30). In almost every sector, work is transformed into an extension of management's information system. This helps bring about a new form of Taylorism, extending management control and creating "a universal technologic with a monopoly on workplace knowledge and operating procedures" (112). Her vision of the informated workplace has workers being pushed toward the fringes and finally out the door, their skills consumed by the fires of Zuboff's cozy electronic hearth. Writing in a similar vein, Aronowitz and DiFazio (1994) argue that the application of information technology to work has moved the deskilling trend up the occupational ladder. Deskilling is not just a feature of manual labor but of scientific and technical labor as well. For an ever smaller number of people in virtually all occupations, the installation of computers in the workplace has created new opportunities for satisfying and well-paid work. But for the immense majority, it has meant subordination, displacement, or irrelevance. Aronowitz and DiFazio conclude, "What could not be accomplished by Taylorism was finally achieved by computerization" (27).

In the newspaper business, as in others, new technology encourages deskilling by offering managers the promise of greater control of the labor process. Starting in the 1970s, technical change, once seen as episodic (and occasionally spasmodic), became routinized and unrelenting. The composing room, for decades the hub of production, has withered away. Converged technologies have blurred the lines between stages of the production processes, undermining craft (and union) culture along the way. At the same time, the newspaper business itself is becoming less distinctive: the employers are national or multinational corporations, not publishers whose roots are sunk deep in the local community.

For the unions representing newspaper workers, the challenge in the last quarter of the twentieth century was how to help their members cope with the twin forces of deskilling and convergence at the same time as the unions themselves risked being overwhelmed by them. The answer was fairly clear: they had to unite. Bringing about that unity turned out to be an enormously complex and difficult task, however, and one that is still not completed. It required overcoming years of craft-based pride and interunion rivalry. It also required careful strategizing as to how not merely to endure the forces of change, but to survive and thrive.

NOTES

1. Fulton's article is typical of this rhetoric. She writes that the Internet is fueling "a Cambrian explosion of innovation," creating "new species" that add on functions to existing communication forms, substitute functions of other forms, and completely transform still other forms (30).

2. For example, Dow Jones, publisher of the *Wall Street Journal* and owner of a business wire service, began repackaging its material to sell to television or on databases (Dennis and Pavlik 1993, 3).

3. Viacom press release, 7 September 1999, at www.viacom.com (accessed 29 October 1999).

4. CanWest originally purchased a half-share in the *Post*. It acquired full ownership of the daily in 2001.

5. Andrée Wylie, the CRTC's vice-chair of broadcasting, asked during hearings on the license renewal, "Will there not be a tendency to standardize output, and therefore reduce the variety of information?" (quoted in Scoffield 2001, A8).

6. Hobsbawm uses the phrase to describe a distinctive upper stratum of the working class: better paid, better treated, and generally regarded as more "respectable" and politically moderate than the mass of the proletariat (1964, 272).

7. Burr (1993) notes that the National Typographical Union decided in 1854 that it would not encourage the employment of women as compositors. In the late 1860s it decided to permit women printers to create their own locals, but only if the male local in the area agreed. A few years later it stopped granting charters to women's locals, instead allowing women printers to join the men's locals. The International Printing Pressmen Assistants' Union, which split from the ITU, was also unwelcoming to women, Burr found (62). The union made a strong link between craft and social role: men were seen as destined to become breadwinners, women were not.

8. Burr argues that one of the reasons the ITU moved so quickly to establish jurisdiction over linotype machines was to prevent publishers from displacing male hand compositors with female typists at the machine's keyboard (1993, 55–56).

9. According to Leab, newspapers at the time still employed as editorial writers men who could set type, if necessary. But while "reporter scabbing" was the most important reason for ITU interest in news writers, two other factors were at play. First, the ITU believed that by organizing reporters it could get better coverage. Second, some in the union saw news writers as simply another group to be organized (Leab 1970, 12–13).

2

Convergence and Corporate Control

North American newspapers trumpet their claim to a local community right on the front page. The typical nameplate gives not just the title of the publication but emphasizes place as well—the *Ottawa Citizen*, the *Chicago Tribune*, the *Toronto Star*, the *Los Angeles Times*. Even the leading U.S. business daily, which bills itself as "the daily diary of the American dream," bears a name that appeals to place: Wall Street, in the heart of the New York financial district.

Unlike in Britain, where the press is divided into national and regional dailies, the pattern in English-speaking North America is one of local newspapers, tied to a particular city or town. Only two genuinely national newspapers operate in the United States and Canada: *USA Today*, founded in 1982 by the Gannett Co., and the *National Post*, launched in 1998 by Hollinger International Inc. Others, chief among them the *New York Times* and *The Globe and Mail*, publish national editions and have national or international circulation lists.[1] But these editions are extensions of the New York or Toronto papers, not freestanding dailies.

The local nature of the North American newspaper is the product of its history. As Rutherford notes, newspapers were founded by local entrepreneurs who "seized the main chance, sometimes aided by political overseers or inspired by foreign examples" (1982, 36). The U.S. press moved to a commercial model and to a daily publication cycle in the middle of the nineteenth century (Emery and Emery 1978); Canadian newspapers followed several decades later (Rutherford 1982; Sotiron 1997; de Bonville 1988).[2] In both countries, daily newspapers flourished

17

in cities and towns, attracting advertisers and readers alike. But the notion that the North American newspaper is a local newspaper has an ideological component as well. This is grounded in the idea that newspapers are every bit as integral to the social, political, and economic life of a community as the local town hall or the fire department. Journalism, produced and circulated locally, is seen as providing a service to local citizens, and newspaper writers, editors, and publishers are servants of that community.

In the last half of the twentieth century, the traditional view of the North American newspaper as a local enterprise became less and less useful as a means of understanding the business. Indeed, the pattern of concentration of ownership among the North American media has transformed the daily newspaper from a publication rooted in its own community into a product of conglomerates with stakes in a variety of media forms. Instead of being ruled by local markets, newspapers are increasingly subject to the disciplines of national and global markets. This escalating level of concentration is one of the key reasons why the unions that represent newspaper workers have had to think about how to come together into new configurations of their own. In the end, they too chose to cut across traditional media lines, to configure themselves more or less in line with the changing nature of their employers.

LINKS IN THE CHAIN

While the history of the press in North America has generally been told as the story of independent, local enterprises, concentration of ownership has been a factor for a long time—at least since the middle of the nineteenth century. Many of the early newspaper chains were family enterprises.[3] Others were part of empires being built by ambitious publishers who wanted to play a role in national affairs.[4] But for much of the nineteenth and twentieth centuries, newspapers were for the most part owned by individual, local publishers. In 1933, the year the American Newspaper Guild was founded, there were 1,911 daily newspapers and 506 Sunday newspapers in the United States. Some 63 national and regional chains owned and operated 361 dailies, mainly in the larger centers of population. Together, the chains controlled about 37 percent of national daily circulation and about 46 percent of Sunday circulation. The six biggest chains—Hearst, Patterson-McCormick, Scripps-Howard, Paul Block, Ridder, and Gannett—accounted for 26 percent of daily and 35 percent of Sunday circulation (Jacobson 1960, 26). At around the same time in Canada, there were 116 daily newspapers, controlled by 99 publishers (Kesterton 1967, 76).

By the early 1960s, chain ownership was a significant feature of the newspaper landscape in both countries. But while some critics, inside government and out, expressed alarm about the growing power of newspaper publishers,[5] the ownership issue attracted relatively little attention from policymakers in North America until the appointment in Canada of the Special Senate Committee on Mass Communication, known as the Davey committee, in 1969.[6]

Scholars and analysts have offered a number of explanations for the lack of critical analysis of the ownership issue. Bagdikian points to the strong business orientation of the daily press, identifying a "peculiar American belief (ironically created more by the media than by any other source) that to criticize big business is to attack American democracy" (1997, 54). This applies equally to public self-criticism by publishers. He also notes that prior to the 1960s, individual newspapers and newspaper chains were privately owned. This meant that their owners did not have to disclose their considerable earnings, a fact they used to their advantage: "For decades American newspaper publishers cultivated the impression that they presided over an impoverished institution maintained only through sacrificial devotion to the First Amendment. The image helped reduce demands from advertisers for lower rates and agitation by media employees for higher wages" (Bagdikian 1997, 11).

Successive waves of newspaper mergers or closings seemed to support the publishers' stance. After peaking in 1909 in the United States (Adams and McKercher 1991, 320) and in 1913 in Canada (Kesterton 1967, 64), the number of daily newspapers declined steadily. Bagdikian writes that while they were closing newspapers, publishers "cried poverty and the First Amendment to fend off antitrust indictments, child labor and wages-and-hours laws, unions, workers' appeals for higher wages, advertisers' complaints of high rates and politicians' accusations of monopoly bias. Each newspaper failure was reported as proof of the imminent collapse of the industry" (73). At the same time, the owners of the newspaper chains tended to justify their existence by portraying them as mutual-aid societies.

> The argument in favor of chain ownership, advanced most energetically by chain owners, rested on a delicate principle called "cross-subsidization." In theory, all member papers benefited from a strong, centralized head office that gave them access to the human and financial resources of the chain and independence from the influence of powerful local advertisers. If one paper was losing money, it could be supported by profits from the others. (Hayes 1992, 134–35)

The idea of newspaper chains as protectors of freedom is common. In his history of the Southam chain from the 1870s to the 1960s, for example, Bruce (1968) describes the company as fending off advertiser influence and helping member papers weather tough times.

Finally, it must be noted that independent and chain publishers, particularly in the United States but also in Canada, responded aggressively—and often on constitutional grounds—to criticism or suggestions they change their ways. When the Hutchins Commission's report reflected public distaste for powerful media owners, Henry Luce, the publisher who founded (and funded) the commission, derided its findings for an "appalling lack of even high school logic" (Hamilton and Krimsky 1996, 134).

The Davey committee began its examination of media ownership from a frankly stated point of view: "The purpose of this committee was not to ascertain whether concentration of media ownership is a Good Thing or a Bad Thing. *Of course* it is a bad thing . . ." (Davey committee 1970, 4; emphasis in the original). Nonetheless, it saw a certain amount of consolidation as a natural, if regrettable, process: "The big trouble with . . . the notion that media diversity equals a higher polity, is that it happens to be in flat defiance of economics. More voices may be healthier, but fewer voices are cheaper" (3). In the real world, the task is to strike a balance. Even though its members might not like concentration of ownership, the challenge facing the committee was to figure out the point at which it becomes more harmful than the alternatives, such as government control or further expansion of the chains.

The Davey committee's count of newspaper ownership in 1968 found that newspaper groups owned 77 of 116 Canadian dailies, or 66.4 percent (16), and controlled 76.9 percent of total daily circulation (21). It also found that while some newspapers were struggling, on the whole the industry was highly profitable. Overall after-tax profits between 1958 and 1968 averaged between 12.3 and 17.5 percent, well above the 10.4 percent profit of manufacturing industries and the 9.2 percent earned by retailing industries (46). Newspaper companies were not plowing those profits back into their publications, however; "They weren't spending much of it on new buildings and new equipment. . . . What they *were* doing was investing in other companies" (47; emphasis in the original). Often, this meant buying up each other's assets. "The logical (but wholly improbable) outcome of this process," the report found, "is that one man or one corporation could own every media outlet in the country except the CBC" (6). Some corporations were making genuine efforts to deliver quality newspapers and broadcast programming, "But the general pattern, we regret to say, is of newspapers and broadcasting stations that are pulling the maximum out of their communities, and giving back the minimum in return. That is what, in contemporary parlance, is called a rip-off" (63).

Faced with figuring out what to do about the problem, the committee came up with a modest set of policy recommendations and a wish list for media owners. The most significant recommendation was the establishment of a press ownership review board to screen all future newspaper takeovers. The board would not have the power to act retroactively; rather, it would ensure that concentration of ownership did not progress further. This recommendation was ignored by government. As a result, "members of the committee had the dubious satisfaction in subsequent years of seeing their forecast of increasing newspaper concentration become a reality" (Desbarats 1996, 65).

FROM CHAIN TO CONGLOMERATE

Over the next decade, concentration of ownership intensified. This was most dramatic in Canada, in part as a side effect of 1965 legislation to protect the Canadian magazine industry from foreign (mainly American) competition. The law prohibited Canadian advertisers from taking tax deductions for ads placed in foreign-owned print media. This doubled the cost of advertising in foreign magazines, keeping money in the Canadian market. In effect, it also prevented foreign ownership of Canadian media, including newspapers.[7] By the time the Royal Commission on Newspapers, known as the Kent commission, reported on the ownership problem in 1981, the share of English-language circulation controlled by newspaper chains had risen to 74.3 percent (Royal Commission 1981, 2). More shockingly, the share of French-language circulation controlled by chains had almost doubled, from 49.2 percent in 1970 to 90 percent by 1980 (3). The commission also found that eight daily newspapers, which together accounted for 15 percent of total circulation in 1970, had disappeared (1). At the same time, ownership was concentrated in fewer and fewer hands. FP Publications, the largest chain at the time of the Davey study, was gone, absorbed by Thomson. Some other, smaller, family-owned chains had also disappeared. Meanwhile, the Thomson company had grown to forty dailies, up from thirty a decade earlier (90), and Southam owned fourteen dailies, up from eleven (92).

The newspaper corporations had not merely added links in their daisy chains of newspapers, however. The commission's report found that they were turning themselves into diversified corporations. It described Thomson newspapers as part of a much larger group of corporations controlled by the Thomson family. Together, they formed "a multi-national mixed conglomerate engaged in many other kinds of business, including wholesaling and retailing, real estate, oil and gas, insurance, travel and tourism, financial and management services, high technology communications, trucking, and so on, many of which have no direct relationship with newspaper publishing" (90–91). As for Southam, the report summed up the company's goal during the 1970s as diversification (93). It quoted Southam's 1976 annual report, which described the company's business as "'communications'—both mass communications and products aimed at small, select segments of the mass market" (93). Southam had expanded steadily into non-newspaper holdings, "from Coles Book Stores Ltd. to Videosurgery Ltd" (93). Sterling Newspapers, controlled by newcomer Conrad Black, was the third-largest Canadian chain in 1980 in numbers of newspapers (eleven dailies and seven weeklies), though not in circulation. Sterling itself was "a minor holding" in an "impressive conglomerate" (94): it was a division of Western Dominion Investments Co. Ltd., controlled by Warspite Securities Ltd., the main holding company of the Black group.[8]

One thing that had *not* changed between 1970 and 1980 was the fact that newspapers earned substantial profits. The Royal Commission used a different index for measuring earnings than the Davey committee: returns on net assets rather than after-tax profit on equity (84). It found that newspaper returns were 37 percent in 1975 and 25 percent in 1978. By comparison, returns in the food industry were 7 percent in 1975 and 10 percent in 1978; returns in retail trade were 25 and 21 percent respectively; and in wholesale trade they were 6 and 5 percent (84).

Like the Davey committee, the Royal Commission proposed a relatively modest set of solutions to the problem of ownership concentration. The key recommendation was legislation that would prohibit significant further concentration of ownership of newspapers (and across other media), and correct "the very worst cases of concentration that now exist" (237) by requiring some corporations to sell some of their holdings. Like the Davey recommendations, these went nowhere. The federal government again took no action on the issue.

Although the Royal Commission studied the result of concentration of ownership, its economic analysis of newspapers focused on the internal operations of the dailies themselves, rather than on the corporations that owned them. It described the daily newspaper business in Canada as a series of local monopolies. In markets with more than one local newspaper, the pattern was oligopolistic, with different newspapers aiming at different market segments (87). This approach fit with the ideological conception of the press as local businesses, subject to the demands and opportunities of the local market. It did not, however, tell the whole story. While the pressures and revenue possibilities in a newspaper's circulation area were indeed crucial to its survival, it is clear that something else had been going on in the 1960s and 1970s—something that promoted not simply consolidation of ownership but diversification into other media (and sometimes, nonmedia) products.

A number of authors (including Bogart 1991; Bagdikian 1983, 1987, 1990, 1992, 1997; and Squires 1993) argue that this crucial development was Wall Street's discovery of newspaper stocks.[9] In Bagdikian's words, investors were let in on "the best-kept secret in American newspapering," the impressively high profits newspapers earned (1997, 11). They did not have to work very hard to uncover this secret: Al Neuharth, then president of Gannett, proclaimed it loudly. Squires writes that when Neuharth took Gannett stock public in 1967, "he presented the newspaper business in general and Gannett in particular to Wall Street in a way it had never been presented to anyone before: he billed it as 'a dependable profit machine in good times or bad'" (1993, 21). More than anyone else, Squires contends, Neuharth shattered the illusion of newspapers as poverty-stricken enterprises kept alive only through devotion to the principle of free speech.

The approach worked. When Gannett offered its stock for public sale, it had twenty-eight newspapers and $250 million in annual revenue. By 1986, when Neuharth stepped down, Gannett owned ninety-three dailies, forty weeklies, fifteen radio and eight television stations, 40,000 billboards, the Lou Harris Public Opinion Poll, television productions, a half-interest in McNeil-Lehrer Productions for television and cable, and satellite operations in thirty-six states. It also earned more than $2 billion in annual revenues (Bagdikian 1997, 73). A company profile posted on Gannett's Web site indicates that by 2000, Gannett's operating revenues were $6.2 billion, and that this "large diversified news and information company" owned ninety-eight U.S. daily newspapers in 2001, up from seventy-four in 1999, and a variety of nondaily publications, including *USA Weekend*, a weekly magazine with a circulation of 21.8 million.[10] With its acquisition of Newsquest in 1999, Gannett had become a major regional newspaper publisher in the United Kingdom, with nearly 300 titles, including 15 daily newspapers. In broadcasting, Gannett owned twenty-two television stations covering 17.5 percent of the United States. Other ventures included a news service; retail advertising, telemarketing, and direct marketing companies; a commercial printing operation; and a media technology firm. It claimed more than 100 Web sites in the United States and United Kingdom, including USATODAY.com.

Gannett has also had what Bagdikian calls a "spectacular record of ever-increasing quarterly earnings" (1997, 73). For eighteen straight years, from 1967 to 1985, each quarterly profit was higher than the one before. "Even to hard-boiled investors, the profit margin on some Gannett papers was astonishing—30 to 50 percent a year" (74). At the 1999 annual meeting, company president Douglas McCorkindale reported that the company had achieved record revenues, record net income, and record earnings per share in 1998. He added: "Since Gannett became a public company in 1967 we've reported record earnings in thirty of those thirty-two years"; a year later, the company reported that 2000 was "the ninth consecutive year of record revenues, profits and cash flow."[11] The economic downtown that began that year ate into 2001 revenues, especially at the company's U.S. newspapers, where advertising spending dropped "disproportionately," according to McCorkindale. Nonetheless,

> stringent cost controls and the hard work and dedication of Gannett employees continued to enable the company to achieve one of the best year-over-year earnings performances in the industry. Our Newsquest properties, benefiting from strong advertising demand particularly in employment classified, made solid contributions to cash flow and earnings per share.[12]

Operating cash flow from newspapers grew 10 percent in the second quarter and revenues rose 17 percent over the same period last year.

Unlike privately owned newspapers, publicly traded companies must disclose information about their earnings. The measure of their success lies largely in the price a share of their stock fetches on Wall Street or Bay Street. In general, the steeper the increase in profits, the higher the share price. This means, however, that despite the local label, publicly owned newspapers operate well beyond the context (or the confines) of a local market. In a genuinely local market, the business of running a newspaper involves selling ads to local advertisers and delivering news to local citizens, and earning a profit for the local owner. Newspapers owned by publicly traded companies, by contrast, are subjected to the disciplines of national and international stock markets, where success demands ever-increasing growth. In these companies, profits extracted from one group or sector may be used to expand profits in another group or sector, across the country or halfway around the world.

In terms of company structure, the trend among media companies in the 1980s and 1990s was toward larger and larger enterprises, and toward enterprises that operate across a number of previously distinct media forms. The story of Conrad Black's Hollinger Canadian newspaper experience exemplifies this trend. In 1999, Hollinger owned or controlled 60 of Canada's 105 daily newspapers,[13] bringing the country close to what the Davey committee saw as the "wholly improbable" outcome of the pattern of ownership concentration it studied in the late 1960s: the possibility that "one man or one corporation could own every media outlet in the country except the CBC" (Davey committee 1970, 6).

Hollinger's earnings rose from $12 million in 1996 to $72.6 million in 1997 and $95.8 million in 1998.[14] The company was not strictly Canadian: through subsidiaries and affiliates, it owned or controlled newspapers in the United States, Britain, and Israel as well as Canada. And although Hollinger produced a large number of newspapers (in 1999, its 296 daily and weekly newspapers had a total daily paid circulation of 4.1 million),[15] the company had been moving into areas that had little to do with the traditional definition of the newspaper. Hollinger chairman Conrad Black's annual letter to shareholders in 1998 described some "promising ventures" by Hollinger Digital, owned by Southam, which Hollinger controlled.[16] The first was American Interactive Media, which rents or sells boxes that adapt television sets to simultaneous broadcast reception and Internet use. The letter noted,

> This fits conveniently into this Company's view of convergence between all telecast and Internet-transmitted images on the same screen, at which point newspaper companies such as ours will be able to initiate their own programming without the expense or regulatory problems of license purchases or applications. The newspapers and associated Internet programming could then cross-promote.

Other digital products Black highlighted in the letter included Trip.com, an electronic travel service, and Canada.com, a search engine and gateway Internet site with a broad array of informational and commercial content.

A year later, Black noted the company's "increasing presence in the transactional Internet business." Canada.com, he reported, was one of the leading sites in Canada. A British gateway Internet site, UKMax, "in the process of a gradual soft launch, shows much promise."[17] Company news releases posted on the Hollinger Web site offer glimpses of a wide range of non-newspaper activities that occupied the company in 1999. These included an agreement with the Bank of Montreal to introduce the Canada.com Mastercard; the launch a few days later of a new and improved Canada.com Web site; an investment in Coventus Inc., an electronic service for business travelers; a joint venture with Boots pharmacies to create a new Internet site, handbag.com, aimed at British women; an agreement with two newspaper publishers in the Chicago area to collaborate on a regional classified advertising Web site powered by InfiNet, the joint new-media venture of Gannett, Knight-Ridder, and Landmark Communications; an investment in StockHouse Media Corp., an Internet financial media group with offices in the United States, Canada, Australia, and Hong Kong; and an alliance between Hollinger's *Chicago Sun-Times* and ApexMail to provide subscribers with free e-mail service.[18]

The chairman's statements and the announcements posted on the Hollinger Web site paint a portrait of a newspaper company that is far removed from the traditional conception of newspaper publishing in North America. Hollinger's reach extended not only beyond the local markets of its newspapers but beyond national borders as well. And rather than acting as an old-fashioned mutual-aid society—where profits from one paper may go toward helping out another experiencing hard times (Hayes 1992, 134–35)—Hollinger used profits from individual properties to either feed expansion or boost its share price. Black identified the price per share in his 1999 statement to shareholders as "the one area that has been a substantial and largely inexplicable disappointment."[19]

Hollinger was, however, primarily a newspaper company; the Canadian dailies it owned were its core business—that is, until the summer of 2000, when Hollinger announced the sale of $3.5 billion of its assets to CanWest Global Communications Corp.[20] The transaction, which created a conglomerate of unprecedented scope in Canada, included 13 major metropolitan newspapers, 126 nondaily community newspapers, Hollinger's Canadian Internet operations (among them Canada.com, Faceoff.com, Careerclick.com, and Carclick.com), and a 50 percent interest in *National Post*, the national daily newspaper Hollinger launched just two years earlier. CanWest's Canadian holdings already included the ten-station Global Television Network, four other non-Global TV stations, a cable specialty channel, and 50 percent of *ROBTv*, the business information specialty cable channel co-owned by *The Globe and Mail*.[21] It owned or had a significant share in broadcasting operations in Australia, New Zealand, the Republic of Ireland, and Northern Ireland. It owned film and television production and distribution companies, advertising sales firms, radio stations and networks, and a range of interactive media properties.[22]

Two other mergers announced within weeks of the CanWest Hollinger deal further reshaped the Canadian media landscape. In September 2000, the telecommunications giant BCE Inc. announced a $4 billion deal to pool its Sympatico Internet portal and the CTV private television network into a new company that would also contain *The Globe and Mail* newspaper of Thomson Corp. and its related Internet and business-TV enterprises. The news release announcing the merger described the new entity as "Canada's premier multi-media company that will combine Canada's strongest media brands."[23] In the same week, newspaper chain owner and printing company Quebecor Inc. emerged as the victor in a $4.9 billion battle to buy Le Groupe Videotron, a Quebec-based cable TV and broadcasting company. Quebecor, whose Canoe.ca Internet portal competes with BCE's Sympatico, beat out Rogers Communications Inc. in the bidding for Videotron's favors (Bonisteel 2000). As a result of these and other transactions, the degree of concentration of ownership of Canadian newspapers has declined somewhat (though the number of independent dailies has not increased). At the same time, however, cross-media concentration has risen to new levels.

Big though they are, the companies created by the CanWest, Quebecor, and BCE/Thomson mergers are relatively small players compared to the giant corporations that have been steadily buying properties across the media sector in the United States. The conglomerate created when Disney took over ABC had revenues of $22.5 billion in 1997 and included five movie studios, twenty-six radio stations reaching almost one in four U.S. households, ten TV stations reaching one in four U.S. households, ten daily newspapers, three magazines, a professional hockey team, Disney resorts (in California, Florida, Paris, and Tokyo), a cruise line, a planned housing development in Florida, three record labels, the ESPN network (co-owned with Hearst), and four TV production companies ([Jaquet] 1998). The $50 billion CBS and Viacom merger created a company that included cable TV networks (MTV, VH1, TNN, CMT, Nickelodeon) and pay channels (The Movie Channel, Showtime, FLIX); a majority interest in Infinity Broadcasting; the largest television group in the United States, including the CBS Television Network; Paramount Pictures; syndication and production operations (CBS Productions, Paramount Television, Viacom Productions, and, subject to CBS's pending acquisition, King World Productions); Simon and Schuster publishers; Blockbuster video; five theme parks; and a "significant and growing" Internet presence.[24]

Topping both these was the January 2000 America Online Inc. takeover of Time Warner Inc., at a cost of roughly $182 billion in stock and debt. American Online was the top Internet service provider in the United States; Time Warner was the world's largest media conglomerate (T. Johnson 2000). Time Warner, with 1997 revenues of $13.3 billion, owned or controlled three movie studios in 1998, along with 625 screens in seven countries, CNN radio, thirty magazines (including *Time* and *People*), four book publishers, CNN International (operating in 210 countries and territories), cable franchises serving 20 percent of U.S. households, and three sports teams ([Jaquet] 1998). America Online boasted more than 20 million subscribers through its AOL and Compuserve Internet services, and the merger gave it broadband access to more than 13 million Time Warner cable subscribers (T. Johnson 2000).

Bagdikian, who has spent much of his career tracking media concentration, contends that corporate giants like these constitute a communications cartel (1997, ix). In the past, he says, it was possible to describe the dominant firms in each separate medium. That is no longer the case.

> With each passing year and each new edition of [*The Media Monopoly*], the number of controlling firms in all these media has shrunk: from fifty corporations in 1984 to twenty-six in 1987, followed by twenty-three in 1990, and then, as the borders between the different media began to blur, to less than twenty in 1993. In 1996 the number of media corporations with dominant power in society is closer to ten. (xii–xiii)

These corporations have acquired "more public communications power—including ownership of the news—than any private businesses have ever before possessed in world history" (ix). Through digital technology and the purchase of subsidiaries—in other words, through corporate convergence and digital convergence—the media cartel can exert power at every step in the communication process, from the creation of content to the delivery of content into the home.

PRESSURE FOR PROFITS

Much of the debate about these new converged corporations has centered on whether (or how) they have altered the practice of journalism, and what that means for a democratic society. Scholars and critics have pointed with concern to the spread of entertainment values to news, the blurring of the lines between reportage and promotion, the way ownership may affect decisions about which stories to cover, and the narrowing of channels of public communication (see, for example, Miller 1998; H. Schiller 1992, 1996; Smythe 1981; Squires 1993; Roberts, Kunkel, and Layton 2001). The question of how convergence affects the labor (and the labor unions) of newsworkers has received comparatively less attention.

Corporate growth requires resources, and there is no doubt that the potential for profits is part of what makes newspapers attractive to investors. This means that newspaper managers face constant pressure to produce ever-higher revenues. Bogart writes that in the 1980s, "corporate managements were impelled to maximize current earnings as a way of boosting the price of the stock" (1991, 52). He explains that part of the reason for optimizing profit was "the corporate owner's many and varied cash needs—not the least of which in many instances is huge debt incurred by companies caught up in the acquisition mania of the 1980s" (93). This meant that newspapers bought by expanding groups "were immediately pressed into service to finance the next deal" (93). Growth targets could be set and achieved in a variety of ways: "by acquiring additional properties, expanding sales, cutting costs, and raising prices" (52). Bogart notes that newspaper advertising rates rose almost automatically starting in the mid-1970s, and at a rate that outpaced inflation. Between 1965 and 1975, newspaper ad rates in the United States went up 67 percent, while consumer prices went up 74 percent. Between 1975 and 1990, ad rates rose 253 percent, while consumer prices rose 141 percent (53). Production costs, meanwhile, showed a different pattern. Between 1965 and 1975, they rose 94 percent, or more quickly than both advertising rates and inflation. Between 1975 and 1990, production costs rose 163 percent, higher than inflation but well below the 253 percent hike in ad rates. Bogart concludes, "In practice rate increases were in many cases being set by the publishers' profit objectives" (53).

Because public companies report their earnings quarterly, Bogart argues, their management focus tends to be on the short term and the bottom line:

> Publishers who worked for publicly owned companies felt the fire at their fannies at every moment. One, faced with a serious local business recession, told his group management, "I'm not going to be able to meet my profits goal this quarter." He was told, "That's not one of your options." (53)

One way to increase profits is to use new management techniques to wring the maximum amount of profit from each enterprise. This has led to a phenomenon described by Underwood (1993) as "MBA Journalism," referring to the growing influence of marketers and managers—people with master's degrees in business administration rather than backgrounds in journalism—on the news. Underwood contends that local newspaper publishers have had little choice but to go along with the trend: "the new capital-conscious, market-driven newspaper companies have found they aren't in a position to just sit on their riches.... Wall Street, as publishers have learned, can be insatiable in the demand for earnings growth and unmerciful in hammering a stock if earnings drop" (41).

Underwood notes that one result of this phenomenon has been an emphasis on "reader-friendly" journalism, supported by marketing programs and management systems that see readers as customers and news as another product in the consumer society. In some cases, this has breached what journalists call "the wall between church and state"—the separation between the newsroom and the business departments of the newspaper.[25] A 1998 *Columbia Journalism Review* examination of the *Los Angeles Times* found that reporters had been divided into teams, each headed by a business-side executive. For journalists, this resulted in an uncomfortably close relationship with people who normally would stay out of the newsroom. According to writer Charles Rappleye, "Throughout the paper, editors are sitting down with delegates from circulation, marketing, research and advertising to develop new sections and new offerings within sections, to establish targets and goals for revenue and readership, and to search for new ways to achieve overall increases in circulation, advertising and profit" (Rappleye 1998, 20).

Underwood (1998) found similar patterns at other U.S. newspapers. He quotes newspaper executives as saying that this kind of practice makes business sense in an era where newspapers are under intense competitive pressure (24). Given that most U.S. newspapers operate in monopolistic or oligopolistic markets, it seems clear that these executives are not referring to competition in the traditional sense of a newspaper war for the readers in a local community. Instead, the competition is for profits, which boost corporate earnings and share prices on Wall Street and Bay Street.

In part because they earned comfortable profits for their owners, the old privately held newspapers often had what can only be termed quirky business practices. Hayes writes that before Roy Megarry became publisher of *The Globe and Mail* in 1978, the business side of the newspaper lagged far behind other Canadian businesses. "Financial record keeping was primitive. A dated IBM 360/30 churned out reams of raw data that were later summarized by the business manager and hand-written onto a one-page spreadsheet. *Hand-written!*" (Hayes 1992, 143; emphasis in the original). The wall between "church and state" was high and wide: "The editorial department was run so separately from the commercial side of the paper that [editor-in-chief] Dic Doyle didn't even have a budget; he simply spent carefully until the year ended or the publisher came to him and told him he had run out of money, whichever came first" (143).

Bogart says the best of the independent newspaper owners "exemplified all the classic virtues of a hereditary aristocracy" (50). At times this meant forgoing profits. He cites the well-known case of the *New York Times* turning down advertisements when newsprint was rationed during the Second World War, so it could print more news. In Canada, Michael Davies, owner and publisher of the *Kingston Whig-Standard*, came up with an innovative strategy when faced with a major drop in advertising during the 1982 recession. According to Fetherling, a number of Southam newspapers jettisoned between 4 and 9 percent of their work force that spring (1993, 293). Davies called his 170 employees together for a meeting and asked them to take part in a nine-week campaign of donating personal time to generate additional revenue. The employees were given a choice: face fifteen layoffs, or sell 3,000 new subscriptions and as much additional advertising as possible. The employees agreed to pitch in on the subscription and ad sales campaign. It worked. There were no layoffs that year. Two years later, Davies, a reformed smoker, decided to refuse to accept any more cigarette ads, a decision that cost the company $50,000 a year (Fetherling 1993, 300).

It would, of course, be a mistake to see independent local publishers as philanthropists first and business people second. As Bogart notes, the independent publisher was as eager as any other business operator to earn a profit, "but generally he was not in need of ready money. To preserve the institution he could afford to think long range. Besides, an improvement in quality might provide the publisher with deeper, nonfinancial satisfactions: an awareness of accomplishment, the admiration of associates and of the public" (1991, 52). Those other satisfactions have become less significant as more publishers become employees of publicly traded corporations. The odds are that the publisher of a local newspaper was sent there by the head office, has few personal ties to the community the newspaper serves, and may not stay there for long anyway. In addition, the publisher is likely to concentrate on carrying out business strategies established at corporate headquarters, with an eye to extracting profits rather than exploring the particular needs and concerns of the community.

Bagdikian writes that Gannett imposes strict financial expectations on its newspapers. A publisher is told exactly how much the paper must produce in each three-month period. This quota has nothing to do with the local market, and everything to do with the company's position on Wall Street. Local publishers who meet their quotas have considerable freedom. "Those who don't are punished. They either lose their jobs or relinquish control to Gannett's regional or national headquarters" (78). Those who succeed also have a shot at rising within the corporation; "the reward is far from their current local community, their 'commitment' to whose future is so often the subject of the full-page ads" (79). Pohle (1984), describing Thomson's takeover of the *Lethbridge Herald* in Alberta, found a similar pattern. The company demanded a stream of paperwork from editors and paid very close attention to budgets. The corporation also used cross-chain, bottom-line figures as guides for the Lethbridge paper, regardless of whether this was appropriate in the local market. Within the newspaper, power was concentrated in the hands of the publisher and managing editor, who were appointed by the head office and led a steady campaign to scale down editorial expenses.

Interviewed during Hollinger's most acquisitive phase, company president David Radler told *Maclean's* magazine,

> I visit the office of each prospective property at night and count the desks. That tells me how many people work there. If the place has, say, forty-two desks, I know I can put the paper out with thirty people, and that means a dozen people will be leaving the payroll even though I haven't seen their faces yet. (quoted in Barlow and Winter 1997, 95)[26]

In the days when newspapers were owned by independent publishers, there was a direct connection between profits and wages. That connection is much weaker today. As Underwood notes, "Not only does the substance of the newspaper become secondary to the planning, prettifying, and promoting of the newspaper, but newspaper executives often must institute tough newsroom management systems in order to bring along newsworkers reluctant to buy into the philosophy of market-oriented journalism" (1993, 27).

THE NEW "LOCAL" PRESS

One of the consequences of the corporate convergences that have been described here has been the decline of the newspaper as a distinctly local enterprise. The "local" press has lost many of the elements that once marked it as a product of its own particular community. Newspapers still hire their own reporters, sell ads to local businesses, and offer home delivery. But instead of being owned by people with ties to their communities, newspapers are owned by corporations whose loyalties and responsibilities lie with their stockholders rather than with local readers. Instead of functioning within the confines of the local economy, local publishers work with company-wide targets on how many people to employ, how much (or how little) to pay them, how much (or how little) room to set aside for news and for ads, what kinds of equipment to purchase,[27] and so on. Increasingly, they see readers as customers or consumers, rather than as neighbors and fellow citizens. As for workers, former *Calgary Herald* managing editor Gillian Steward says corporate managers see reporters and photographers "as expendable costs rather than valuable resources" (Steward 1999).[28]

At the same time, corporate convergence has blurred the edges of what was once relatively easy to define as the daily newspaper business: the production of "a printed account of timely and important information distributed within a specific market on a regular basis" (Sohn, Ogan, and Polich 1986, 3). The corporate owners of daily newspapers see themselves in the business of producing and distributing not news but "information"—an elastic term that can cover products ranging from CanWest Global's carclick.com, to Disney's movies (and assorted spinoffs), to Gannett's telemarketing and retail advertising groups.

It should come as no surprise that Linda Foley, president of The Newspaper Guild sector of the Communication Workers of America, sees consolidation of ownership as the "number one worry" for her union. The challenge for organizations that represent newsworkers, she says, is "to figure out is how can we maintain a voice" (Foley 1998).

NOTES

1. Indeed, *The Globe and Mail* proclaims itself "Canada's national newspaper" on its front page.

2. It is useful to define commercialization as the point at which the balance of a newspaper's revenue tilts toward advertising and away from subscription or other funding sources. In the 1870s, advertising in Canadian papers accounted for less than 50 percent of revenue. By 1918, however, it had risen to 75 percent (Sotiron 1997, 58, 62).

3. By 1880, for example, the Scripps family owned newspapers in Detroit, Cleveland, Cincinnati, Buffalo, and St. Louis (Emery and Emery 1978, 209). The Southam company began in the 1880s as a family business with newspapers in Hamilton and then Ottawa, and printing plants in Toronto and Montreal. By 1923 it also owned

daily newspapers in Calgary, Edmonton, Winnipeg, and Vancouver (Kesterton 1967, 78). As Vipond notes, cross-media ownership was a feature in Canada in the 1920s, when newspapers opened radio stations in most major cities across the country (1992, 44).

4. For example, William Randolph Hearst's political and economic ambitions were too large to be satisfied by his *San Francisco Examiner,* and led him to purchase newspapers in New York, Chicago, and Los Angeles (Emery and Emery 1978, 266)

5. Concern about concentration of ownership and decreased newspaper competition resulted in the appointment of a Royal Commission on the Press in Britain in 1947. A few countries, including Sweden and the Netherlands, experimented with subsidies to keep competition alive (Desbarats 1996, 64). In the United States, the 1947 Commission on Freedom of the Press, known as the Hutchins Commission, examined the public responsibilities and character of the U.S. press.

6. The committee reported, "strangely enough, no exhaustive comprehensive study" of media ownership had been conducted in Canada until it took up the question (Davey committee 1970, 15).

7. The 1965 change in the tax law drew mixed reaction from the Canadian Daily Newspaper Publishers Association. While some publishers approved, others feared it might lower the eventual value of their newspaper businesses. Still others saw it as an infringement by the state on their rights as free-enterprise publishers (Desbarats 1995, 82).

8. Financial statements for Sterling were not public; however, public data were available on some of the companies Western Dominion controlled, including Hollinger Argus Ltd. and Argus Corp. Ltd. These two companies had gross assets of more than $900 million in 1980, and their revenues that year exceeded $90 million (Royal Commission 1981, 94).

9. Bogart attributes the growth of media companies in recent decades to a coincidence of two factors: the difficulties inheritance laws posed to passing along a newspaper to the next generation, and "an incredible escalation in the market value of newspapers and television stations" (1991, 49).

10. See Gannett company profile at www.gannett.com (accessed 23 July 2001).

11. See highlights of annual meeting, 5 May 1999; and corrected fourth-quarter earnings, 8 February 2001, at www.gannett.com (accessed 23 July 2001).

12. See 2001 second-quarter earnings report, 17 July 2001, at www.gannett.com (accessed 23 July 2001).

13. See "trivia" link at Canadian Newspaper Association Web site, www.cna-acj.ca/newspapers/facts/trivia.asp (accessed 23 July 2000).

14. Chairman's letter, 1998 Hollinger Annual Report, 9 March 1999, at www.hollinger.com (accessed 29 October 1999).

15. Hollinger International Inc. home page, at www.hollinger.com (accessed 15 July 1999).

16. See chairman's letter, 1997 Hollinger Annual Report, at www.hollinger.com (accessed July 1998).

17. Chairman's letter, 1998 Hollinger Annual Report, 9 March 1999, at www.hollinger.com (accessed 29 October 1999).

18. See Hollinger news releases for 17 August, 15 September, 28 September, 19

October, 20 October, and 25 October 1999, at www.hollinger.com (accessed 29 October 1999).

19. The statement said Hollinger fell victim to short sellers in 1997 and, "despite the excellent results described and an unbroken series of analysts' recommendations, languishes somewhat below where it was a year ago"; see Chairman's letter, 1998 Hollinger Annual Report, 9 March 1999, at www.hollinger.com (accessed 29 October 1999).

20. Hollinger news release, 31 July 2000, at www.hollinger.com (accessed 15 August 2000).

21. This meant that the owners of the two rival newspapers—BCE/Thomson, which owned *The Globe and Mail*, and CanWest, which owned 50 percent of the *National Post*—were equal partners in a spinoff broadcast product of one of the newspapers. The federal competition bureau announced in the fall of 2000 that it would not challenge the CanWest takeover of Hollinger's assets, but it convinced CanWest to terminate its partnership in *ROBTv*. See Competition Bureau news release, 3 November 2000, at www.strategis.gc.ca (accessed 24 July 2001).

22. See "Backgrounder," 16 November 2000, at www.canwestglobal.com (accessed 24 November 2000).

23. News release, 15 September 2000, at www.Thomson.com (accessed 26 July 2001).

24. News release, 7 September 1999, at www.viacom.com (accessed 29 October 1999).

25. Journalists see this as crucial to the public service mandate of journalism: it lets them do their work without thinking about commercial considerations.

26. When Hollinger bought the *Regina Leader-Post* and *Saskatoon StarPhoenix* in 1996, it immediately laid off 170 people, or more than one-third of the work force (Miller 1998, 93)

27. In the 1980s, for example, a number of Thomson newspapers switched to a particular computer system to handle electronic layout of pages. The reason: Thomson's head office decided this was the best system to use (McKercher 1991).

28. Steward wrote her column to help explain why *Calgary Herald* workers went on strike in November 1999, after attempts by the Communications, Energy and Paperworkers Union to negotiate a first contract with Hollinger failed. The main issue in the dispute was not wages but job security and what the union saw as threats to the professional integrity of newsroom workers. Hollinger immediately brought in replacement workers and continued to publish the newspaper. The company eventually broke the union.

3

Convergence, Technology, and Labor

If corporate convergence has dramatically redrawn the broad outlines of the North American newspaper business, a second form of convergence has taken apart and reconstituted the labor process within the newspapers themselves. This is technological convergence, brought about through the application of digital technology to work. The introduction of computers in newspaper publishing in the 1960s set in motion a series of transformations that first blurred the lines between what were once discrete steps in the production process, and then collapsed the separate stages into one another. As Pacific Press put it in a 1995 application to the provincial labor relations board, "the skills needed in many areas of the operation [have] converged and met on the computer."[1]

In addition to changing how a newspaper is put together, technological convergence poses a fundamental and philosophical challenge to the labor unions representing newspaper workers. Starting in the late nineteenth century, a range of printing trades workers broke away from the International Typographical Union to establish their own unions, with jurisdictional lines that reflected specific and distinct sets of skills. In the days before the computer, newspaper unions and their employers had relatively little difficulty identifying appropriate bargaining units—a process which, as Murray notes, is the cornerstone of union structures (1995, 171). Though there was sometimes competition over which union would represent which group of workers, the division of labor within the newspaper plant was tied to the use of distinctive skills and specific tasks. New technology undermined not just those skills, but the division of labor (and of labor unions) within the newspaper plant. This raised the prospect of jurisdictional disputes over ever-shrinking jurisdictions.

Technological changes and corporate convergence can each be tracked separately, but they are not separate phenomena. Rather, they are complementary features of the capitalist system of manufacturing. As Braverman observes, one of the fundamental characteristics of this system is the use of increasingly sophisticated machinery and administrative techniques to assert control over work (1974, 45–58). In the newspaper business, technological innovations have presented different challenges to the various unions at different times. For some craft unions, the introduction of new technology raised the specter of imminent extinction, their skills transferred into increasingly sophisticated machinery. For other unions, digital technology has offered a more complex set of possibilities: expansion of skill in some areas, contraction in others. But the overall tendency since the 1960s has been toward eliminating step after step in the production process, and shedding the workers who used to perform those steps.

NEWSPAPER LABOR IN THE PRECOMPUTER AGE

Hadley describes the history of technological innovation in the printing trades as featuring periodic, sudden upsets, followed by decades of relative stability (1995a, 5). Not surprisingly, the history of unions in the printing trades has followed a similar pattern. The task of turning written material into type was accomplished in the early years of printing by skilled, literate craft workers. Letter by letter, they set lines of type into a composing stick, then used blank slugs to "justify" each line, or make it the same length as the others. The lines of type were transferred into a galley. Printers made a "proof" or a preliminary impression of the galley so they could read it over and correct for errors in spelling, typography, or spacing. Once the corrections were made, the type was set into page form and locked into place in a metal frame on a hard, smooth surface known as "the stone." Because the type was hand-cast and of varying age and quality, printers had to do a great deal of "make-ready" work, fixing and adjusting forms and plates to ensure a clear, uniform impression. Printers then applied ink to the type, and, using substantial force, squeezed a single sheet of paper against the form to make the final impression (see Baker 1957, 2–5).

In the nineteenth and early twentieth centuries, a series of mechanical advances—the rotary press, powered by steam and later electricity; the linotype machine to cast type; photoengraving, which allowed for improved illustrations—transformed newspaper production. More and more, it resembled factory work, following the model of a production line. The unions' view, proclaimed most loudly and successfully by the ITU, was that the work belonged to the individual worker, not to the employer. And the union, not the employer, decided which printers would work, and when. "No union ever had the extent of job control that the ITU did," Walsh notes (1985, 35). Lipset, Trow, and Coleman agree: ITU "laws" determining conditions of employment, maximum length of the work week or work day, control of composing room work, and so on, were non-negotiable in local contracts and strictly enforced (1956, 24). This meant that to a considerable extent, the workers ran the composing room.

The production process established in the early twentieth century endured with remarkably few changes until the 1960s.[2] The *London Free Press*, in a limited-edition souvenir publication (1966) marking the opening of its new plant in the mid-1960s,[3] offered a detailed description of this production cycle. Though some North American newspapers were experimenting with computerization in the 1960s, the *Free Press* of 1966 was not: the word "computer" does not appear in the text of *Communication in the Community*, and none of the pictures shows a computer terminal. The book offers, therefore, a clear snapshot of how newspapers were put together in the days before digitization.

The new *Free Press* building cost $6.5 million and housed the newspaper and CFPL Radio, both owned by the Blackburn family. In trumpeting how modern and up-to-date the facility was, the commemorative book emphasizes speed of production: "The most important single advantage gained by this capital outlay is time—measured in minutes. News is highly perishable. Publishing a newspaper is a never-ending race against time. This big (160,000 square feet) building was designed with that in mind—no wasted motion—no wasted time."[4] It says, "valuable minutes have been gained here and there" in the entire production cycle, highlighting in particular the construction of a "modern" composing room, improvements in casting of printing plates, and a $1.5 million high-speed press. But while the plant and equipment were indeed new, fast, and efficient, the technology in which the *Free Press* invested in 1965 was not. Instead, it represented refinements on innovations that had appeared much earlier, around the turn of the century.

The production process in the 1960s began in the newsroom, where reporters phoned in stories to the rewrite desk or wrote them on typewriters. In doing so, they used essentially the same technology as their predecessors, shown in a newsroom photograph taken in 1923, though they used more of it. (In the 1920s, for example, the newsroom's only telephone was in a booth in a corner of the room; by the 1960s, reporters had their own phones and the rewrite desk staff used phones with headsets.) Reporters did their research in person or by phone, and drew background material from clipping files in the newspaper library, where by 1966 librarians had 12,000 files on people and 25,000 on subjects.[5] Some reporters sent in news by teletype from bureaus at city hall and the police station. News from the wire services also came in by teletype. Teletype machines were introduced in Canadian newspapers in the 1920s (Kesterton 1967, 120).

When reporters were finished writing their stories, they handed them to the editors on the news desk. The job of editors is to "sort and scan the written stories, selecting and evaluating, trimming some and seeking more information on others. Checking, checking and re-checking" (*London Free Press* 1966). The editors did this work by pencil on paper. Other editors decided where the story would go in the newspaper and what headline it would carry.[6] As they finished with a story, the editors put it on a conveyor belt that ran along the newsroom ceiling. This took copy to the composing room.

Meanwhile, *Free Press* photographers stayed in contact with their editors by two-way radio, a technology perfected during the Second World War. They took pictures on film, and most photographers developed their own film in the newspaper's darkroom. Prints selected for publication went to the engraving department, where they were rephotographed by special cameras through screens that broke up the picture into a pattern of dots. The screened negative was placed on a coated, light-sensitive magnesium plate and exposed to high-intensity light. The exposed plate was then etched in an acid bath, washed, and dried. This process, a variation on half-tone photographic printing, had been around since the 1860s,[7] though the full impact of pictorial journalism was not felt until the 1920s (Emery and Emery 1978, 235). The *Free Press* engraving department was also equipped to handle color reproduction, a later refinement on the half-tone process. The newspaper had been printing some elements in color since the late 1930s.

Advertisements for the paper came through two departments, display and classified. In the display department, advertising sales people signed up clients and made sure they got what they wanted in the final ad. Individual advertisements were put together by copy service specialists—artists, ad layout and typographical design staff—shown in a photograph as working by hand, with pencils and paper. A department known as "dispatch control" kept track of advertisements, acting as "an important production liaison between advertising and composing room, keep[ing] record of ad insertion dates, colour positions and maintain[ing] extensive files of ad illustrations." The photograph of this department shows rows of metal filing cabinets, indicating that this clerical work was also done on paper.

The process of placing the ads in the paper was done by ad layout people working with a "dummy," or a plan for the next edition. The layout people drew boxes on the dummy showing where the ads would go. Leftover space was the "news hole," to be filled by the editors. Some display ads came in as "mats"—thick, soft cardboard sheets carrying the impression of the advertisement's typography and illustrations. These were used to make metal casts for the press.

Classified ads were handled in a separate department by ad-takers, who recorded by hand the name, address, and phone number of the advertiser, plus the classification, price, and code for each ad. The ad moved by conveyor belt from the ad-takers to a control room to be checked. It then sped by pneumatic tube to the composing room to be set in type. The commemorative book notes that in addition to the ad-takers, classified staff included "street salesmen, telephone salesgirls, paper marker, clerk, secretary, copy service person, two supervisors and manager."

Ads and news met in the composing room, "the biggest and busiest staging area in the newspaper production line," and "a big funnel through which everything must flow to get into the next edition." The caption of a photograph of the *Free Press* composing room taken in 1912 points out five linotype machines along the back wall, the first such machines the newspaper purchased. The "spacious new composing room," by contrast, had two dozen typesetting machines. Six of these contained a relatively recent innovation: they were equipped to operate from prepunched perforated tape; according to Kesterton (1967, 121), these appeared in Canada in the 1950s. The rest were operated by a compositor who sat at a keyboard and retyped the news or advertising copy, casting it into metal type.

Printers set stories in type, then sent them to a "dump" in the middle of the composing room, where proofreaders checked the type for mistakes and ordered corrections. Stories were then matched with their headlines, which were cast in metal on different machines, and moved to page forms. Compositors putting together pages put the ads in first, then filled the rest of the space with news and pictures, following directions sketched on the "dummy" by the editors.

Once a page was full, the frame was locked and it went to the stereotype department. There, a cardboard mat was placed over the form and squeezed in a press that exerted 400 tons of pressure. The mat, which now bore the impression of the page, was put in a semicylindrical casting box and used to make a curved printing plate that would fit on the press. The plates, each weighing forty-seven pounds, were sent to the press room along a roller-track conveyor belt, where pressmen picked them up and attached them to the press.[8]

The pressmen had two other important jobs: they adjusted by hand the control valves on pipelines that fed ink to the press, and they prepared the rolls of newsprint for the press. The printing process that combined stereotyping and the rotary press was developed in London and spread to the United States in the 1860s (Emery and Emery 1978, 145). The electrically powered rotary press was standard newspaper technology by the time the *Free Press* bought its first one in 1905. The new presses bought in 1966 were bigger and faster, and had refinements like automatic web-break detectors and sophisticated switches for controlling ink flow, but they used essentially the same processes as those built almost 100 years earlier.

When the presses began to roll, the inked printing plates applied type to rolls of blank paper threaded through the presses. The pages were folded and cut, and finished newspapers rolled off the press and into the mailroom. The caption for a picture of the *Free Press* mailroom in 1934 says it took "stamina, strong backs and a staff of fourteen employees" to move the papers from the conveyor belt to the mailing tables, where they were counted in bundles, hand-wrapped and tied, and carried out to waiting trucks. The modern mailroom of 1966, by contrast, was "highly mechanized." Conveyor belts kicked out every twenty-fifth paper, to make it easier to count bundles. Mailers made up bundles and steered them onto conveyor tables running down the sides of the room.[9] At the far end, machines tied the bundles, and mailers then slid them down spiral chutes into waiting trucks. The trucks took the bundles to drop-off points. There "carrier boys, independent young businessmen who are the vital final link in the newspaper distribution system," broke up the bundles and delivered papers to readers' doorsteps. Home delivery was coordinated by the circulation department, which kept track of customers and created small plates to print address labels for carriers, news dealers, and individual mail subscribers.

As this description shows, the production process of newspapers in the precomputer era was labor-intensive, complex, and required many separate steps. The task of putting words and images on newsprint required a lot of repetitive action: stories were typed on paper and retyped as they were cast into metal; photographs were developed, then rephotographed to be turned into engravings. Making the printing plate meant converting flat pages of metal type to cardboard mats and back to metal again, this time as curved plates that fit on the press. All these tasks were carried out by groups of skilled workers, each responsible for a small step leading to the final product.

Cumbersome though it was, the production process of 1966 was efficient and successful: the newspaper printed 124,000 copies per day in five editions, serving readers throughout southwestern Ontario. It had deep roots in its community;[10] the *Free Press* marked its 100th anniversary in 1949 with a 232-page edition, which it claimed was "the largest ever printed in Canada up to that time." By the 1960s, the company had outgrown the existing plant it had occupied since 1931, when its circulation was 38,850.

In hindsight, it is clear that the printing process the *Free Press* trumpeted as new and improved used new equipment but not new technology. The *Free Press* of 1966 was simply a bigger and faster version of the *Free Press* of 1956, and one with a few more bells and a few louder whistles than the *Free Press* of 1946. Indeed, a compositor trained in the 1920s on linotype machines would probably have had little difficulty adapting to the linotype machines installed at the new plant in the 1960s. The one exception was the bank of linotypes that had been modified to set type from perforated tape. These offered the potential of eliminating a step in the production process, particularly for copy from the wire services. As Zerker explains, "One reporter could write a story, and one operator could transmit the message, which automatically perforated as many teletypesetters as were linked to the point of origin" (1982, 246). She adds that the use of tape, "paper or magnetic, makes all typesetting machines compatible with computers" (248). The *London Free Press* had yet to take that step. But in the mid-1960s, other North American newspapers were starting to. They were experimenting with technologies that over the next few decades would radically transform the production process for newspapers, and would pose major challenges to the unions representing newspaper workers.

COLD TYPE AND COMPUTERS

In the early 1960s, a series of innovations began to offer new ways of producing the daily newspaper. The first of these was the development of what is known as "cold type," defined by Zerker as "the replacement of a mould of a letter type for a photograph of the desired letter" (1982, 246). Cumbersome phototypesetters were displayed at a Chicago graphic arts show in 1950,[11] and more sophisticated models appeared quickly. The second development was the attempt to merge electronic computers with mechanical devices. Zerker writes that early in 1963, the American trade press was reporting that some newspapers were using digital computers for typesetting (248). By the 1990s, cold type and the computer had changed every facet of newspaper production, from reporting and editing, to selling (and billing for) ads, to running the presses, to managing the mailroom.

These changes did not happen at once, and they did not occur in every newspaper at the same time. Some newspapers leapt at new technologies; others proceeded very slowly indeed. Swartz and Swimmer (1981) point out that in Ottawa, two competing broadsheets, the *Ottawa Journal* and *Ottawa Citizen*, faced some major decisions in the late 1960s: whether to shift from "hot" to "cold" type; whether to move to an offset printing press, and whether to move out of their downtown offices to a location with better highway access. "Both papers," Swartz and Swimmer write, "made these decisions in 1968, with the *Citizen* making all the right choices—a suburban location with ready access to the Queensway expressway, 'cold' type and an offset press—and the *Journal* making exactly the opposite, and erroneous, choices" (107). Nine years later, in 1974, the *Journal* still had not installed computer video display terminals, known as VDTs, for writing, editing, and typesetting (111). Instead, it negotiated a technology package with its ITU compositors that gave them complete jurisdiction over VDTs—should they ever be introduced—and offered protection against layoffs. Two years later, when the newspaper decided to install VDTs after all, it asked for massive changes in the ITU agreement, including the elimination of the 1974 technological change clause (113). Over months of difficult negotiations, the ITU eventually agreed to relinquish its jurisdiction over VDT use by reporters, editors and the classified ad department, though not over VDT use for wire copy. On 25 October 1976, the newspaper locked out all its unions. The other unions—stereotypers, pressmen, mailers, and Guild clerical workers—eventually settled. The ITU never did. Swartz and Swimmer describe the case as "a failure of management,"[12] and suggest that the troubled labor relations were part of a broader pattern of weak management that eventually contributed to the failure of the *Journal* (126–27).[13]

Between the 1960s and 1990s, newspapers took different routes toward technological change, but almost all of them ended up at more or less the same place: with production plants in which the dominant technology is digital, and in which the multiple steps between editor's desk and mailroom have been collapsed and, ultimately, eliminated. Pacific Press, a division of Southam and publisher of the daily *Vancouver Sun* and *Vancouver Province*, chronicled how technological change had affected its operations in a 1995 application for labor union consolidation. Like the *London Free Press* example from 1966, the Pacific Press story offers a template for understanding the broad pattern of technological change that occurred across the industry.

In applying to the British Columbia Labour Relations Board for an order to consolidate its seven bargaining units into one, Pacific Press explained how new technology has led to a convergence of skills across bargaining units. As a result, traditional distinctions between the bargaining units "have blurred and overlapped."[14] Pacific Press installed its first computers in the composing room in the 1960s.[15] Compositors used them to produce a perforated tape which drove the linotype machines. In addition, some wire service material—stock market information from The Canadian Press, for example—came into the composing room electronically, where it was reproduced as computer tape and again fed into the linotype machines. These developments reduced the amount of keyboarding done by compositors, who were members of the ITU. During this decade, Pacific Press also set up a data center to operate a mainframe computer that formatted classified ads, produced labels and distribution information for the mailroom, and produced bills and payroll checks. Because the data center's activities covered work under the jurisdiction of three unions—the Guild, the compositors, and the mailers—its staff was drawn on a proportional basis from these three groups of workers (32).

In the early 1970s, Pacific Press introduced a number of innovations aimed at automating and digitizing an increasing proportion of the work. In the classified ad department, it installed IBM Selectric typewriters. New optical character readers in the composing room "read" the text produced on these typewriters and converted it to perforated tape. This meant that compositors no longer retyped classified ads; instead, they used the perforated tape to drive the linotype machines (33).

The newspapers also began moving from hot metal production to cold type. Pacific Press installed a phototypesetter that converted characters entered by the optical character scanners into columns of text, which were then printed out on photographic paper. This meant that compositors no longer needed to use linotype machines to set this material in metal type. Instead, they were given the job of pasting the columns of type onto forms known as layout boards. The Pacific Press application describes the job of paste-up as "very labour intensive" (33). A new computer brought into the composing room, replacing the one installed in the 1960s, eliminated some of that labor-intensive work. This one produced "full-page pagination" (33) of classified ads, meaning that the computer-driven phototypesetter printed out entire pages of classified ads on photographic paper, eliminating the work of pasting up classified ads. Compositors still had to paste up display ads, news pages, and other parts of the paper (33).

In the engraving room, the change to cold type meant that engravers no longer needed to etch plates of photographs and illustrations. Instead, they produced screened photographic images, which were then pasted on the layout board (33). Cold type composition also altered the procedure for making printing plates. Pasted pages of cold type were converted into a plate using a photographic process that printed a raised image of the page on a photosensitive polymer plate. From there, the plate went to the stereotype department, where it was used to make the cardboard mat, from which the curved metal printing plate was cast. According to the Pacific Press application, these developments eliminated the need for certain skills possessed by stereotypers and engravers (34). The introduction of cold type and polymer plates also produced jurisdictional disputes.

Between 1972 and 1976, Pacific Press and the unions negotiated a number of items designed to simplify the process of technological change and lessen the potential damage to the unions. The first was a job protection agreement negotiated in the round of bargaining in 1972, ensuring that no regular employees would lose their jobs as a result of technological change. At the same time, the employer agreed to conditions on reducing its labor force by attrition (34). In 1976, management and the unions, bargaining as a joint council, came up with a mechanism for resolving jurisdictional disputes (34).

Technological change moved into the newsroom in 1975, with the installation of a Talstar mainframe computer and a series of video display terminals. Reporters wrote their stories on the computer instead of on a typewriter. Editors worked by computer too, correcting copy written by local reporters and working with wire-service stories that came directly into the mainframe. Once the editors were finished with a story, they sent it electronically to the composing room, where it was printed out in hyphenated and justified columns on photographic paper, cut, and pasted on the layout sheet by the compositors. Previously, compositors used linotype machines to set edited stories in type. The Pacific Press application notes that when the Talstar computer eliminated the need for compositors to type a considerable amount of material into the computer, "the compositors responded with a wildcat strike and a grievance claiming jurisdiction over work being performed by editorial staff" (35).[16] The compositors also objected to a plan to connect the wire service feed directly to the composing room computers, a step that would end the need for compositors to convert wire service material to tape (36).

The final major technological change of the decade signaled the end of one form of craft work at the Pacific Press papers: the job of stereotyping, which had been carried out by members of Local 885 of the International Printing and Graphic Communications Union. Starting about 1976, Pacific Press began to invest in technology that enabled it to place polymer plastic plates directly on the press. It did this in two steps: first installing di-litho plates, which converted a letter press to a form of offset press, then moving to a process that used plastic printing plates. This meant that the newspaper no longer needed to use the combination of stereotype mats and curved, cast metal plates. Pacific Press assigned the new technology to the engravers. The stereotypers challenged it, and eventually lost. The application adds, "This led to the demise of the stereotypers at Pacific Press" (37).

By the start of the 1980s, the production process was remarkably different from what it had been ten years earlier. A compositor trained in the 1920s, who would have adapted quickly to the *London Free Press* of 1966, would have been completely baffled by the *Vancouver Sun* just a dozen years later. He would have found that the printers, whose craft had been to produce a remarkable volume of metal type at high speed, no longer produced very much type at all, and none of it was metal. Instead, they worked with razor blades and wax-like glue, pulling sheets of computer-generated type off the phototypesetter, slicing it into columns, and sticking it onto a layout sheet. But while the work of compositors had undergone a radical shift, they were by no means the only workers affected by new technology. The number of tasks performed by (and the skills required of) engravers had also been reduced. The stereotypers had been eliminated.

Though it occurred fairly swiftly, this conversion did not happen easily. It produced a significant amount of labor strife. Between 1967 and 1978, there were seven rounds of collective bargaining. Four of these resulted in strikes/lockouts: a three-day strike by the Guild in 1967; a twelve-week shutdown in 1970; a three-day shutdown in 1972, and a lengthy strike/lockout from November 1978 through late June 1979.[17]

Not all of these were the direct result of technological change, though the disruptions brought about by new technology played a role in many of them. According to Fraser and Angel's research for the Royal Commission on Newspapers (1981), technological change was the key factor in 1972. Jurisdictional disputes arising from technological change caused a brief shutdown in 1975. The question of manning, or how many people were needed to run the presses, was a critical factor in 1978. Indeed, the Royal Commission researchers found that between 1970 and 1980, "there was almost continuous conflict at Pacific Press" (Fraser and Angel 1981, 32).

In the early 1980s, Pacific Press decided to move more of its display advertising work to the computer. It installed a Xenotron computer and terminals in the composing room, where compositors entered display ads. The computer was hooked up to the phototypesetter, which printed out the completed ad for pasteup. Pacific Press also replaced its Talstar mainframe with a centralized CSI data processing system. According to the company, none of these changes affected employee numbers, though they did provoke more jurisdictional disputes (Pacific Press application, 38). The compositors claimed jurisdiction over creating and using computerized formats, classified pagination, display ads, and "longhanding," or typing codes into a computer system to direct the output of text. The arbitrator who handled the complaint ruled that the employer could assign creation of formats as it saw fit. Because the Guild classified ad staff determined where ads should be placed, paginating those ads should be assigned to the Guild. On the display ad question, the arbitrator said that both the Guild and ITU units had a claim to input the ads, but because of the creative element involved, the task was awarded to the Guild. As for longhanding, the arbitrator ruled that this should be assigned to whoever input the original keystroke (38–39). The compositors took the case to the B.C. Court of Appeal seeking a judicial review. They also contacted the Industrial Relations Council, asking that the arbitration award be set aside. Neither strategy succeeded (39).

In 1985 Pacific Press began to take advantage of desktop publishing technology, which made it possible to carry out a wide assortment of publishing functions from a single computer terminal. An operator working at an Apple Macintosh computer could receive electronic text and images over a network, combine them, and send them to the phototypesetter—again over the network—to be printed as a single unit. By the end of the decade, Macintoshes replaced all the Xenotrons in the composing room. Desktop units were installed in the editorial department starting in 1987, producing graphics for designated newspaper pages. They were used in the advertising department to create display ads, and in the promotions department (40).

In the engraving department, a Howtek system was installed that could speed the processing of color pages. Color pictures could be scanned or electronically entered into the Howtek, which separated color photographs into four colors and transferred the result to film. This allowed editorial department staff to see low-resolution versions of the photographs on their computers for page layout purposes. When the page was "printed" to the Howtek, the computer substituted high-resolution images and exposed the separation onto film. The company noted that the Howtek "relies on manual intervention in the process, and a certain degree of knowledge is required to operate the system. Other systems are now available which automate the entire separation process" (40). Nonetheless, the Howtek cut another step in the production process, eliminating the need for engravers to shoot four separate films to create a color plate. In the late 1980s, the company added Autokon scanners to replace the large cameras previously used to create screened, half-tone images. These scanners also required manual operation but could scale, correct, and screen photographs. "Since their introduction more simple scanners and software automate much of the manual steps required," the Pacific Press application stated (40).

In 1990, the company installed an Ethernet communications network that linked the mainframe and stand-alone computers. This allowed for movement of electronic text and images back and forth among the various computers at Pacific Press, and to laser printers and phototypesetters. By 1991, all the Macintoshes in the composing room and the phototypesetters were on the network. (The Macintoshes were also linked to scanners and laser printers.) Promotions went on the network in 1991–1992, editorial graphics in 1991, and creative artists in 1992–1993. At about the same time, the mainframe computers serving the classified department, reader sales and services, business offices, and editorial systems were also linked to the network (41).

In 1991, Pacific Press opened a satellite production plant in the Vancouver suburb of Surrey. This was part of a long-term plan to move all press work to the suburbs and nonpress work to new quarters in downtown Vancouver. At first, the Surrey plant printed just the *Province*; the *Sun* was still printed in downtown Vancouver. Staff working in Vancouver electronically transmitted images of the pasted-up photocomposed pages of the *Province* to Surrey, where they were made into printing plates. The plant used Flexo presses, which have "a more efficient inking system" and require lower manning levels on each press. The company assigned some maintenance work on this new system to the pressmen's union. The machinists union challenged this assignment, prompting another jurisdictional dispute (41).

In 1993, the company installed 100 Macintosh computers, equipped for desktop publishing and connected to the Ethernet, in the editorial department (43). These allowed editorial workers to edit and position editorial material on a partially paginated page and send it directly to the phototypesetter. Editors worked from an electronic dummy produced by the advertising department, filling spaces around the spots slotted for the ads. The pages went to the phototypesetter, which printed them as laid out. Compositors then pasted in the ads and the photographs. This system eliminated a great deal of the cutting and pasting of news and editorial material that had been handled by the compositors.

Also in 1993, the company installed a VAX mainframe computer in the mailroom to control stacking and bundling. This system was equipped to receive daily reports from the reader sales and service department about the number of papers, routes, loads, and bundle sizes. It also kept track of the number of inserts that must go in the paper, and co-ordinated the loading of each truck. "Before these technological changes," the Pacific Press application explained, "the mailers manually coded the stacker and built the loads. The VAX system eliminated the last vestiges of hand-tied bundling, as the computer can direct the stacker to build irregular bundles" (44). Pacific Press planned to assign the work of instructing the computer to build loads for a specific truck to the driver of that truck. The mailers filed, and won, a jurisdictional claim (44).

Another jurisdictional dispute around this same time centered on the use of ad control scanners. This one involved three unions: the Guild, the compositors, and the engravers (44). Compositors and Guild staffers were also involved in a more complicated dispute over who would create mockups of ads—known as "spec ads"—that Guild sales representatives could take to potential advertisers as a way of drumming up business. The compositors claimed that making up ads was their job, and they refused to handle Guild-generated ads that had been sold "on spec." The labor relations board called this an illegal strike (45).

In 1993 Pacific Press decided to consolidate all its production operations for both newspapers at Surrey, selling off its downtown plant on Granville Street. At first, the company planned to buy used printing presses for the Surrey plant. But when the cost of newsprint rose, the company decided to buy new presses, which not only were more efficient but used less newsprint. The presses the company would eventually buy could read data encoded in photocomposed images electronically, and could preset ink and water levels. This meant that fewer pressmen would be needed to run the press (46). But in order to use the presses, Pacific Press said, the partial pagination system then in use had to be upgraded to a full pagination system—in other words, to one that would produce completed pages of text, photos, and ads to be sent to a single phototypesetter.

In 1994, the newspaper began buying electronic cameras for news photographers. These stored an image on a disk rather than on film, eliminating any need for film processing and half-tone production. The combination of full pagination and electronic cameras affected the work of three unions. The Guild-staffed photo lab was closed in 1995 and the nine people who worked there were reassigned (47). The compositors no longer had to paste up photographs or display ads. For engravers, work with the Howtek system, which had been installed less than ten years earlier, would also be eliminated.

In early 1996, Don Ross, vice-president of financing for Pacific Press, gave the B.C. Labour Relations Board an update on technological developments in the year following the filing of the consolidation application. He said that full pagination of color pictures would occur by the spring of that year. Plans also called for a new ad tracking system in February 1996, and a new ad billing system and classified system in March 1996.[18] He predicted that the number of compositors at Pacific Press would likely drop to fifty once full pagination was installed (79). By comparison, 450 people worked in the composing room in the 1960s.[19] The number of engravers—twenty-two at time of the hearing on the application—was expected to drop to twelve with full pagination.[20] In 1978, the newspaper had thirty-three engravers (Fraser and Angel 1981, 26).

Though the story of technological change at Pacific Press is specific to that company, it fits patterns that can be found at other newspapers in North America. The strongest of these trends is the steady push to compress and eliminate steps in the production process, and to eliminate the need for the workers who once made their living carrying out these tasks. Where the *London Free Press* of the 1960s opened a new plant with the goal of shaving minutes off each stage in the production cycle, the newspapers of the 1990s, in Vancouver and elsewhere, sought to transfer as much work as possible to the computer. In addition, the pace of technological change at Pacific Press was relentless: workers barely had time to adjust to one new device before the next generation arrived.

Technological change did not happen easily: the unions at Pacific Press, which had a reputation for solidarity and toughness, fought hard at almost every step. Their campaigns followed the same kinds of patterns that would be tried at newspaper after newspaper, across the continent, during the 1960s and 1970s. One technique, used with vigor by the ITU, was to pursue grievances and disputes over jurisdiction, challenging company plans to assign (or reassign) work affected by new technology. Pacific Press reports that there were "numerous" disputes over technological and related organizational change during these years, and at least seventeen adjudications. Nine jurisdictional disputes were still outstanding when the company filed its application for bargaining unit consolidation (30). The Pacific Press unions, which had a solid history of joint council bargaining, had come up with a mechanism for resolving interunion jurisdictional disputes back in the 1970s: a mediator-arbitrator acceptable to both parties could be called in to settle conflicting claims. But as the work shrank, the unions found themselves competing "for the same technologically changed work" (55).

A second tactic pursued by the unions was to seek job guarantees. The Pacific Press workers achieved these in the early 1970s, negotiating a clause ensuring that no regular employees would lose employment as a result of technological change. Later in that decade, the ITU negotiated lifetime job guarantees for 290 printers, in exchange for giving up their so-called reproduction rights—their right to set in type material that was already set in type (38).[21] The job guarantees are perhaps best seen as the price the company had to pay for its workers' consent to technological change. Ultimately, both sides knew the goal was to displace workers with equipment. But the job guarantees meant this would happen by attrition, not by layoff.

Braverman would see the changes at Pacific Press as striving toward the capitalist ideal: the domination of "living labor" by "dead labor," or the skills and knowledge of workers by automation (227). The last thirty years at Pacific Press have seen a steady transfer of skills to computers, and the concurrent deskilling of several groups of workers. The stereotypers are no more. The compositors, once the powerhouse of newspaper unions, have been steadily and severely affected. The remaining compositors are now clustered in the advertising department, where they compose display advertisements. The engravers have seen their skills (and their numbers) reduced. Some of the functions formerly performed by mailers have been automated. New presses include electronic devices that mean fewer pressmen will be required.

In the newsroom, new technology has had more mixed results. Digital cameras have eliminated the photo lab and the jobs of photo technicians, and reduced the requirement for photographers to master the skills of developing film. At the same time, online databases and the Internet have given new tools to reporters. As Koch notes (1991), reporters now have access to information that may be equal to or greater than that possessed by their sources. With word-processing programs, they have gained enormous flexibility in self-editing or rewriting stories without having to retype them in full. The news desk, meanwhile, has become the production hub of the newspaper. According to Russial, editors have been simultaneously reskilled and deprofessionalized, a term he defines as "the white-collar analogue of deskilling" (1989, 15). Editors retain their professional knowledge and their monopoly in its application, he argues, but they have lost much of their discretionary capability in the face of production imperatives. For each page they produce, they have to complete a series of must-do production tasks. Pressed for time, the traditional aspects of their job—described by the *London Free Press* in 1966 as "sort[ing] and scan[ning] the written stories, selecting and evaluating, trimming some and seeking more information on others. Checking, checking and re-checking"—are the ones most likely to be sacrificed.

In a 1985 guide produced by the Associated Press Managing Editors (APME), an editor with the *Aiken Standard* described "the ideal situation" for newspapers: a computer system in which completed pages "go directly from editor to the press" (Hunter 1985, 3). This, he added, is "the logical extension" of the wave of newsroom computerization that began in the 1970s. Hunter and other authors expressed disappointment that it had taken longer than expected to achieve this ideal.[22] APME reports in 1987 and 1988 were more optimistic. The 1987 report was called *Meet the Future: A Report on Pagination and Other Mystical Things*, a title ascribing semidivine qualities to new technology. It quoted one editor who described pagination as "the most revolutionary production change since the introduction of the linotype" (4). These handbooks, produced by and for the newspaper industry, set out very clearly the direction of production in the coming decades: more computers, more convergence, fewer production workers. With the news desk as the production hub, the composing room, engraving department, and perhaps even part of the pressroom would converge in cyberspace—and wither away in the real world.

BEYOND THE PRINTING PRESS

The Pacific Press case and the newspapers described in the APME reports are still grounded in the conception of newspapers as editions produced on paper by companies that run their own presses. In an age of convergence, however, both these ideas—the newspaper as words on paper, the newspaper as the product of the printing press—are being interrogated.

The marriage of newsprint and telecommunications has offered newspapers a new way of reducing labor costs: sharing presses. If the digital content of printing plates can be transmitted electronically from newsroom to pressroom, the content can be transmitted across town, or across the country. In Canada, Ottawa's French-language daily, *Le Droit*, set the pattern. In a dramatic restructuring in 1989, the newspaper installed a new pagination system, which eliminated its composing room. It also contracted out its printing, which eliminated its press room (Pane 1994, 138). The net effect was to reduce the staff by half. Pages of *Le Droit* are transmitted electronically to a printing plant in Quebec, and the newspaper is then trucked back across the Ontario–Quebec border to Ottawa. This kind of production is becoming increasingly common. Indeed, one of the factors that enabled Hollinger to launch its *National Post* was that it could use the presses at its dailies across the country to print the newspaper. Smaller dailies with joint ownership have begun sharing printing plants too.

Starting in the 1990s, newspapers began launching online editions that offer readers the potential of the "paperless" newspaper—or, perhaps more accurately, the "press-less" newspaper. In Canada, more than 95 percent of the Canadian Newspaper Association's 105 members had "hot links" on the CNA Web site in 2001.[23] The same pattern is seen in the United States, where 93 percent of print publications had Web sites in 1999 (McNamara 2000, 25). These ranged from fairly simple offerings, designed mainly to stake out a small patch of "turf" in cyberspace, to large and complex Web sites, complete with electronic classified ads or searchable archives of back issues. Most, however, offered only selected bits and pieces of the print version of the paper.

In 2001, led by the *New York Times* and the *Globe and Mail*, newspapers began taking the idea of electronic newspaper delivery one step further, offering to e-mail complete electronic replicas of the print editions to subscribers. *Globe and Mail* publisher Phillip Crawley told the union representing newsworkers at the paper that he expects the digital election will supplement print circulation, not reduce it. "The reach of it will be mostly beyond our current delivery network," he said (*SONGsheet*, November 2001, 1). But clearly, the potential is there for larger numbers of subscribers to bypass the presses altogether. Indeed, the "labor" of receiving the electronic newspaper would be done by the readers, using their own home computers as a private, nonunion printing press.

For newspaper workers and their unions, the last forty years have been a time of change, an era when two faces of convergence—among corporations and among technologies—have altered virtually every aspect of newspaper work. This has not happened easily, simply, or smoothly. At times the technology has not performed as managers hoped. At times, the unions have succeeded in fending off the installation of new equipment; at other times they have welcomed it. Remarkably, until very recently, much of this change has occurred with relatively little impact on the public face of the newspaper; it still arrives at (most) readers' homes every morning, as it did in the 1920s, the 1940s, or the 1960s. And for many newsworkers, the reassuring thud of newspapers landing on doorstops has been the one constant in an era of relentless and accelerating change.

NOTES

1. Pacific Press Inc., application for consolidation of bargaining units to B.C. Labour Relations Board, 12 June 1995, 27; hereafter "Pacific Press application." The company is now known as the Pacific Newspaper Group.

2. So did the union structure. The final union to be founded was the American Newspaper Guild, which in 1933 became the national union for reporters and editors.

3. The publication of souvenir editions marking major developments in a company has been a fairly common practice in the newspaper business.

4. Pages in the book are not numbered.

5. The newspaper also kept all its back issues on microfilm—and, according to the book, was the first Canadian newspaper to do so.

6. Editors of the precomputer era memorized an elaborate counting system to ensure the headlines would fit their allocated space, and would appear in the type size and font the editors desired.

7. In 1869, Quebec publisher Georges-Edouard Desbarats helped found the weekly *Canadian Illustrated News*, believed to be the first periodical in the world to carry half-tone photographs (Phillipson 1988, 587).

8. After the day's papers were completed, the plates went back on the roller-track belt and were sent to the basement, where they were melted down. The molten metal was pumped up to the stereocasting pot for reuse.

9. Some newspapers were mailed out to individual subscribers. A special machine stuck mailing labels on the individual copies.

10. Kesterton includes the *Free Press* on a list of eight Ontario newspapers founded prior to 1858 that are "probably the ones most deserving of mention." These papers enjoyed long lives, were pioneers in their communities, and played a prominent role in the political and social movements of the day (1967, 11).

11. According to Zerker, these worked by assembling and justifying a line of type matrices, as in metal casting. The letters in the matrix were lifted from their storage

position so that a beam of light could be projected through film and onto the matrix, producing a negative of the characters (1982, 246–47).

12. This is the title of their chapter in the Royal Commission on Newspapers volume on labor relations in the newspaper business (1981).

13. Thomson newspapers, which bought the *Journal* in 1980 through its acquisition of FP publications, shut it down in August 1980, on the same day Southam shut down the *Winnipeg Tribune*. The move, which gave Thomson a monopoly in Winnipeg and Southam a monopoly in Ottawa, precipitated the appointment of the Royal Commission on Newspapers.

14. Pacific Press application, 2. Parenthetical page references to this document follow in the text.

15. The application does not give the precise year.

16. The arbitrator, drawing on a similar case affecting the *Victoria Times-Colonist*, ruled in 1977 that where the predominant focus of the VDT work was to develop and edit editorial copy, that work belonged to the Guild. Where the predominant focus was the accurate transcription of hard copy received from outside, that work belonged to the composing room. The compositors also fought the direct connection of wire service material to the composing room computer. They lost that case in 1978 (Pacific Press application, 36).

17. See Pacific Press application, 60–62; and Fraser and Angel 1981, 32.

18. Don Ross, testimony before B.C. Labour Relations Board, 6 February 1996, 5.

19. Ross, testimony before B.C. Labour Relations Board, 11 October 1995, 51.

20. Ross, testimony, 6 February 1996, 85.

21. The Royal Commission on Newspaper researchers referred to this as "bogus type" (Fraser and Angel 1981, 39). It was a common form of ITU featherbedding, in this case through duplicating work that had already been done. The purpose was to keep employment of ITU printers as high as possible.

22. Hunter says a number of factors slowed the process. Direct-to-plate production requires expensive new central computers and subsystems, some of which had not been fully developed. Digital pictures required an enormous amount of storage space, which in 1985 was expensive. Finally, the key attraction—the savings on labor costs—was slow in coming. Many newspapers justified the cost of computer systems in the 1970s by showing the resulting reduction in so-called back-shop (composing room) costs. "But," Hunter notes, "pagination has been coming along in stages, and savings in the back shop have not seemed as apparent as with front-end systems." It is only when newspapers reach the final stage of pagination, when entire pages of pictures, ads, and text go directly to the printing plate, that substantial labor savings are produced (Hunter 1985, 3).

23. See "The Ultimate Online Guide to Canadian Newspapers," at www.cna-acj.ca (accessed 21 September 2001).

4

Mergers and More Mergers

In November 1959, fifty-six stereotypers went on strike at the *Portland Oregonian* and the *Oregon Journal*. The immediate cause of the strike was technological change: the Newhouse-owned *Oregonian* planned to install a new, German-made plate-casting machine that would reduce the number of stereotypers needed to make printing plates. The Portland action was noteworthy in several respects. The other unions at the newspapers refused to cross the stereotypers' picket line, and the papers suspended publication for a time. But the managements of the papers soon brought in out-of-state strike breakers, some of them armed, and announced that from then on, the newspapers would operate as an open shop in all areas (*Guild Reporter*, 27 November 1959, 3). This fortified the union opposition, and before the end of 1959 the unions had set up their own newspaper, the *Portland Reporter*, which would endure for almost five years.[1]

But perhaps the most significant action was taken in early 1960, when the unions set up an interunion newspaper strike committee headed by the International Typographical Union's Rene Valentine (*Guild Reporter*, 8 April 1960, 1). This committee brought together the so-called mechanical or craft unions[2] and the American Newspaper Guild, an industrial union that represented newsroom workers at the papers (Kuczun 1970, 281),[3] to jointly plan and coordinate strike activity.

Four months into the strike, the leadership of the unions came together for a meeting of the Allied Printing Trades Association of Phoenix. Though it was not a member of this group, the Guild was invited to attend. The meeting produced an extraordinary result: an agreement among the international presidents to pursue closer ties through some sort of federated organization (*Guild Reporter*, 25 March 1960, 1). This raised the prospect of creating "one big union" in the printing trades. It was an idea that was both breathtakingly simple and enormously radical, reversing seventy years of labor history that had seen the creation of more and more unions, specializing in smaller and smaller portions of the production process.

There had been earlier instances of cooperation between the Guild and the craft unions, and some talk of unity. The Guild had a longstanding pattern of refusing to cross the picket lines of other newspaper unions. Jacobson (1960) says the Guild harvested the fruits of interunion cooperation in 1950, in its seventy-one-day strike against Scripps Howard's *New York World Telegram and Sun*. The Guild got some financial help from the Council of Industrial Organizations and the United Mine Workers. More crucially, members of the craft unions refused to cross Guild picket lines in New York, claiming that their safety would be endangered by going to work. This effectively shut down the paper. This strike, Jacobson concludes, taught the Guild a lesson about "the paralysing force of labor unity" (164). Walsh notes that the Guild and the printing trades unions talked informally about unity later in the 1950s—at AFL-CIO conventions in 1957 and 1959, and at a 1959 meeting of the Allied Printing Trades Association—but nothing came of these discussions (1985, 42–43). A few months before the beginning of the Oregon strike, the Guild's annual convention, held in New York, heard a call for unity from the president of the powerful New York ITU local known as "Big Six." Francis G. Barrett acknowledged that the printing trades had made an enormous mistake when they "separated and divided themselves into separate craft unions." He urged the newspaper unions, including the Guild, to merge into a single, large body in which each existing union would have its own department. "The United Front of Capital must be met by the United Action of Labor," Barrett said (*Guild Reporter*, 10 July 1959, 13). Again, nothing came of the idea.

In 1960, however, the goal of "one big union" took center stage. Leaders of the Guild and the ITU met in April and released a joint statement committing themselves to the principle of unity. It read in part, "A unified organization of all workers in the printing, publishing and related trades, we believe, would create a strong force for the ultimate progress of employees and the industry which employs them." Significantly, the statement was less clear on exactly what unity meant: "Whether such unity takes the form of a merger, an amalgamation of existing unions, or a new organization; whether it begins with a combination of two unions or several—are details which should not hinder us in pursuit of our goal" (*Guild Reporter*, 22 April 1960, 1). According to the *Guild Reporter*, the joint statement by William J. Farson, the executive vice-president of the Guild and its highest-ranking full-time officer,[4] and ITU President Elmer Brown meant "they were agreed on a goal of 'one big union' in the industry, whatever form it ultimately takes" (27 May 1960, 1). In June, Guild leaders held meetings with the International Printing Pressmen and Assistants Union, "the first between the officers of the two unions since the formation of the Guild" (*Guild Reporter*, 27 May 1960, 1).

Talk of "one big union" was a key theme at the Guild's 1960 convention in Chicago. The convention endorsed a report from the union's international executive board recommending that Guild officers pursue unity talks with the other unions and report to the convention in a year. The report also urged Guild locals to work for solidarity with other unions at the local level and to participate to the fullest possible extent in interunion councils, allied printing trades councils, and city and state bodies. It described that year's unity discussions and the growth of interunion cooperation as signs of "dramatic progress" toward achieving one of the Guild's constitutional purposes, "to promote industrial unionism in the newspaper industry" (*Guild Reporter*, 15 July 1960, 1).

The ITU's Elmer Brown, invited to speak at the Guild convention, stressed that unity was necessary to survival. Given the growing power of the corporations that owned the newspapers, he said, "we are down to the alternative of amalgamation or annihilation" (*Guild Reporter*, 15 July 1960, 3). Brown conceded that the unions themselves had to share some of the responsibility for their current difficulties: "These separate unions have failed to unite for the common benefit of all; each has tried to advance its own interests, too frequently with little or no regard for sister organizations." The solution, however, was clear: "One strong organization of employees in the industry can fight off the attacks upon our free, democratic organizations more effectively than can the several crafts, trades and associations making up the printing trades unions" (*Guild Reporter*, 15 July 1960, 3).

Farson told convention delegates that he planned to propose the creation of a working committee of all the unions to draw up a blueprint for a single, unified organization. He recalled that at the previous year's convention in New York, where Big Six's Barrett issued his own call for unity, he had expressed doubts about whether genuine interunion cooperation could be achieved soon at the international level. The situation had changed, however: "Today, the international officers of each of the craft unions have committed themselves to work for all possible unity among the unions. . . . I can assure you they are sincere, and mean what they say." Farson attributed the change of heart to a number of factors, including the Portland strike, developments in printing technology and new leadership in some of the unions.

> But above all there is the realization, so dramatically underscored by Portland, that in the year 1960 the unions in the newspaper industry can no longer afford to go their own separate ways, unthinking and alone. We know now—all of us— that our own self-interest demands unity, and until there was that realization, there could be no unity. (*Guild Reporter*, 15 July 1960, 3)

When the ITU held its annual convention later that summer, it returned the favor the Guild had shown its president by inviting Guild president Arthur Rosenstock, a *New York Times* librarian, to speak. Like Brown at the Guild convention, Rosenstock presented unity as an idea whose time had come. "In the year 1960 the unions in our industry can no longer afford to go their separate ways," he said, adding that the newspaper business was not unique in this respect. "Everywhere management is pooling its resources to fight labor. In turn, unions everywhere are concentrating their forces, as they must" (*Guild Reporter*, 26 August 1960, 5).

But while Rosenstock enthusiastically endorsed the idea of "one big union," he characterized the phrase as "a symbol of unity, not a blueprint." He outlined the same plan to the ITU as Farson had to the Guild: the creation of an interunion committee to draw up that blueprint. He also noted that the ITU's Brown had come up with the idea of an amalgamated union in which each of the formerly independent unions would become a department of the bigger union, ultimately merging into functional divisions corresponding to divisions within the industry. Said Rosenstock, "That proposal merits close study of all the unions in the industry. It parallels in many ways our own thinking" (*Guild Reporter*, 26 August 1960, 5).

If Rosenstock's comments to the ITU were optimistic about unity, Brown's were even more so. "Merger of the newspaper unions could best be described as a spontaneous reaction by the leaders of the various crafts," he told the convention. "But it has been pressured by the membership itself." Brown predicted that unity would be a reality within five years (*Guild Reporter*, 9 September 1960, 1).

He was wrong.

Seven unions initially participated in formal talks on unity: the Guild, the ITU, the pressmen, the photoengravers, the stereotypers and electrotypers, the bookbinders, and the lithographers. Over the next year, they were joined by the United Papermakers and Paperworkers and the International Plate Printers, Die Stampers, and Engravers Union, bringing the total to nine. The unions appointed an interunion working committee to draft a plan for merger. Though it met a half-dozen times in 1961 and 1962, it failed to produce a working draft on consolidation. Indeed, only the ITU came up with a written proposal to circulate among committee members. By the end of 1962, the talk of "one big union" had died down.

None of the participants in the talks ever offered a public explanation of exactly why the movement failed (Walsh 1985, 51). The *Guild Reporter* simply stopped reporting on it. It seems clear, however, that the unions were divided on how closely connected they wanted to be to each other, and fearful that they would give up more than they would gain in a merger. Some unions, including the Guild, feared a loss of identity in a merger with the larger and more numerous craft unions. In addition, several unions found the ITU's attitude during the unity talks to be patronizing. Walsh quotes the Guild's Farson as saying in a later interview that the ITU president repeatedly used the phrase "come on home" in promoting the idea of unity (55). This phrase was a reminder of the ITU's historic position as the parent of printing unions, but it also put the other unions in the role of runaways or disobedient offspring, who were now being invited to return to the parental home—and, possibly, to parental control. For unions who had found it necessary to break away from the ITU, the idea of "coming home" to the ITU was far from reassuring. Walsh quotes the president of the pressmen's union, Anthony DeAndrade, to the effect that, one by one and for different reasons, the unions stopped attending the meetings of the interunion working committee. His union, for example, refused to sit at the same table as the lithographers, whom the pressmen accused of raiding (51). The photoengravers, bookbinders, and stereotypers decided they favored a federation of printing unions, not a merger, and lost interest in the unity talks (51). In less than two years, the drive toward "one big union" had not only stalled; it had broken down.

One significant merger did, however, result from the talks of the early 1960s. In 1964, the 40,000-member Amalgamated Lithographers of America merged with the 20,000-member International Photoengravers Union to become the Lithographers and Photoengravers International Union (*Guild Reporter*, 24 January 1964, 2).

DEFINING MERGERS

The failed unity drive of the early 1960s struck notes the unions would play again and again in subsequent decades. Changing technology, especially changes that eliminated workers or forced unions to compete over jurisdiction, would prompt all unions at one time or another to question their security. The combination of technological change and concerns about growing corporate power made it inevitable that the unions would seek out each other as allies or even partners. At the same time, though, the unions had to think seriously about whether unity was available for a price they were willing to pay.

Clearly, one critical problem in the failed 1960–1962 merger talks was a lack of agreement on what "one big union" actually meant. The literature on labor union mergers shows that there are, in fact, several forms of unity. Chaison (1986) identifies three types of mergers: absorption, in which a larger union takes over a smaller one; amalgamation, in which two or more unions of roughly equal power join forces; and affiliation, in which the unions unite but maintain their own identity. Other scholars have identified other forms—commensalistic mergers, in which the merging partners are unions that organize the same kinds of workers; symbiotic mergers, in which unions represent workers that are technically interdependent; mergers for scale, in which the work the members do has no apparent connection, but the merging unions see benefits in expansion (for a discussion of types of mergers see Chitayat 1979 and Walsh 1985.) In 1960–1962, the ITU's Brown saw "one big union" as an amalgamated union divided into departments. Other unions envisioned a federation—in other words, an alliance rather than an organic merger. The Guild's Farson was even more vague: for him "one big union" was mainly a metaphor, a symbol of a desired end rather than a detailed plan.

Another reason for the failure was that a multiunion merger, whatever form it might take, was simply too ambitious an idea. As the unions were learning, a merger between two unions is a substantial undertaking. One simultaneously involving seven or nine unions was next to impossible.

But like the leaders of many other unions,[5] the heads of unions in the newspaper business had a good sense of why mergers were worth pursuing. In a study of trade union mergers in Canada, Coady (1976) identifies a number of causes of trade union mergers. These include increasing concentration of corporate ownership, fragmented and decentralized union membership, and continuing technological change. All three threaten union survival. All three applied in the case of the newspaper unions, though they would apply far more strongly in 1970 than in 1960, and in 1990 than in 1970.

Chaison (1986) argues that union mergers occur only when the motivations to merge are greater than the barriers to merge. This sounds almost absurdly simple, but it confronts the reality that merger is a complicated solution to a complex and sometimes contradictory set of problems. Chaison notes the conventional wisdom that mergers are caused by membership decline and financial difficulty. But his data on mergers refute this idea: one in three unions that end up being absorbed by or amalgamated with another union grows prior to merger, and more than one in four of the unions absorbing other union declines in size before merger (45). Like Coady, Chaison sees technological change as one of the most significant motivating factors behind union mergers: "Technological change threatens the employment of union members and thus jeopardizes the survival of the union as a representative institution. Mergers are aimed at absorbing the impact of technological change rather than preventing its introduction or continuation" (47). Other motivating factors include narrow or overlapping jurisdictions (a problem often exacerbated by technological change), a need to increase bargaining power, and protection against raids by other unions. Changes at the level of the employer—such as mergers among companies, reorganizations, or diversifications—may also prompt union mergers (47–52). All of these have been factors in the newspaper union mergers of the last few decades, though the impact of technological change and its jurisdictional consequences were only beginning to be felt in the early 1960s.

Although the participants in the "one big union" talks of the early 1960s believed closer ties would be beneficial, it is clear that the motivations to merge were not strong enough to overcome the barriers. Chaison says possible barriers include internal opposition (which is especially significant if it comes from the leadership of the union), opposition from labor federations, or institutional differences between the merging unions. In 1960–1962, the first factor was clearly at play. Some of the craft unions decided they preferred a federation rather than a merger and dropped out of the interunion unity committee. The third was also critical: there were enormous organizational, structural, and cultural gaps between these unions, including between the Guild and the ITU. Over the next few years, these structural and cultural differences would cast a chill over relations between these two unions that would take many years to thaw.

FROM "ONE BIG UNION" TO "PIGGYBACK UNIONISM"

Though their members worked side by side for the same employers across North America, the Guild and the ITU were very different organizations. The ITU had a long history of organization and a hard-earned and enviable tradition of solidarity. The Guild teetered uncomfortably on the cusp of professionalism and trade unionism. As Jacobson notes,

> At one time it was believed that newspaper writers were a working group not organizable into a trade union, especially one using orthodox labor union tactics and procedures. This belief was based on the notion that news reporting was not a vocation but a profession—and a trade union of professionals would be an anomaly. (1960, 3)

Though the Guild's membership had been divided since the late 1930s between editorial workers and those in the various business offices, Guild culture has traditionally been dominated by journalists: independent, competitive people who are wary of rules, suspicious of trade unions, and likely to see themselves as intellectuals rather than as members of the working class.[6] The ITU, by contrast, took pride in representing the elite of the working class, and saw itself as custodian of the craft.

A second area of difference had to do with the importance of a union card. Membership in the Guild was not necessarily a requirement of work. Rather, it was often a function of whether a reporter joined a newsroom that had already been organized. Membership wasn't necessarily portable either. Reporters could move from a Guild newspaper to non-Guild newspaper, and back again. The ITU, by contrast, was built on a monopoly on craft, a closed shop, a rigid set of ITU laws, and a "traveling-card" system allowing members who moved from place to place—even across national borders—to retain their union status. ITU members owed their jobs as much to their union as to their employer, a situation that reinforced the power of the union and the loyalty of the membership.

There were other differences as well. The two unions had, for a time, belonged to rival labor federations: the Guild to the CIO, the ITU to the AFL. They had different organizational structures, different ways of dealing with members, different dues structures, and different political and electoral systems.[7] Crucially, they had different attitudes about how to react to new technology and to each other's strikes—differences that became increasingly problematic in the years after the unity drive broke down. Though there had been exceptions, the Guild's tradition was to refuse to cross picket lines set up by other newspaper unions. This made sense from both a fraternal and a strategic point of view, given that the Guild lacked the level of workplace control enjoyed by the craft unions. A Guild strike simply did not pose the same kind of threat to the publisher as a strike by the ITU, which could almost certainly shut down a paper. The Guild hoped that if it supported, say, a pressmen's strike, the pressmen would be more likely to support a Guild strike. The ITU's bylaws, by contrast, required that once a contract was signed, the members had to strictly observe it—and that meant crossing another union's picket line.

During the early 1960s, a few high-profile strikes in Canada and the United States put enormous stress on the relationship between the ITU and the Guild. In Toronto, the ITU walked off the job at three newspapers—the *Telegram*, *Star*, and *The Globe and Mail*—on 9 July 1964, in a disastrous strike that eventually cost the union its certification at the papers. Five members of the Guild walked out with the compositors, and were soon joined by six more. By the end of September, forty-two Guild members were refusing to cross the line (Zerker 1982, 281). This was but a small proportion of the membership, and not enough to affect production. Some of the other unions were even less supportive. The pressmen and stereotypers stood by their contracts and showed up for work, though many found the act of passing their colleagues on the picket lines "shameful and embarrassing" (281). The photoengravers, who were engaged in a jurisdictional dispute with the ITU at the time, signed a new four-year contract just days after the compositors walked out.

In response to a request from the ITU, the Toronto and District Labour Council approved a motion to encourage its members and all Toronto citizens to boycott the struck newspapers.[8] In a particularly painful display of lack of solidarity among unions in the printing field, the presidents of five Toronto-area locals—the pressmen, photoengravers, paperhandlers, bookbinders, and the Guild—abstained.

In Baltimore, the Guild went on strike for recognition at the Baltimore Sunpapers in April 1965. The printers and drivers initially refused to cross the Guild picket line. But in May, the ITU international advised its Baltimore members that they should live up to the terms of their contract—in essence, ordering them to cross the Guild line and return to work. They did so on 25 May 1965, along with the pressmen, stereotypers, photoengravers, and mailers. The paper resumed publication and the Guild was forced to call off its strike a week later.

The ITU's change of heart was a severe blow to the Guild. ITU president Elmer Brown then went on to rub salt in the wound. His recall notice to the Baltimore local said the printers's obligation to the ITU should "outweigh lesser considerations," the Guild strikers apparently among them. In addition, Brown gave an interview to the *New York Times* in which he accused the Guild of abusing the ITU's good will: "It's a pretty expensive philosophy to support some picket lines," he said. "We have made overtures to other unions to join us in some sort of federation for closer cooperation, but they would rather get on our back and ride. They keep us broke getting things for them" (quoted in the *Guild Reporter*, 28 May 1965, 6). The head of the Guild unit in Baltimore complained that Brown had "played footsie" with Baltimore management. The ITU responded with an attack in the *ITU Review* newsletter complaining that other unions were dissipating "our members, our funds, and our prestige . . . by piggyback unionism," and accusing the Guild in particular of strike-breaking or raiding in close to a dozen cities, including Toronto and Portland (quoted in Walsh 1985, 58). The accusation of "piggyback unionism" was particularly hurtful: the phrase suggested not only that the Guild was a burden on the ITU, but that the latter was the stronger player—strong enough to carry freeloaders. The phrase represented a 180-degree turnaround from the talk of unity and joint action heard from ITU leaders in previous years.

A few weeks later, the Guild's international executive board released a lengthy statement analyzing the state of relations with the ITU. Though it was tough on the printers, suggesting the union leadership's "bitter attack on the Guild" in the *ITU Review* sought "to justify its actions in Baltimore by calling attention to Guild actions in Toronto and elsewhere," it conceded that both unions had made mistakes.

> In the year since our last convention, unions in the newspaper industry have learned the high price they must inevitably pay for failing to respect each other's picket lines. This has been demonstrated as rarely before in our history. . . . Make no mistake about it. We were wrong in Toronto. The ITU was wrong in Albany and Baltimore. These are facts of life that our two organizations must face. But three wrongs don't make a right. There must be no more Torontos, Albanys and Baltimores. Only the publishers benefit. Instead there must be the kind of co-operation at both the local and international levels that the Guild and the ITU and other newspaper unions have repeatedly endorsed but all too often have failed to achieve. (*Guild Reporter*, 30 July 1965, 12)[9]

An accompanying article analyzing the specific details of the ITU's charges reacted vigorously to a section of the ITU statement that read, "Has the Guild ever aided the ITU or an ITU local in a struggle for a contract or to win a strike? The answer is simply one word—NO." The *Guild Reporter* replied, "The correct answer, of course, is YES, and often" (*Guild Reporter*, 30 July 1965, 13).

The statement concluded with a call for a meeting between the leaders of the two unions to clear the air. The ITU agreed, and the two unions began talks aimed at working out a reconciliation. These ended at an impasse. Walsh writes that the ITU proposed that the Guild affiliate with it. The Guild would pay the ITU one dollar per month per member, but would have no voting privileges. This was unacceptable to the Guild. It countered with a proposal for a joint council and equal partnership with the ITU, an offer unacceptable to the ITU (Walsh 1985, 59–60). Neither side was willing to budge. While locals of the two unions would continue to work side by side in newspapers, sometimes in harmony and sometimes not, almost ten years would pass before the two unions would resume formal talks aimed at uniting the Guild and the ITU.

DEALING WITH NEW TECHNOLOGY

One of the critical factors in the bad blood between the newspaper unions in the late 1960s and 1970s was changing technology, which affected the ITU far more quickly and adversely than it did the Guild. Both unions saw automation and the computer as threats to their members. But the Guild tended to be more open to negotiation on new technology, and more willing to accommodate. The ITU, by contrast, tended to dig in its heels, at times quite aggressively, using jurisdictional claims to shore up its position.

When it came to tracking new technology, Guild members reaped substantial benefits from their in-house newspaper. The *Guild Reporter* of the early 1960s devoted an enormous amount of space to stories reporting on which newspapers were installing computers—and where—and warning about the dangers of automation to Guild members and other newspaper workers. For example, a lengthy feature published on 21 June 1963 surveyed the state of the technology across the United States and Canada: "Automation, a year ago something for automobile and railroad unions to worry about, is establishing a rapidly growing bridgehead on Guild newspapers. Starting, in most cases, in the business office, it is moving inexorably toward processes performed by the editorial and advertising department" (4). The article reported that the *Washington Post* was about to install a computer that would hyphenate and justify classified ads and editorial copy, "an operation that increases productivity by an estimated 40 percent." This meant the *Post* would become the first Guild paper with a computer for editorial and advertising copy. At the non-Guild *Los Angeles Times*, reporters were punching tape to drive composing machines as they typed their copy. At the *Toronto Star*, computers would soon take on the billing of ad accounts on a newspaper with the second largest classified ad volume in the world. The paper planned to computerize circulation billing and accounts payable a bit later. The article said the Toronto Guild had negotiated contract protection against staff reductions resulting from automation, including retraining, relocation procedures, and augmented severance pay. These safeguards had not come into play yet, because the computer had brought about an initial staff increase rather than a reduction. "Eventually," though, "as the computer takes over an increasing burden, the staff will shrink. But this reduction . . . will be spread over two to four years and is expected to be by attrition rather than layoff." At *The Globe and Mail*, where the business office was not covered by the Guild, seven clerical employees were laid off when a computer moved in. At the *Chicago Sun-Times*, electronic photocomposition machines, known as photons, had been installed to set and make up ads. "While they do not yet affect editorial operations, a management official has told the Guild they are adaptable to editorial use and may one day result in a reduction in copy readers," the *Guild Reporter* article said. At the *San Francisco Chronicle*, a machine called a Univac would handle billing and accounts, undertake sales analysis, made credit checks, compute newsprint consumption, and control automatic purchase orders, among other functions. Other uses, including an automated clipping library (known in the newspaper business as a morgue), were expected to develop. At The Associated Press, nineteen stock-market tabulators were laid off when a computer was installed. Nine were displaced in a similar manner at United Press International (*Guild Reporter*, 21 June 1963, 4).[10]

This article and the many others like it that appeared in the pages of the union's newspaper served two functions. The first was an informing function—simply to make sure members got information about what was happening in newspaper shops across Canada and the United States. The second was an educational function, an attempt to make connections between equipment that was being installed here and there and what the union saw as the implied agenda of the publishers, individually and collectively. To that end, the union invited technology expert John Diebold, president of the Diebold Group, to talk about automation at its 1963 convention.[11] He sketched out the likelihood that within a few years, editors would do most of their work electronically, dummying pages on a computer screen, sizing headlines, and cropping pictures to fit a layout.

> The whole editorial process will use information retrieval machines for the morgue—it will have wire services coming in, reporters typing stories into the system, but a constant availability of the information at any desk in the editorial office, availability of any of the information so you can look at what the

sports pages look like as of this moment, and you can dial it in and see, if you want to determine the relationship of one story to another. (*Proceedings* 1963, 146)

This means that editors would not have to commit pages to type until the very last minute, he said. In the short term, the computers would drive linotype machines; but "not too far off from now," type would go "directly to engraving plates for use on the press" (164).

Diebold warned that these technological developments were inevitable, which meant that both the Guild and the publishers had to think seriously, and soon, about how to handle them. In a question-and-answer session after his talk, Diebold said most unions had taken too narrow a view of technological change.

> I think the unions by and large have a very defeating attitude in this, in that unions have looked at this as a question of eliminating jobs. The social changes can be much greater. . . . You are totally changing the way in which we do work and the role of work in society, and the role of a union is going to change as a result . . . All kinds of basic new questions are raised about the rights of the individual, and the unions are not asking them and ought to be. They would be a much more vital part of the society if they did. (*Proceedings* 1963, 152)

Diebold recommended that unions engage in a continuing dialogue with management on issues like retraining and how to revise organizational structures to cope with technological changes that blur craft lines. Craft lines, he added, "are going to cause more and more and more trouble in the future. . . . They are going to be more and more artificial" (154).

While some convention delegates made light of Diebold's comments—one asked him, "Do you think there is a possibility the President of the American Newspaper Guild may some day be a machine?" (153)—others in the union were working to add language to the Guild model contract on technological change.[12] This included clauses forbidding dismissals as a result of technological change, and requiring employers to give the Guild six months' notice on new equipment that would result in job changes. The changes were aimed at solidifying the Guild's position with employers. As James White, speaking for the collective bargaining committee, told the annual convention the next year,

> Every Local should insist on language in its contracts protecting the Guild's jurisdiction and assuring jurisdiction over any new work such as is now performed in Guild jurisdiction, or, without raiding any work justifiably the jurisdiction of other unions, jurisdiction over new processes which lend themselves to performance in Guild jurisdiction. (*Proceedings* 1964, 73)

The flurry of Guild activity in the early 1960s on what it called the automation problem was directed at finding an accommodation between technology and the work of its members. The Guild, like the publishers, tended to see computers as multipurpose machines that could be used for writing, editing, billing, and other tasks, not as digital analogues of typesetting machines. Its position on technological change could perhaps best be characterized as cautious, but not overtly hostile. In addition, as the new language on jurisdiction shows, it realized that some changes might in fact benefit the union's membership.

The ITU took a markedly different view. It had encountered overwhelming success seventy years earlier, when its assertion of jurisdiction over the linotype meant shorter hours, higher productivity, and higher pay for a rapidly increasing membership. This time, it hoped for the same result. But the new equipment the newspapers were installing in the 1960s was aimed not at mechanizing various parts of the production, but at collapsing successive stages of the production process.

Zerker says the Toronto branch of the ITU became aware of this in the 1950s, when photocomposition was introduced in commercial print shops. The union's 1955 convention responded by asserting expanded jurisdiction over phototypesetting, which put it in conflict with the pressmen's union and raised fears that the ITU would raid the latter's membership (1982, 243). The pressmen responded by attempting to broaden their own jurisdictional claim into areas the ITU leaders saw as theirs. Zerker notes, "In the nature of that contest, with the dangers of technology undermining all the crafts, neither would be the winner" (244). At the same time, the ITU was engaged in another conflict over phototypesetting, this time with the photoengravers union.

As typesetting machines driven by perforated tape began to appear in newspapers in the 1960s, the ITU took a page out of its own history and set up a computer training program, similar to the linotype training program decades earlier. It also pursued a strategy of "controlled automation," aimed at ensuring that publishers who wanted to introduce new technology had to obtain union approval first (Sleigh 1998, 93). This time, though, the union had to deal with a bewildering and rapidly changing array of machinery, not with a single new process for setting type. Zerker, analyzing contracts signed by the Toronto branch of the ITU, notes that the union tried to be as specific as possible in the jurisdiction section of its contracts. Ultimately, this was a hopeless task: "at the rate that changes were occurring in printing technology, it would have been impossible to foresee and write terms which would cover every eventuality" (251). Near the end of the long negotiations that would eventually lead to the disastrous 1964 Toronto ITU strike, the union tried to claim jurisdiction over computers. This was an extremely sensitive subject: even Big Six, which was then heading toward a 114-day strike that would in the end help kill three of New York's six dailies, "preferred to act with timidity and caution" on the computer question (265).[13] Computers, of course, were multipurpose machines. The publishers in Toronto and elsewhere had no intention of giving jurisdiction over computers to a single union—especially not to a union with a reputation for militance, and most especially not to a union whose members would in all likelihood be the first ones deskilled by the new equipment.

As computerized typesetting spread throughout the newspaper industry in the 1960s and 1970s, ITU membership began to fall and the union searched for strategies to deal with new technology. One was the determined attempt to make or defend jurisdictional claims, which often put it in conflict with other unions as well as management.[14] Another was an effort to negotiate job protection for members, with attrition rather than layoffs as the mechanism for reducing newspaper staffing. In 1972, Pacific Press and its joint council of unions negotiated job guarantees ensuring that no employees would lose their jobs as a direct result of technological change (Pacific Press application, 34). In 1974, the *Washington Post* negotiated a deal with its ITU compositors similar to the one reached at Pacific Press two years earlier (Sleigh 1998, 92). Also in 1974, Big Six negotiated an eleven-year agreement with the *New York Daily News* and *New York Times* that provided a wage increase and lifetime job guarantees for union members displaced by computerization. Labor arbitrator Theodore Kheel described the contract as "a turning point for the entire newspaper industry" (quoted in Sleigh 1998, 93). Sleigh argues, however, that the publishers' apparent generosity was not a sign of weakness, but a recognition that this would be the ITU's last hurrah. The settlement shifted the balance of power in the newspaper unions away from the ITU. The strategy of controlled automation "had fallen to the guarantees of lifetime jobs" (93).

ONE PRETTY BIG UNION?

Though the ITU had fallen on hard times, it was still a union to be reckoned with. In 1975, it had about 72,000 members—down from 94,500 in 1961 and dropping quickly. (The next year, its membership would fall to about 66,000.) Still, it was twice the size of The Newspaper Guild.

Between 1950 and 1970, Guild membership had grown from 23,750 to 32,000 (Kuczun 1970, 257, 305), where it hovered for many years.

The ITU also had a new leader, A. Sandy Bevis, a more accommodating individual than the tough-talking and sometimes arrogant Elmer Brown. A genuine thaw in relations between the unions began in 1974, when Charles A. Perlik Jr., the Guild's first full-time president, invited Bevis, who at the time was the ITU president-elect, to come to the Guild annual conference. Bevis could not make it that year, but asked for a meeting with Perlik, which was held in the fall of 1974. A few months later, the two unions issued a "declaration of principles," a joint statement that stressed cooperation and announced the appointment of a fact-finding task force whose first job was to shape a common collective bargaining policy. The leaders also agreed to an air-tight no-raiding pact. Said Guild president Perlik,

> It is the first time in modern memory that the Guild has signed an agreement with the ITU or with any other union for that matter. Aside from the objectives it seeks, this agreement is one more signal that the dark suspicion, the bitterness and the rancor that have troubled our relationship in the past are rapidly falling away. (*Guild Reporter*, 14 February 1975, 1)[15]

That year, Bevis became the first ITU president to speak to a Guild convention since 1960 (*Guild Reporter*, 25 July 1975, 1). He told delegates that each union had to face the reality that they were increasingly working in what had traditionally been the other's territory.

> Our spheres of interest and influence continue to tighten and to overlap, so the areas of confrontation between our two unions will continue to grow. We are literally being forced by the changes in our industry into a position where we must make a decision—a choice.... [W]e can decide to fight each other tooth and nail for every new member or for every new electronic device—wearing ourselves out, depleting our treasuries and destroying our effectiveness as labor unions—or we can make an intelligent choice to join forces and work together for the benefit of our two great unions and for the increased welfare of all those people working in the printing and publishing industry who look to us for help and leadership. (*Proceedings* 1975, 36)

For Bevis, the solution was simple: it was time for the two unions to merge. Guild members were less enthusiastic about the idea. Indeed, president Perlik seemed to tap into that anxiety by presenting a vision of bottom-up merger to the connection delegates: "Merger will come when, and only when, the grass roots of our two unions want it and want it badly" (*Guild Reporter*, 25 July 1975, 1).

At the 1976 Guild convention, Perlik said the joint task force set up the previous year would look at the constitutions, policies, and practices of the two unions, with an eye to dovetailing them where possible. Bevis, again invited to speak, pushed for more, asking for a merger agreement within the year. He made the same appeal at the 1977 convention:

> The ITU can't go it alone in this age of technology, conglomerate ownership, one-newspaper towns and all of the forces that are aligned against us, and we think you feel the same way—you can't go it alone or you can't make the progress you should make and have the protection you must have in order to survive as a viable trade union organization. (*Guild Reporter*, 15 July 1977, 4)

This time, the Guild agreed to pursue a merger seriously. In 1977, each union appointed a high-profile merger committee, which began holding joint meetings that fall. Meanwhile, the ITU demonstrated that it could act on mergers, not just talk about them, by signing a merger agreement with the International Mailers Union,[16] which had split from the ITU in the 1940s.

By the end of the year, both unions felt that many problems were still to be resolved, but progress had been made. The *Guild Reporter* published an eight-part look at the ITU, aimed at making sure members knew as much as possible about their potential partner. The ITU elected a new president, Joe Bingel, in 1978. Like Bevis, he supported a merger with the Guild. The merger committee met on and off in 1978, 1979, and 1980, and reported progress on some issues like the officer structure of the new union. But the pace was slow. In 1981 the unions committed themselves to reaching a deal in time for their annual conventions that year. In April, when it became clear that this would not happen, the merger talks collapsed. Walsh writes that timing was not the real issue: "The truth was that the two sides weren't getting anywhere. As their joint statement put it, discussions would cease 'until new and fresh looks and approaches can be brought to bear on our unresolved problems'" (Walsh 1985, 124). At the ITU convention that summer, the union held a referendum on a merger timetable, calling for third-party assistance, if needed, to get the job done. It passed and the talks resumed.

By the fall of 1982, four and one-half years after the first joint meeting in 1977, the two sides had a deal. They would create the Media Employees' International Union, ITU/TNG, a new body with an organization and structure that drew on elements from both unions. The union would have an elected, lay governing board, a feature from the Guild's structure, and an elected board of full-time union officers, an ITU feature. For the first four years, the four top jobs would be evenly divided between ITU and Guild executives. The first general president would be from the ITU; the second from the Guild. After that, the president would be elected by the full membership. Key features of the merged union included the use of union-wide collective bargaining goals, a $10 million defense fund (combining the assets of the two unions), a policy of respecting picket lines, and the use of simple majority votes for questions before international bodies. Guild dues would eventually rise to ITU levels. The union would be headquartered in Colorado Springs, home of the ITU, but would have satellite offices in Washington, the home of the Guild, and in Canada. Locals of the two unions would not be forced to merge, but could do so if they wished (*Guild Reporter*, 21 September 1982, 1).

The entire Guild leadership supported the deal, and a ratification convention was set for early 1983. Support was less solid at the ITU: although a majority of the five-member executive liked the deal, there were some critics. One of these was the ITU secretary-treasurer, Thomas Kopek, who used his column in the union's monthly *Typographical Journal* magazine to pick away at the deal. In August, he wrote that the most critical question to ask in any merger is, "Will merger provide increased work opportunities for the typographical union members?" (*Typographical Journal*, August 1982, 4). In September, he mused on a speech the president of the Communications Workers of America, Glenn Watts, gave to the ITU convention that year:

> Although President Watts was careful to avoid an appearance of meddling in our internal affairs, I could not help wondering why we have been engaged for years in attempting to put together a clutch of relatively small unions rather than make the quantum leap into an existing large one. If it is true that we are entering an age where only those who have the heavy artillery will survive, and I believe that to be the case, then we should look to opening talks with one of the truly large internationals and protect our people. (*Typographical Journal*, September 1982, 4)

In October, he again raised the possibility of a merger with the CWA, and attacked the specifics of the Guild merger:

> The question is not: merger. The question is: *This* merger. . . . Now we have a merger document allying us with a smaller union, having fewer assets but with more problems than our own. . . . Analyze the essential elements and you must conclude we will have been taken over "lock, stock and barrel" by a 27,000 member union rather than by one of 650,000 members." (*Typographical Journal*, October 1982, 4)

In December, Kopek made his opposition brutally clear: "Simply put, the Guild moves into our home, runs the show and pays less rent" (*Typographical Journal*, December 1982, 4). That same month, Robert McMichen, the first vice-president of the ITU, also came out against the deal, writing in his *Typographical Journal* column that the merger agreement "has been proven to be unsound, unworkable and therefore is unacceptable" (5).

Things really began unraveling in December, when Kopeck gave the Guild new figures that reduced the ITU's estimated membership by between 15 and 20 percent. This raised questions about whether the new union would be financially viable. There were also disagreements over projections of operating costs for the new union. The uncertainty prompted the Guild to postpone its merger ratification convention and send the deal back to the drawing board (*Guild Reporter*, 20 December 1982, 1).

The merger committee came up with a revised agreement that modified the dues structure slightly in favor of the ITU, revised the estimated membership, and changed the name of the new union to the Media Workers International Union, ITU/TNG. The Guild's twelve-member special merger committee approved the deal unanimously in early April, and the international executive board did the same in a roll-call vote on April 20. The ITU's twelve-member special merger committee gave what the *Guild Reporter* called "near-unanimous" approval (*Guild Reporter*, 22 April 1983, 1). McMichen, writing for his own ITU members, claimed that 25 percent of ITU's merger committee refused to endorse the revised agreement (*Typographical Journal*, May 1983, 5). At the Guild convention that July, delegates approved it by a margin of 96 percent. A referendum was scheduled for September.

The deal fell apart, finally and forever, at the ITU convention in San Francisco that August. The five-member ITU executive committee went into the convention divided three-two over the deal: president Bingel and vice-presidents Allan Heritage and Robert Wartinger supported it; treasurer Kopeck and vice-president McMichen opposed it. The ITU invited the leadership of the Guild to attend the convention, and the merger proponents hoped their enthusiasm would help seal the deal. But Bingel also invited someone else to speak: Jackie Presser, president of the renegade International Brotherhood of Teamsters. Bingel told delegates that three weeks before the convention, he had a meeting with Presser, during which "we identified common ground of our two great unions, and discussed some mutual objectives."[17]

While Guild leaders sat in the audience, the Teamsters leader told the

ITU delegates they would be better off becoming part of "the Teamster family" rather than merging with the Guild (23c).

> I am not opposed to the Guild. I hope that someday the Guild is part of the International Brotherhood of Teamsters. I do not say that to be facetious. . . . But when you get down to the bottom line, the Guild looks to the Teamsters and to the rest of the labor organizations when they go to the bargaining table and I do not think there is a union in this room that cannot tell you or would not say that we of the Teamsters are strong. (24c)

Presser added that after he was invited to speak, he did a survey of print industry organization and was surprised by the number of unorganized printing shops and newspapers across the country. The Teamsters want to organize them, he said, and add them to the list of 150 or so printing companies with Teamsters contracts. To make matters more complicated, the head of the Big Six local, Bertram Powers, told the convention that he no longer supported the Guild–ITU merger either. He said the ITU and the Guild should both negotiate a three-way merger with the newly formed Graphics Communication International Union, or GCIU (95c).[18]

On a 122–86 standing vote, convention delegates rejected the Guild merger (*Guild Reporter*, 15 August 1983, 1). That was that. The presidents of both unions announced that the deal was null and void. There would be no referenda, and no merger.

In her analysis of why the merger failed, Walsh identifies more than a dozen obstacles to merger, though most are interconnected (1985, 180–85). It seems clear that the root causes of the failure were an uneven commitment to the merger over the nine years of talks, and a breakdown of unity within the ITU executive. As Walsh points out, the shape of the merger changed over the years it was being negotiated. At the beginning, it looked as though the larger and more powerful ITU would absorb the Guild. Guild concerns about this possibility go a long way toward explaining why it took two years for the talks to get started. But as the talks wore on, the Guild's membership base remained relatively stable and the ITU's dropped.[19] An ITU absorption of the Guild began to look less and less likely, and by 1980 the merger looked more like a union of equals. But this raised a new set of problems: if neither was absorbing the other, then the merger document had to come up with a way of genuinely reconciling two very different partners. Linda Foley, who became president of the Guild in 1995 as it merged with the Communications Workers of America, says it was extraordinarily difficult for the Guild and ITU to work out an agreement by which they would share power. After all, she notes, these unions had worked together in newspaper plants for years, and had not always got along: "When you get into a power-sharing arrangement, then it becomes a very delicate balance. And that's ultimately what threw it over, I think" (Foley 1998).

By the end, the union fearing absorption was the ITU. Once the most powerful of the newspaper unions, it had been battered by new technology that deskilled its members. It wanted a partner, but feared the loss of its identity.

James Cesnik, editor of the *Guild Reporter*, suggested in a bylined post-convention analysis that some specific points in the merger were hard for the ITU to bear. These included an end to dues-based support for the ITU home for retired printers; an end to the $500 ITU mortuary benefit; changes in the level of strike payments; and a dues structure that would see former Guild members paying lower dues for a time than former ITU members (*Guild Reporter*, 26 August 1983, 1, 4–5). Certainly, Jackie Presser of the Teamsters tapped into ITU fears on these points in his speech to the convention. The Teamsters, he said, "do not want to sell your property . . . do not want to close your training centres . . . do not want to deny your pensioners." He promised that if the ITU joined his union, "we will give you a national division. You will be recognized as the ITU under our banner" (quoted in *Guild Reporter*, 26 August 1983, 5).

Walsh suggests that part of the ITU's reluctance stemmed from a longing for the past, when it was "the colossus of newspaper unions," and an unwillingness to confront the present: "It yielded grudgingly and gradually to a shift from craft to an industrial union. But to the majority of members, as evidenced by their remarks at conventions, it was still a craft union in an industrial union age" (1985, 180). Reluctance at the grassroots level was reflected in an increasingly bitter division among its leadership. After the convention, vice-president Bob McMichen, who opposed the Guild merger but favored making a deal with the GCIU, announced that he would run for president that fall against Joe Bingel. Bingel, faced with an executive committee that not only helped kill the Guild deal but was after his job, decided in September 1983 to open immediate talks with the Teamsters.

A PARTNER FOR THE ITU

This move launched the ITU on the most turbulent period of its long history. In the executive committee elections that fall, McMichen drew more votes than Bingel. But Bingel contested the election and remained in office during the appeal. He wanted to continue talking to the Teamsters while the appeal was decided. McMichen fought bitterly against this and sought to open talks with the GCIU. Bingel's ITU faction signed a merger agreement with the Teamsters in March 1984, before the leadership issue was settled (*Typographical Journal*, April 1984, 3). Over the next couple of years, factions within the union tore at each other over the merits of an alliance with the Teamsters. The U.S. Department of Labor got involved, as did the AFL-CIO. An injunction prevented executive members from discussing the Teamsters merger in the ITU's magazine, the *Typographical Journal*,[20] or from setting up a referendum on merger with the Teamsters, until the makeup of the executive council was decided (*Guild Reporter*, 14 September 1984, 4).

McMichen and the anti-Teamster faction eventually won control of the executive in a rerun election supervised by the U.S. Department of Labor. At their 1984 convention, the ITU delegates directed the leadership to reach a merger agreement with the GCIU or another AFL-CIO union by January 1985, or submit the Teamsters proposal to the membership for a vote.

Unlike the Guild negotiations which dragged on for years, the GCIU and ITU reached a deal in near-record time. Like the failed Guild merger, it was an agreement for an organic merger—this time into a union of printing crafts workers with more than 200,000 working members (*Guild Reporter*, 22 March 1985, 1). And like the ITU–Guild merger, it fell apart before a pair of simultaneous 10 April referenda could be held. This time, it wasn't the ITU that pulled out but the GCIU. The GCIU board voted in February to send the merger proposal to referendum, even though it had some questions about the deal. It set up a special meeting on 12 March to decide whether it would recommend that its members endorse the proposal. The board decided at that meeting against recommending approval. The union's secretary-treasurer explained that the union had felt rushed by the deadline set by the ITU convention for conclusion of a merger proposal. "A certain number of important operational, legal and financial matters were not fully clarified" (*Guild Reporter*, 22 March 1985, 1). Almost immediately after the referenda were cancelled, Jackie Presser of the Teamsters was back on the scene, declaring his determination to seek a membership vote on a Teamster–ITU merger.

Leaders of the ITU offered a range of explanations for the failure of the GCIU deal. Those who favored the merger claimed that the deal was sabotaged by the Teamsters and their supporters within the ITU. According to president Bob McMichen,

When unions within the same industry attempt to work out mergers that would strengthen their members, the Teamster leaders do what they can to bust up the talks, then circle around like buzzards and sharks, moving in to rip off some flesh. That's exactly what happened in the ITU/GCIU talks. (*Typographical Journal*, March 1985, 3)

Second vice-president Bill J. Austin offered his own analysis of why the GCIU board rejected the merger:

> I've got some ideas on the subject. They include the incredible amount of misinformation and pressures put on the board members by the Teamsters and their ITU agents; the feeling by some board members that the ITU was getting the better part of the deal in the agreement; unresolved internal GCIU politics; concern they'd be buying a peck of trouble from the Teamsters if they followed through. (*Typographical Journal*, March 1985, 6)

Kopeck, a leader of the pro-Teamster faction, argued that the membership should have the right to choose between two offers representing two different philosophies.

> One road (GCIU) leads to organic merger, thus ending the ITU as an international union. . . . The other road (IBT [Teamsters]) places the ITU under the wing of the Teamsters as an autonomous division to be known as International Typographical Union. There are those who sincerely favor one path over the other and they deserve the right to make a choice. (*Typographical Journal*, March 1985, 4)

With the GCIU out of the running, the Teamsters urged the ITU to forge ahead with a referendum on its deal. But by then, much of the enthusiasm for the Teamsters merger had waned. The big attraction of the Teamsters had been size and power: the union had more than a million members, including truck drivers in the newspaper business, and a reputation for ferocity that some ITU leaders hoped would help preserve the ITU. By the mid-1980s, these attractions no longer compensated for some less attractive features of the union. The Teamsters were still outside the AFL-CIO.[21] A number of Teamster leaders had been convicted in the 1970s and 1980s of irregularities in handling pension funds. One union president, James Hoffa, had disappeared in 1975 and was believed to have been murdered. In April 1985, just as the ITU was looking seriously at the Teamsters, Teamster president Jackie Presser pleaded the Fifth Amendment fifteen times when testifying before the President's Commission on Organized Crime.[22] In the spring of 1985, the three anti-Teamster members of the ITU executive wrote joint columns for the

Typographical Journal offering a close analysis of the Teamster constitution. They concluded that the promise to the ITU of an "autonomous division" had far less substance than it seemed. They warned that the supposed clout of the Teamsters was not supported by its organizing record, characterizing the union as "a neighborhood bully with a good public relations man" (*Typographical Journal*, May 1985, 3, 6). It was clear that the Teamsters' attempts to undermine the GCIU deal had alienated many. And there were fears of Teamster raiding of ITU staff and locals.

The referendum on the Teamster merger went ahead in the summer of 1985. It was defeated by a margin of two to one (*Typographical Journal*, October 1985, 3). This sent the ITU back to the GCIU for one last effort at making a deal. Again, the GCIU general board was unwilling to rush to meet a deadline set by the ITU (*Typographical Journal*, May 1986, 3).

In July 1986, two other unions visited ITU headquarters to talk about a merger: the Communications Workers of America and the International Association of Machinists. According to Morton Bahr, president of the CWA, the idea of courting the ITU did not come from the CWA itself but from a higher source. Bahr said in an interview,

> I received a call from the then-president of the AFL-CIO, Lane Kirkland, and he asked me if I'd come down to see him. He said, "I need you to take the International Typographical Union into the CWA because if you don't do it, the Teamsters (who were not in the AFL-CIO at the time), will be successful in raiding them." My gut reaction was, "Why in the world would I want the ITU?" . . . He said, "There are a group of unions in the broad media and entertainment industries"—remember, this is 1985—"who should be merged. Some have tried to merge with each other and have not been successful, but they will ultimately merge under somebody else's umbrella, and that umbrella should be the CWA." (Bahr 2001)

Bahr complied with the request.

The CWA arrived at ITU headquarters on 3 July with an outline of a merger in hand. ITU officials visited the CWA in Washington on 9 July. The Machinists' union president visited the ITU on 17 July and invited ITU leaders to visit his headquarters. Kopek was delighted with the prospect of having two suitors, and claimed credit for the idea, reminding members that in 1982, he had "anticipated further negotiations with both unions" (*Typographical Journal*, August 1986, 4). But within two hours of the departure of the Machinists' union leader, the ITU executive council agreed to send the CWA offer to referendum.

After twelve years of looking for a partner, the ITU finally succeeded. Its 1986 convention committee on merger put forward the deal with the

Communications Workers of America, a union with more than 600,000 members, mainly working in the telephone and telecommunications business. Again, the ITU was split. The deal was approved at convention by the narrowest of margins: 14,266 in favor and 14,042 opposed (*Guild Reporter*, 22 August 1986, 1). But in a referendum later that year, the ITU membership overwhelmingly endorsed the merger, by a margin of more than four to one.

Under the merger, the ITU became the Printing, Publishing, and Media Workers sector of the CWA. It retained a substantial degree of autonomy, including its own bylaws and control of its own funds and pension plan. The Union Printers Home would continue as a separate entity, though efforts would be made to make it self-sustaining. And the traveling-card system, which allowed ITU members freedom to move from employer to employer, would remain intact (*Typographical Journal*, August 1986, 18–22). At a press conference in December 1986, McMichen said that joining a union of CWA's "size and sophistication" meant that his union would be "better equipped to move into the twenty-first century and beyond" (*Guild Reporter*, 19 December 1965, 6). CWA president Bahr said he did not expect to run into jurisdictional disputes with the other unions, adding that he hoped to work with both the Newspaper Guild and the GCIU on joint organizing campaigns for "wall-to-wall" representation.

THE GUILD STANDS ALONE

Between the early 1970s and the mid-1980s, the shape of the unions representing workers in North American newspapers had been radically altered. One by one, printing craft unions found partners. On the "mechanical" side, the photoengravers', lithographers', and bookbinders' unions joined in the early 1970s into the Graphic Arts International Union. Shortly thereafter, the unions representing pressmen and stereotypers created the International Printing and Graphic Communications Union (*Guild Reporter*, 13 January 1978, 1, 4–5). In 1983, these two unions joined to create the GCIU. With a combined membership of 200,000 members, this union became a substantial player in the printing industry.

The ITU's record was considerably more mixed. It had failed at three merger attempts (with the Guild, the Teamsters, and the GCIU) and succeeded at two. One success came early and easily: the absorption of the mailers union in the mid-1970s. The other, with the CWA, occurred after a decade of struggle that sapped the union's vitality and tore its leadership apart.

The rapid set of mergers on the craft union side reflected the rapid pace with which new technology strode through the newspaper plant. During these decades, the installation of computers affected not just typographers but engravers, stereotypers, mailers, and pressroom workers as well. The effect of this new technology was to fold previously discrete steps in the production process into each other. With their memberships increasingly working in each other's traditional areas of jurisdiction, mergers made sense.

The Newspaper Guild found itself in a very different situation. It had been slow to warm to the idea of a merger with the ITU in the mid-1970s. In part, this was due to the fact that the Guild was not facing the same kind of technological imperatives as the craft unions. It was, however, very concerned about what it saw as the growing concentration of power among its employers. By the early 1980s, Guild leaders and members were overwhelmingly in support of an alliance. When the ITU deal fell through, the Guild found itself on its own.

In 1983, a few months after the devastating final collapse of the merger agreement with the ITU, the *Guild Reporter* ran a special section commemorating the fiftieth anniversary of the union. In a column entitled, "And What of the Guild Tomorrow?" president Perlik reminded members that despite the failure of the ITU deal, the considerations that led the two unions to seek unity "are as compelling as ever, if not more so."

> Those considerations, in sum, boil down to the elemental fact that individual unions can no longer afford to go it alone in the news industry against management fortified by increasingly sophisticated technology, increasingly concentrated economic power and increasing aggressiveness at the bargaining table. If we hope to counter that power, we must unite our forces. That means that even if merger with the Typographical Union is no longer just around the corner, it had better not be very far down the road, both for their sake and ours. And it means, of equal importance, steps toward merger with the Graphic Communications International Union.... I don't know, and it doesn't too much matter, in what order those mergers take place—the ITU with the GCIU, for example, and then the Guild with the new union, or the Guild with the GCIU and then the ITU—but I do know that merger, in whatever sequence, is imperative. (*Guild Reporter*, 16 December 1983, A1, A7)

NOTES

1. The *Portland Reporter* began as an eight-page weekly (*Guild Reporter*, 12 February 1960, 1). The International Typographical Union provided most of the mechani-

cal equipment to produce it and owned almost a quarter of its stock. In February 1961, the paper became a daily and stayed in business until September 1964 (Kuczun 1970, 280-81).

2. These included stereotypers, compositors, pressmen, photoengravers, and, somewhat later, paper handlers, who belonged to a separate local of the pressmen's union (*Guild Reporter*, 8 April 1960, 1).

3. The Guild's officers later pointed out that the Portland strike contained an object lesson on the weakness of editorial-only units. Their report to the 1961 convention said, "If the Portland local had been organized over its entire jurisdiction, greater success in halting publication of the struck papers would have resulted. And if the local had contained representatives from circulation, advertising, commercial, etc., production of a strike newspaper unquestionably would have been simplified and expedited" (Officers' report to the twenty-eighth annual American Newspaper Guild convention, quoted in Kuczun 1970, 281).

4. At the time, the job of president was not a full-time position.

5. In a Canadian study, Mawhinney (1989) found that between 1967 and 1987 two out of three small unions, defined as those with 500 members or less, disappeared from the Directory of Labour Organizations in Canada, mainly through mergers.

6. Indeed, Heywood Broun's 1933 column, which helped prompt the organization of the Guild, mocked journalists for being "peculiarly susceptible to such soothing classifications as 'professionals,' 'journalists,' 'members of the fourth estate,' 'gentlemen of the press' and other terms which have completely entranced them by falsely dignifying and glorifying them and their work." Broun wrote that journalists fail to "look upon themselves for what they really are—hacks and white-collar slaves." The reporter's view of unions, he added, goes like this: "Unions? Why, that's all right for dopes like printers, not for smart guys like newspapermen!" He added that meanwhile those "dopes," the printers, earned 30 percent more than journalists, thanks to their union (reprinted in *Guild Reporter*, 16 December 1983, A2).

7. The ITU was known for its unique two-party structure. The Guild had no such formal party system. In addition, the presidency of the ITU had long been a full-time job. The Guild presidency was not.

8. The ITU also wanted the council to ask Toronto citizens to boycott firms that dealt with the newspapers, and to refuse to cross the picket lines. The motion approved by the council dealt with the newspaper boycott only and stopped short of asking its affiliated unions to honor the picket lines (Zerker 1982, 288).

9. In Albany the other newspaper unions, including the ITU, crossed Guild picket lines in the fall of 1964 (*Guild Reporter*, 30 July 1965, 12).

10. The *Guild Reporter* article is accompanied by "before and after" pictures of the AP office. The "before" picture shows at least twenty tabulators sitting at a long table working on the stock charts. The "after" picture, captioned "the machines take over," shows a sterile computer lab with four people tending machines (*Guild Reporter*, 21 June 1963, 4).

11. Diebold was doing research on the use of computers for the owners of the Chicago newspapers. He had given a similar talk earlier in the year to newspaper editors. See *Proceedings of the ANG/TNG Annual Convention*, 1963, [n.p.,] 144-45; hereafter "*Proceedings*."

12. The model contract is the basis for negotiations by Guild locals. Though it has no force in and of itself, it sets standards for what the parent union and its individual locals expect in their dealings with employers.

13. The agreements that eventually ended that strike had the effect of freezing in place the technology then in use at the remaining three New York daily newspapers (Sleigh 1998, 90). This was, however, a temporary solution.

14. Pacific Press reports that in making technological and organizational changes, it encountered "numerous disputes and grievances about jurisdiction and at least seventeen adjudications." See Pacific Press Inc., application for consolidation of bargaining units to B.C. Labour Relations Board, 12 June 1995, 30; hereafter "Pacific Press application." The bulk of these dealt with the ITU.

15. The ITU signed a similar no-raiding pact later that year with the graphic communications union (*Typographical Journal*, July 1975, 3).

16. Mailers take newspapers off the presses, add inserts, and bundle papers for delivery.

17. *Typographical Journal*, September 1983, convention proceedings supplement, 22c. Parenthetical page references follow in the text.

18. This union was the result of a merger between the Graphic Arts International Union and the International Printing and Graphic Communications Union that occurred on 1 July 1983, just a month before the ITU convention. Both partners were themselves the result of a series of mergers. The GAIU was created through a merger among the photoengravers, lithographers, and bookbinders in the early 1970s. The IPGCU was the result of a 1973 merger between the pressmen's and stereotypers' unions.

19. When the two groups began formal talks, they estimated the membership base of their merged union would be 85,000. When the talks ended, this had shrunk to 67,000 (Walsh 1985, 183).

20. The May 1984 edition of the *Typographical Journal* ran with blank pages after columns by the executive were pulled because of the injunction.

21. They were expelled in 1957 for corruption and did not rejoin the national labor federation until 1988.

22. A column by the three anti-Teamster members of the ITU executive noted that among the questions Presser refused to answer were: Is violence an acceptable means by which the Teamsters organization controls its members? Did he know about corruption by Teamster officers? Did he have "ghost" employees on his own Cleveland local union payroll? Did he have knowledge of Teamster ties to organized crime? (*Typographical Journal*, June 1985, 3).

5

A Partner for the Guild

The 1980s were both hard and good times for The Newspaper Guild. The union got bad news on many fronts. Its hard-won merger with the printers' union had been stomped into the dust on the floor of the ITU convention. But the developments that prompted the Guild to seek a merger in the first place—key among them the growing concentration of ownership in the media business—were more worrisome than ever. In 1985, in the wake of a number of high-profile corporate mergers, the international executive board renewed a call for legislation to limit the concentration of newspaper ownership.[1] Guild president Charles Perlik told the 1985 convention,

> What is significant here is not just the continued accumulation of newspapers by chains, or even the continued concentration of newspaper control in a small number of powerful chains. It is the maturation of a long-growing trend toward cross-media conglomerates—mammoth corporations grinding out newspapers, television and radio broadcasts, and now even films—and with it, inevitably, the entry of the financial wheeler-dealers, prepared to compete with the big chains themselves in takeover attempts, hostile or otherwise, of all these tempting media properties. (*Guild Reporter*, 9 August 1985, 7)

On the technology front, the Guild had avoided the kinds of layoffs other newspaper unions experienced in the wake of technological changes that deskilled workers and compressed the production process. But the union was concerned about the health consequences of prolonged computer use. Almost every issue of the *Guild Reporter* from the late 1970s and the 1980s contained some sort of story on the perceived dangers of VDTs, from radiation to eyestrain to repetitive stress injuries.

Politically, the Guild and other unions suffered the consequences of the rise of the new right. U.S. President Ronald Reagan shook organized labor deeply when he broke the 1981 air traffic controllers' strike by bringing in permanent replacement workers. Morton Bahr, president of the Communications Workers of America, says that action "led to a destabilization of collective bargaining" across the country (Bahr 1998, 41). Governments, first in the United States and later in Canada, adopted pro-business economic policies that undermined union security. A number of states rushed toward so-called right-to-work legislation. Overall U.S. union membership declined: by 1986, only 17.1 percent of nonagricultural workers belonged to labor unions, down from 30.4 percent in 1946 (Murray 1995, 164).[2]

But there was some good news too. During the early and mid-1980s, the newspaper industry registered solid gains in circulation and advertising (*Guild Reporter*, 7 June 1985, 1), though the growth did not keep pace with potential readership (Bogart 1991, 36–39). In Canada, overall union density continued to grow, to 37.7 percent in 1986 (Murray 1995, 164). Guild membership, which had dipped below 32,000 in 1982, was on the rebound, heading toward 34,000 in 1985 and almost 36,000 in 1987 (Work Directions Inc. 1993, 22). A healthy economy fueled prosperity among media owners, which in turn meant prosperity for the Guild and its members.

Around 1989, that era of relative comfort came to an end.

Recession hit the North American economy that year—and hit especially hard at its newspapers. The newspapers had been steadily cranking up advertising rates since 1975 in an effort to raise earnings and, ultimately, share prices (Bogart 1991, 53). With the recession, ad lineage—and, as a result, advertising revenue—began to drop precipitously.[3] Readership was declining too, as was household penetration, a measure of circulation. Editors and publishers began to worry about surveys showing that young people were turning to television as a source of news, and that baby boomers were feeling less guilty than they used to about watching television (Boswell 1992, 8). The newspapers responded with hiring freezes, accelerated efforts to restructure production processes, an emphasis on marketing that at times contradicted news judgment, and flashy "relaunches" that, according to John Miller (1998, 9), offered more sizzle than steak. By 1992, even the trade press was wondering about the future of the daily newspaper. The Canadian journalism review *Content* asked in a cover story that spring whether newspapers were "a vanishing breed" (March/April 1992).

It was amid this atmosphere of uncertainty and discomfort that The

Newspaper Guild began to confront not just its own future but the future of the industry in which its members worked. The critical self-examination did not come easily or naturally to the union, though clearly it was time to set a strategic plan. In the end, convergence was the idea that caught the imagination of the leadership, and set the union on a new path.

ONCE BITTEN, TWICE SHY

The Guild had put enormous energy, effort and hope into negotiating the merger with the ITU. It took years of work, and many false starts, to reach the 1983 merger agreement. No one thought the deal was perfect, but from the Guild perspective it was good enough—in part, perhaps, because the Guild knew that time was on its side more than on the ITU's. Nonetheless, the collapse of the deal was a blow, and a humiliating one at that: it happened very much in public, and at the hands of a prospective mate who, in effect, had brought another suitor to the wedding. In the wake of those events, it should come as no surprise that Guild leaders were edgy about the whole idea of merger.

Nonetheless, a significant portion of the membership believed that the circumstances that made the ITU merger make sense—a need to increase bargaining clout, an attempt to counter the growing power of the publishers, a sense that new technology required new approaches to the labor process—still counted. Three years after the collapse of the ITU talks, a Guild poll of members found the membership was split on the issue of merger. Just over 18 percent supported the concept of merger strongly, and another 24 percent were "somewhat" supportive. Eighteen percent felt the idea was "not good at all" and another 11 percent responded that they were "not very much" in favor of a merger. Twenty-eight percent of respondents chose not to answer the question (*Guild Reporter*, 26 November 1986, 6). Asked which union, if any, they would prefer as a merger partner for the Guild, 23 percent of respondents listed the ITU, which was then in the process of joining the CWA. Ten percent favored the Teamsters and 9 percent preferred the Graphic Communications International Union (GCIU), the product of a recent merger among unions in the printing trades. Seven percent listed other unions. "As a group, these other unions had a common characteristic: none have their principal jurisdiction in the newspaper industry" (*Guild Reporter*, 26 November 1986, 6).

The analysis of the poll characterized the stance of the Guild membership on merger as "wait and see." It found that the type of merger partner most likely to garner membership support was another of the traditional news industry unions. But the merger partner would likely have to demonstrate three key characteristics. First, it would have to be a large and wealthy union—seen as crucial to satisfying the 21 percent of Guild members who supported a merger on the grounds that it would "strengthen the Guild." Second, it would have to let the Guild keep some sort of distinct identity—seen as crucial to countering fears of members about losing the "unique character of the Guild." Finally, it would have to have a demonstrated record of success in organizing the unorganized—crucial to meeting Guild concerns about strength and the need for growth (*Guild Reporter*, 26 November 1986, 6).

This "wait and see" attitude prevailed for several years. In April 1989 Guild leaders convened a "futures forum," primarily to study the prospects and advisability of merger with another union.[4] The forum was to allow for a freewheeling discussion. No votes were taken but a committee was struck to draw up a list of elements the Guild would consider essential in any proposal for merging or affiliating with another union. That list was to go to the union's international executive board, who would act as a committee on merger, prior to that year's annual convention (*Guild Reporter*, 5 May 1989, 1).

The *Guild Reporter* estimated that sentiment at the forum ran "roughly two to one in favor of actively pursuing merger or affiliation with another union in the news industry" (*Guild Reporter*, 5 May 1989, 6). In the months before the forum, the union collected twenty-four responses in a poll of locals. These responses ran about three to two in favor of a merger. The CWA ranked first in order of preference as a merger partner, followed by the GCIU. The GCIU was certainly interested: in March, more than a month before the Guild's "futures forum," its general board voted unanimously to pursue "exploratory talks" with the Guild (*Guild Reporter*, 5 May 1989, 6).

Chuck Dale, who became president of the Guild in 1987, urged forum participants to proceed with caution on the idea of a merger.

> "I do not believe we should press forward quickly," he said. "I do not believe a merger with another union—in or out of the industry—should be ruled out in the future, but I do believe that any steps should be taken cautiously, conservatively, slowly and quietly. A bidding war, a romancing of the Guild by interested unions, is not in our own best interest at this time." (*Guild Reporter*, 5 May 1989, 6)

Some at the forum focused on fostering interunion cooperation rather than a merger. Other participants, however, saw a merger as not only a necessity but an inevitability. The *Guild Reporter* quoted Bruce Meachum, a Denver administrative officer, as saying, "Merger is inevitable, and now is the best time. We're healthy, but under increasing attacks from publishers. . . . We ought to formulate an offer to the CWA or the GCIU and see what they say." Dale and others at the forum argued that before looking for a partner the Guild should decide what kind of partner it wanted. The president said, "We can't be going down three or four paths at the same time" (*Guild Reporter*, 5 May 1989, 6).

A few days after the forum, the union's international executive board appointed a subcommittee to develop a list of "essential elements" the Guild would need in a merger. By that summer, the board had nineteen. The list, presented to the annual convention, included:

- TNG remain a separate division within an affiliate, with its own budget, convention, executive board (to include separate seats for representatives elected in Canada), geographic district councils, legal counsel and publication.
- Any partner be an AFL-CIO and CLC affiliate and be in compliance with CLC Guidelines-Standards of Self-Government.
- The Guild's role be clearly defined in decision-making on matters outside its own division.
- TNG maintain its own strike fund and rules regarding strikes and payment of benefits.
- A separate Guild collective bargaining program be maintained and TNG's human rights program be maintained or satisfactorily merged with that of the partner.
- TNG's education, research and information programs be blended with those of the partner.
- Locals be encouraged but not required to merge with proximate locals of the affiliate. (*Guild Reporter*, 4 August 1989, 7)

This list is telling, in several respects. It suggests the Guild was willing to merge, but only if it did not have to give up anything significant in the deal. It wanted to keep its own identity, its own governing structure, its own budget, and its own rules on strikes and strike pay. This was a marked change from the union's position in the 1983 ITU merger agreement. Then, the Guild was prepared to enter into a partnership that would have created a brand new union out of two existing ones, drawing on elements from each. That merger would have required the Guild to change many of the ways it had traditionally gone about its business, from the governing structure to the dues charged to its members. After having its fingers burned in the ITU merger, however, the Guild apparently was reluctant to reach that far again. But perhaps it wouldn't have to.

The wish list is significant in another respect: without naming any names, it suggested that the union was indeed narrowing its list of potential merger partners. The requirement that the merger partner "be an AFL-CIO and CLC affiliate and be in compliance with CLC Guidelines-Standards of Self-Government" might be read as a not-so-subtle reminder about the history of the International Brotherhood of Teamsters.[5] The list also raised questions about whether the GCIU, the other big player in the newspaper industry, might be a suitable partner. The GCIU was the product of a series of mergers: the photoengravers, lithographers, and bookbinders joined into the Graphic Arts International Union (GAIU) in the 1970s; the pressmen's and stereotypers' unions into the International Printing and Graphic Communications Union (IPGCU) in 1973; the GAIU and the IPGCU into the GCIU in 1983. Duncan Brown, formerly an organizing coordinator with the GCIU in Toronto and now a GCIU vice-president, says the GCIU approach "has always been for organic mergers" (Brown 1998). Given the diversity of its membership, the union felt that the only way to make mergers work was to insist on unity: to ensure that GCIU members would be GCIU members, regardless of which union they belonged to in the past. For the Guild, however, the kind of mergers that created the GCIU—and that presumably would be expected of the Guild if it wanted to join the GCIU—would mean sacrificing the independence the union itemized on its list of essential ingredients for merger.

But if the GCIU would not be able to fulfil the required wish list, where did that leave the Guild? After all, its 1986 poll of members found that the type of merger partner most likely to be acceptable to the membership was another of the traditional news industry unions. By 1989, there were no "traditional" news industry unions left *except* the GCIU. The ITU was by then part of the CWA, a union most newspaper workers viewed as a telephone workers' union. Within the CWA, however, the ITU had been able to retain a substantial degree of autonomy: it had its own sector, it elected its own officers, and it controlled its own finances. In other words, it had just about exactly the kind of autonomy the Guild saw as desirable in a merger.

The poll of locals commissioned before the "futures forum" found that the CWA was the merger partner of choice. But that poll was small: just twenty-four locals, or about one-third of the total. In addition, it found that a sizeable minority—two out of five—disliked the idea of any kind of merger at all. Without strong pressure to change coming from either the leadership or the membership, and in the absence of an ideal suitor, the merger question remained on the agenda, but not at the top of Guild concerns.

FORGING A STRATEGIC PLAN

In 1992, as the full impact of recession ate into Guild membership and the union's resources, the Guild decided it was time to develop a strategic plan to guide it through the next four years. It commissioned a Boston firm, Work Directions Inc., to examine the union and its industry. The study included a survey of locals, an analysis of a membership poll conducted by the Wilson Center, and interviews with 166 local and international leaders, activists, and staff. The result was a set of far-reaching recommendations aimed at reinforcing the union's traditional strengths and promoting expansion into new areas. Twenty-two of the twenty-three committee members overseeing the plan endorsed its recommendations, sending it to the 1993 convention.

The lone dissenting vote on the committee was cast by Gail Lem of the Southern Ontario Newspaper Guild, who found the plan lacking in two key respects. Lem felt the recommendations should have included the hiring of an organizing specialist and the adoption of a plan specifically to guide organizing efforts. She also felt it should have included "more specific recommendations to resolve the Canadians' concerns" (Work Directions Inc. 1993, 12). As we will see in the next chapter, some Canadian locals, most especially Lem's, were becoming increasingly impatient with both the structure of the Guild and the level of service and support it offered locals in Canada. These concerns would eventually result in three Canadian locals, including the powerful Southern Ontario Newspaper Guild, leaving the Guild to join Canadian unions.

The strategic plan is worth examining in some detail. It reveals a union struggling to maintain its bargaining power in an industry undergoing rapid change. It is also the portrait of a union on the cusp of change. The plan begins by identifying a series of what it calls external pressures on the Guild. The newspaper industry—which employed 85 percent of Guild members at the time (Work Directions Inc. 1993, 33)—was shrinking, in terms of numbers of dailies and in employment. This did not mean the newspaper industry was dying. Rather, it was "consolidating and restructuring as part of an evolving information industry" (15). Fewer and fewer Guild members were working at independently owned newspapers. Instead, they were working for increasingly sophisticated employers that were, for the most part, publicly held corporations with wide-ranging investments in media, information, and marketing.[6]

"Driven by the pursuit of high returns, employers have vigorously pursued anti-union and cost-cutting strategies," the report said (14). In an effort to cut costs and produce their products more quickly and flexibly, newspapers were imposing new technologies and work processes in "all phases of newspaper production" (20). Meanwhile, employers in the United States were taking advantage of what the report calls weakened union rights. "The result is that over the past dozen years, the Guild has lost power" (14).

In terms of numbers, the report found that total employment in the newspaper industry in Canada and the United States began to decline in 1989 (21). So did Guild membership, which slid from a high of close to 36,000 in 1987 to about 33,000 by 1989, and to 32,000 in 1992 (22).[7] The numbers were not disastrous—the union still had more members than it had in the early 1980s—but the moderate decline was a concern. Of equal concern was the finding that Guild members were more likely than in the past to be working under expired contracts. In 1993, 103 of the Guild's 224 contracts, or 46 percent, had expired. This was up significantly from 34 percent in 1977. Meanwhile, it was taking longer and longer to negotiate new contracts (23). The report said these findings indicated that the Guild had lost bargaining leverage.

Financially, the Guild's books were in good shape. In part that was the result of two episodes, in 1979 and 1985, when higher dues were triggered under the constitution (24).[8] In 1979, 1990, and 1991, international expenses outpaced revenues, primarily due to higher defense fund expenses. In 1992, the Guild reduced its international staff from thirty-three to twenty-six to trim its expenses (25). By the end of that year, revenues and expenses were balanced (24).

The report concluded that the Guild was facing a critical strategic choice: how to define itself in an industry that was being transformed from the newspaper business to an information industry. The solution was to redefine the Guild's identity and jurisdiction as the union for workers "in the evolving news and information industries in the United States and Canada" (35). This was a significant shift in how the Guild's members saw themselves, their employers, and their union. Instead of a union of newsworkers, mainly in the newspaper business, the Guild would become a union of information workers, working in a range of industries. In large part, this reflected a response to a change in the industry: just as the newspaper business had transformed itself into the information business, so would the newspaper workers' union be transformed.

The report made a number of recommendations on improving internal

Guild operations and enhancing the union's power vis-à-vis the employers. Several recommendations focused on doing a better job of what the union had already been doing.[9] The one with the most far-reaching consequences was a recommendation that the Guild immediately begin exploring merger options and return to the union with a recommendation no later than the 1995 Guild convention.

The report cited three reasons for the Guild to explore a merger. The first was an evolving industry structure, "with owners investing across the information/media sectors, changed products and markets, and employers who are far more aggressive and well organized." The second was a shift from print to electronic distribution of news and information. This meant that the Guild "must develop stronger alliances with unions representing workers in those sectors controlling electronic modes: telephone, computers, satellite, broadcasting and cable transmission." The final reason was the need for additional resources. The Guild was constrained by a small membership base spread out over seventy-eight locals. "The right kind of merger will bring economies of scale to provide additional resources to Guild locals in areas such as corporate research and analysis and organizing" (103).

Though the report did not use the word, these reasons for pursuing a merger are all linked to the idea of convergence. Neither the diagnosis of the Guild's situation nor the prescribed solution focused on traditional patterns, such as organizing newspaper units that had not yet been organized, or building solidarity among newspaper unions through things like joint bargaining or uniform contract expiry dates. Rather, it reflected an awareness that the Guild should be forging links with workers across the information sector, including telephone and telecommunications workers, broadcasters and computer workers. With corporate convergence and technological convergence, it seems, the time had come for unions in the information business to undertake a convergence of their own.

The 1993 convention endorsed the strategic plan. Interestingly, coverage of debate on the plan in the *Guild Reporter* played down the merger aspect, focusing instead on the plan's other recommendations. This probably reflected the fact that the union's leadership was still feeling a bit gun-shy about the issue. But with the plan in place, the union was now launched on the business of finding a mate.

NARROWING THE FIELD

Starting in the fall of 1993, president Dale and other Guild officers met with delegations from a number of potential partners, including the

Teamsters, the United Steelworkers of America, the GCIU, and the CWA (*Guild Reporter*, 29 May 1994, 1). Fairly quickly, the union dropped the Teamsters and Steelworkers from the list. Though the *Guild Reporter* did not say why, it appears that neither fit the profile the Guild had been developing over the previous several years of an ideal merger partner. The Teamsters, though back in the AFL-CIO fold, were still too much of a loose cannon. The Steelworkers, though large and powerful and interested in mergers, were apparently too far removed from the Guild's core business. And neither had much knowledge of or experience with the shift to electronic distribution of news and information. This left two unions: the GCIU and the CWA. On 23 September 1994, the *Guild Reporter* profiled both in a matching pair of stories, under a front-page joint banner headline saying "CWA, GCIU have evolved with advancing technologies." The two unions emerge as strikingly different choices.

The GCIU is "a union experienced in both merger and society-shaking technological change," the profile said, adding, "In the GCIU's eyes, in fact, merger and technological change are inextricably linked, a part of its past and its future." The profile took readers through the founding of the printing trades unions in North America, noting that in the late nineteenth century the unions underwent technological change just as dramatic as that of the current era. It chronicled the spate of mergers than began in the 1960s and eventually led to the creation of the 200,000-member GCIU. The profile pointed out that the new union has been aggressive in developing resources and programs in technology, health and safety, collective bargaining, and other areas. It concluded with a quotation from GCIU president Jim Norton: "As we head into the twenty-first century, the challenges of yesterday are the challenges of today—new technology, higher skill demands, increased training and retraining, organizing the unorganized. Remember the lessons of the past and look ahead to the future" (6).

The profile of the CWA described it as one of the youngest and fastest-growing unions in North America and noted that it was often "misidentified" as a telephone workers' union. Though it does indeed represent phone workers, CWA "is on the cutting edge of organized labor's expanding role in the information revolution." More than 500,000 of its 600,000 members "are in the four converging communications industries—publishing, telecommunications, computers and entertainment." The profile said the CWA began as a company union at AT&T. When the Wagner Act outlawed company unions in the mid-1930s, a number of independent telephone workers' unions were created. These formed a national federation in 1938. The federation won a national agreement with AT&T in 1946 but collapsed the next year. The federation, the profile explained, was a collection of independent locals, not a genuinely national union. This meant it was vulnerable to pressure from the employer. Following the federation's failure, the phone workers regrouped in 1947 to create a national union, the CWA, with 162,000 members.

The profile said the CWA had become "one of the most successful unions anywhere in achieving equal pay for equal work, full health care, [and] elimination of discriminatory practices both in the industry and in the union." It also had "a remarkable record" in organizing new workers and expanding outside the scope of telecommunications. It noted that at the time of writing, the CWA represented 34,000 state workers in New Jersey, 100,000 public and health care workers across the country, 12,000 police and jail workers in Texas, and 6,400 teaching and graduate assistants at universities in New York, Indiana, and California. CWA has also merged with a number of communications unions: the ITU, the United Telegraph Workers (which represents technical workers at The Associated Press and United Press International), and the National Association of Broadcasting Engineers and Technicians (NABET), representing 9,000 engineers and technicians at NBC, ABC, and independent television stations and cable TV production companies. The profile described the NABET merger as "further recognition by both unions of the converging union interests in the converging information industries." As with the GCIU profile, the last word went to the union's president:

> "The full potential of this emerging industry is still to be defined," says CWA President Morton Bahr in a call to his own and other unions to answer the challenges posed by the breathtaking changes taking place in the creation, presentation, distribution and availability of information, and the expanding audience for it. "Just imagine the possibilities!" (*Guild Reporter*, 23 September 1994, 6)

The GCIU and the CWA each had much to offer the Guild. But each represented a different path. If the Guild merged with the GCIU, the result would be a stronger but more narrowly focused union. Between them, the Guild and the GCIU would have the potential to represent almost every unionized worker in the print media, in Canada and the United States, with the exception of members of the former ITU. (It was abundantly clear by the mid-1990s, however, that with the spread of electronic typesetting, the ITU was less and less of a player in the publishing business.) Between them, the Guild and the GCIU also would have the potential to organize the large group of newspaper workers who were still unorganized. And if the white-collar Guild joined forces with the trades workers in the GCIU, the merged union would be in a stronger position at the bargaining table. In a strike, it would be more likely to have the power to shut down a newspaper than either union operating alone. In addition, while the merged union would be large, the Guild might be less likely to get lost in a union of 230,000 than in an enormous union like the CWA.

Many of these very attractions, however, had a downside. Yes, a merged GCIU-Guild would be stronger—in newspapers and the print media. But given the future sketched out in the strategic plan of 1993, Guild leaders were wondering about the wisdom of tying their future too tightly to the print media. Between technological convergence and corporate convergence, no single medium, or media business, was as distinct as it had been. And it was clear that electronic distribution of news or information, in some form, was likely to be the growth area. In addition, the Guild was hoping to do further organizing among broadcast workers—it already represented workers at the CBC—or workers in the so-called new media. Both groups had a great deal in common with news-workers in the print media but almost nothing in common with newspaper production workers.

At the bargaining table, a merged GCIU-Guild would have more clout and a stronger strike weapon, especially in jurisdictions where employers could not bring in replacement workers. But given the convergence of telecommunications and publishing, there were questions about how strong this weapon really would be. If a strike took reporters off the streets, the publisher could draw on the wealth of wire copy and news agency material that would continue to come into the building over the telecommunications system. If the same strike also shut down the printing plant, it was likely that the publisher could transmit material electronically to another plant operated by the same corporation. And given the growth of newspapers on the Internet, communications workers of all sorts had to confront the possibility that their traditional jobs—translating information into ink on paper—were increasingly being transformed into jobs where the work meant putting bits and bytes onto electronic networks that could drive the printing press or serve as content for a Web site. The GCIU therefore represented a paradox. On the one hand, it was the safe choice: another union operating in the same business, a known commodity, and a union with a record of bringing off mergers successfully. It was also a choice that spoke to history and tradition. In an age of convergence, however, this choice might turn out, in the long run, to be not so safe after all.

A merger with the CWA, by contrast, would represent an enormous leap for a small international union like the Guild. For one thing, it was strictly an American union, without a Canadian presence.[10] For another, it was almost twenty times the size of the Guild. In addition, while GCIU members worked in a set of crafts with which the Guild was, at least, familiar, the CWA membership was much more diverse. The bulk of CWA members were skilled technical workers of one sort or another, many of them in the telecommunications and telephone business. These members had little conception, and no inside knowledge, of news work.

If the appeal of the GCIU was the prospect of building on the past and continuing a tradition of print media trade unionism, the CWA's appeal was based on building toward the future. But this too had its risks. Would there be a good fit between a union of journalists with its own professional culture and a union of technicians? Would the two sides be able to build a sense of solidarity?

Linda Foley, who was secretary-treasurer of the Guild at the time of the merger talks,[11] says one of the biggest considerations was a prospective partner's ability to accommodate the Guild's needs for autonomy within a merged union. "The GCIU, because of their culture and because of the way they had evolved, was unable to recognize the Guild culture within the union," she says (Foley 1998). The GCIU was trying to create a genuinely unified union out of a number of independent-minded members. The pressmen's union in particular had wanted its own separate sector within the GCIU, but was required to give up that idea. "They were kind of in a quandary. They wanted very much for us to merge with them," says Foley. But this would have meant giving the Guild something the GCIU would not give its own pressmen. "That would have been impossible for them, politically." Even if the GCIU had been willing to give the Guild its own sector, Foley says she doubts whether the Guild would have joined:

> We were interested in seeing whether we could work out a merger with the GCIU but the truth is we never really felt that was where we wanted to go in 1995 because of the technology and the way things are today. For us to merge with a union that was just in print didn't make any sense. In that year our largest local was a broadcast local, the Canadian Media Guild, [whose members are employed by] the CBC. So to merge with a union that was just in print wasn't as attractive as merging with a union like the CWA. (Foley 1998)

In addition, the fact that the former ITU was now part of the CWA was a consideration. The Guild had been serious about merging with the ITU back in the 1980s and even though that deal fell through, there was a sense among the printing unions that the Guild and the ITU should somehow be together. "The printers came into CWA and that was in no small part why we looked at the CWA as a merger partner," Foley explains (1998). If the Guild joined too, then the long-held dream of uniting these two unions would be fulfilled. Finally, Guild leaders were impressed with how the CWA had responded to the potentially disastrous effects of the AT&T breakup in 1984. At the time, CWA represented 550,000 telecommunications workers. But with the splitting off of twenty-two Bell operating companies from AT&T and a federal policy of deregulation that promoted open competition in the phone business, its previously secure position at AT&T was undermined. The union fought back on several fronts: waging a strike at AT&T in 1983 that won its members a degree of protection during the switch; running organizing drives at the new companies; fighting plans to contract out jobs; pursuing, at one point, forty-eight separate negotiations at the former Bell system; and expanding organizing drives into new areas (Jeffrey Miller 1988, 60). By 1998, its telecommunications membership stood at 400,000, while its public-sector membership had grown to about 100,000.[12]

MAKING THE CHOICE EASY

By the fall of 1994, the leaders of the CWA and the Guild had come to an agreement. According to CWA president Bahr, it was all pretty easy.

> What made it work, I think, was in the way we both approached it.... We've had several mergers of sizeable unions before the Guild, and I've approached it with the support of our executive board with the understanding that each union that merges with us has a long and proud history, and that the merger agreement has to meet the needs of the smaller union as well as assurances that the culture and long-held practices would be respected.
>
> And so when I met with Chuck Dale for the first time to explore the possibilities, I said, "Chuck, why don't you take a sheet or two sheets of paper and write down all the things that you'd need in a merger, and then we'll go over it and I'll tell you what we can do and what we can't do." He kind of looked at me as if I was giving him a Wizard of Oz story, but that's the way we approached it. And we were able to accommodate virtually every important need that they had. So it started off very friendly, and it remained friendly. (Bahr 2001)

Dale was convinced, and told his members that the CWA was head and shoulders above the rest: "there are no other unions out there that meet all the goals TNG has set for itself" (*Guild Reporter*, 18 November 1994, 1).

In October 1994, the international executive board adopted a merger resolution. It sketched out in broad strokes how the Guild would stand in a CWA merger, and explained why CWA was the most attractive prospect:

> Just as we evolved from a union of editorial-only employees to one representing employees in all newspaper departments to a union with members in virtually all facets of the news industry, we must now continue that evolution to become part of a larger organization representing workers all along the Information Superhighway.... We also must seek a merger that will fulfil our mandate to forge stronger ties with unions in broadcast as well as other areas of the media industry.[13]

At the same time, the resolution said the CWA was willing to preserve the unique identity, purpose, and character of the Guild, creating a division or sector specifically for it. The Guild would retain control over its contracts and collective bargaining and would "continue to exercise the great degree of autonomy that has been a hallmark of our international union." In addition, the merger would not be rushed: it would begin with a period of affiliation. This would give the two unions time to get to know each other. It would also give the Guild time to reorganize its Canadian membership, something the union pledged to do as part of its strategic plan. A full merger would occur down the road.

In an apparent attempt to calm the concerns of members about the merger, the 18 November 1994 issue of the *Guild Reporter* included interviews with Bill Boarman, head of the Printing, Publishing, and Media Workers sector of the CWA (the former ITU) and Ken Moffett, assistant to the president of the NABET sector of the CWA. These two leaders spoke frankly and candidly about the downside of joining a giant like the CWA, but concluded it was worth the effort. Moffett was quoted as saying the 10,000-member NABET had to get used to dealing with the bureaucracy of a union with more than 600,000 members: "There are various layers for everything. It's not that we can't get quick action on things, but we're not used to that. But it's the best thing to happen to us. If we're going to grow this union, this is the way to do it" (7). Boarman and Moffett both said there had been problems melding the financial operations of their unions with the CWA.

Boarman said that in addition, until the ITU joined it, CWA was not accustomed to dealing with newspaper employers. "They were used to dealing with corporations like AT&T, Bell Atlantic, Pacific Telesis and the like. But we're working through the problems." He added there is an upside of belonging to a large union: "all the resources, the research capability, legal assistance, strike benefits and so on. That has a big impact on the local level" (7). Both leaders stressed that CWA's willingness to create special sectors for their unions had helped their unions preserve their identities. Said Moffett:

> I know that what a lot of people fear in a situation like this is that their union will lose its identity in a merger. Well, in some mergers, the little union does get swallowed up. But what [CWA President Morton] Bahr has done with the sectors is to save the identities of the ITU and NABET. It's the best of all possible worlds, we've maintained our identity and our traditions and we've had full access to the tremendous resources of the CWA. (7)

Over the next few months, negotiators from the Guild and the CWA sat down to work out the fine points of a merger and to draft an agreement. They came up with a plan for a two-year period of affiliation. If both sides were happy, formal merger would occur in 1997. The agreement was adopted by the Guild's international executive board in April 1995 and sent to the union's convention in Boston that June for approval. A referendum of members was set for September. Under the Guild constitution, the merger agreement had to be approved by a majority of members in both Canada and the United States. Both groups approved. When all the ballots were counted, 90 percent of Guild members were in favor of the deal (*Guild Reporter*, 29 September 1995, 1).

In large part, the high approval had to do with the fact that the agreement came remarkably close to meeting the list of "essential ingredients" for merger that had been adopted at the 1989 convention. The merger text, published in a special four-page edition of the *Guild Reporter* on 11 August 1995, showed that the Guild would have a substantial degree of autonomy. It would be a sector of the CWA, with its own bylaws (the former Guild constitution), its own staff, and its own set of officers (2). The president of the Guild would become a vice-president of the CWA. The Guild would send delegates to the CWA annual convention, but would also hold its own sector conference prior to it (3). The Guild would retain its own legal counsel. It would continue to publish the *Guild Reporter*. It would retain its own dues structure and its collective bargaining program. It would maintain its own defense fund (4). At the same time, it would be able to take advantage of the expertise of the CWA's staff, including its researchers, organizers, lobbyists, and legislation experts. Participation in the CWA defense fund would be phased in

(4). The Guild headquarters would move from Guild-owned offices in Silver Spring, Maryland, into offices in the CWA headquarters in downtown Washington, D.C. The Guild would, however, have its own suite, separate from other CWA sector offices or general CWA staff (2). Finally, while locals of the two unions would be encouraged to merge with each other, there would be no requirement for them to do so (2).

Foley (1998) says that the CWA's willingness to support Guild autonomy made sense. "We're not a threat to the 600,000 other members of the CWA in the sense that it doesn't disrupt the culture of the CWA to let The Newspaper Guild have its own sector and have its own thing," she explains. "The rest of the CWA can continue doing what it's been doing and we just become a part of that. It's almost like, 'Why didn't we think of that before?'"

While the merger agreement calmed Guild fears of being swallowed up by a large union, it emphasized that the purpose of merger was not simply the preservation of a special identity. Rather, the merger was a way of responding to changes within the industries that would affect members of both unions. As the introduction to the agreement said, "The changing nature of information industries and the convergence of various communications technologies throughout North America make it imperative that the Unions continue to evolve as viable forces and strong representatives of workers who are at the heart of those industries."[14]

The merger agreement claimed that the act of union would significantly enhance bargaining power for the hundreds of thousands of people working in the communications, publishing, graphic arts, media, broadcasting, cable television, and news industries, and would "also create a better climate for our unions to deal with the 'convergence' and technological changes that are upon us" (1). To that end, the merger document included a commitment to create a council on convergence at the international level, drawing on all CWA sectors involved in the communications and information industries. Once that structure was in place at the top level of the new union, the CWA would promote the creation of similar councils at the local level to develop public policy positions and strategies for union education, political activism, research, organizing, and collective bargaining (3).

Foley says it was important to have the concept of convergence in the merger agreement itself, for two reasons. "We made convergence a real *raison d'être* of the merger agreement, which not only helped sell the merger with our people but also sent a signal to employers—this is what we're doing." Salesmanship mattered: after all, Guild members had to be convinced that this was the right deal for them. But good salesmanship depends on having a product to sell. In this case, it was the idea that the unions weren't just sitting back and watching while technologies converged and the newspaper business transformed itself into the information business; they were reorganizing to put themselves in a better position to deal with it.

MAKING THE MERGER HAPPEN

Less than three months after the referendum approving the merger document, the CWA and the Guild put on a joint conference in Washington entitled, "The Information Superhighway: Exploring Strategies for Workers." The conference was designed to showcase the capabilities of the newly combined unions and to focus attention on their shared interests in a time when the previously separate industries of telecommunications and media work had converged. It was also intended to bring together local representatives of the CWA and the Guild. Close to 300 attended.

In preparation for the conference, Guild and CWA researchers put together a report highlighting issues the information highway creates for workers and families: things like access, intellectual property rights, health and safety, and the trend of employers toward creating a contingent work force of people hired on short-term contracts.[15] CWA researchers also put together a set of profiles of major employers in the converging information industry.[16] These reports provided Guild and CWA members with information about their industries, pointing out a community of interest. They also served a second purpose for the Guild delegates to the meeting: they highlighted the quality of the research a merged union could produce. Following the conference, the union compiled a summary of sessions, which it distributed to the presidents of locals across North America in early 1996. Again, this reinforced the message about the benefits of CWA membership.

In the opening address to the conference, CWA president Bahr sketched out the patterns of corporate and technological convergence that had characterized the last ten years. He added that the change in CWA's relationships with other industry unions was "just another consequence of convergence" (Bahr 1995). But the CWA is not interested in simply responding to developments in the industry, he said. "Since it seems clear that we will be working for the same employers in a very few short years, CWA must develop a much stronger and closer relationship with all of the entertainment and media unions." Bahr also emphasized the need to develop plans to stay ahead of what he described as inevitable and continuing change in the telecommunications, information, media, and entertainment ("TIME") industries. He noted that mergers, acquisitions, partnerships, and breakups were creating new players in the industry and changing the roles of old ones. Bahr reminded delegates that he was elected head of the union in 1985, at the time of the AT&T breakup. "Practically overnight we went from an industry that was almost 100 percent organized to an industry that was about 35 percent organized," he said. The breakup offered CWA a chance to rebuild its own operations so it could organize new groups of workers. "In looking back, we know that if we had not changed, our membership base would have eroded to the point where CWA today would be looking for a merger partner in the name of survival," he said. But the union regrouped, experimented with new methods of fighting back against employers, new bargaining relationships, and new organizing strategies. "The point I want to make is this: convergence presents many new challenges and uncertainties. But convergence also offers many new opportunities and openings for us. We are at the ground floor of a burgeoning new industry that is still taking shape" (Bahr 1995).

Bahr also stressed that if the industries are converging, so is the work performed by CWA members. The lines that once separated craft, professional, technical, and office work are slowly evaporating: "We are not even certain what this industry will look like next year, much less five years from now. . . . As more employers merge and combine forces, how can our members possibly hope to survive in this new environment unless *we* merge and *join* forces?" (Bahr 1995, emphasis in original). Convergence, he concluded, is just another chapter in a long history of change that has affected the CWA from its beginnings: "We have survived and prospered from technological change in the past. We are learning how to change today to grow with the converging information industry of tomorrow."

The conference introduced Guild members to the leaders of other CWA media sectors (the former ITU and NABET) and to scholars, government regulators, and other union leaders confronting the effects of digitization on work. It concluded with an effort to launch local convergence councils drawing on all sectors of the CWA. Foley says the conference was useful in more than one respect. "Our whole goal here was not just to educate people about what we need to do to meet the challenges in our industry but also to make them have a comfort level with the new union that they were about to [join]" (1998). Over the following two years, Guild leaders and members had time to grow comfortable with the CWA. "The transition period was really helpful because it allowed us to get a peek at what it was going to be like," Foley says. "The CWA let us in on everything." During that time, the leadership encouraged CWA vice-presidents in the field to contact Guild locals, and Guild locals to get involved in what the CWA districts were doing. The *Guild Reporter* promoted CWA programs in its pages. Guild members began receiving the CWA's newsletter. "The more they saw the CWA, the more comfortable they got," Foley says.

At the end of the transition period, Foley was sworn in as a CWA vice-president at the 1997 CWA convention. More than 100 Guild members attended as CWA delegates. It was an emotional moment.

> When I was sworn in, we arranged it so the Guild people would come up to the front of the hall while I was speaking. When they did that, they got this overwhelming response from the rest of the delegates—1,000 or 1,500 people cheering. They left there feeling very welcomed, and very much a part, at every level, of the CWA. (Foley 1998)

"ONE BIG UNION" REVISITED

By the end of 1997, the Guild had managed to bring to life an idea leaders and members had been talking about as early as 1960: the creation of "one big union" for printing and publishing workers. In its final form, this big union has turned out to be vastly different from the one envisioned in the early 1960s. Then, the talk was of creating a single union bringing together as many as nine printing trades unions, including the Guild. When it became clear that this was too ambitious a goal, the Guild turned its efforts toward merging with the union with which it had the closest ties in the workplace: the ITU. Though that marriage fell apart at the altar, the Guild and the ITU are now under the same roof, as sectors of the CWA. But no one would mistake the CWA for a printing and publishing or newsworkers union. Rather, it represents a wide range of workers in the communications sector—telephone, telecommunications, broadcast, and wire service technicians, for example—as well as workers in various parts of the public and private sector, including nurses and airlines reservations agents. The other print sector unions, meanwhile, have formed their own big union, the GCIU. Says Bahr,

> The new president of the GCIU, George Tedeschi, is an old friend of mine from New York. We've known each other for twenty-five years. We have very friendly

relations with him. I think George knows that at some point they're going to have to look around for a partner, and we hope it will be us. But that's a decision they'll ultimately have to come to. (2001)

For the Guild, the benefits of the merger seem clear. In an era of technological convergence and the rise of the multimedia conglomerate, it has become part of a union that has the size, flexibility, and vision to pursue labor convergence across all areas of communications work. It is able to share in the financial, research, human, and political resources of the CWA, while preserving a significant degree of autonomy and its own identity.

But there has been a cost: the merger was unable to fend off entirely the growing demands for autonomy voiced by a number of Canadian locals. The act of coming together with the CWA also meant a coming apart in the Canadian arm of the Guild. While the U.S. communications workers belong to labor unions that are more united than ever before, their Canadian colleagues have wound up not in "one big union" but in two.

NOTES

1. The union had endorsed a call for legislation preventing ownership concentration in both Canada and the United States at its 1979 convention. It also endorsed the Canada Newspaper Act proposed by the Kent commission (*Guild Reporter*, 26 April 1985, 1).

2. The decline was striking during the late 1970s and 1980s. In 1976, 27.9 percent of nonagricultural workers were unionized. This dropped to 22.6 in 1981 and 17.1 percent in 1986. The numbers bottomed out at around 15 percent by the early 1990s (Murray 1995, 164).

3. For example, Canadian newspaper ad revenues plunged from $2.2 billion a year in 1990 to $1.6 billion in 1995, a drop of 27 percent (Miller 1998, 11).

4. The mandate of the forum was quickly expanded to look at the union's budget. The union's general fund had run at a record $181,545 deficit in 1988. The forum was told that the deficit for 1989 would be lower than that, but not by much (*Guild Reporter*, 5 May 1989, 1).

5. By this time, the Teamsters union was back in the AFL-CIO, but many still thought of it as a renegade union.

6. The report found that newspaper companies have diversified into a number of areas: news programming/syndication, news and information, books and magazine publishing, TV and radio (broadcast and cable), marketing, entertainment programming, retail and travel, business services, equipment, and transportation (17).

7. Membership decline was a U.S. phenomenon, not a Canadian one, however. Canadian membership in the Guild continued to grow, largely though organizing.

This meant that Canadians accounted for 19.2 percent of Guild membership in 1993, up from 13.6 percent in 1982 and 15 percent in 1987 (111).

8. The union's constitution triggered higher dues whenever the International Defense Fund dipped below its set point. (See Article XVIII of The Newspaper Guild constitution, adopted by the sixtieth annual convention, July 1993.)

9. Internally, the first recommendation was to work with Canadian leaders to strengthen Guild unity. Others called for improvements in policymaking and efforts to ensure financial viability at the local and international levels. As for increasing the Guild's bargaining power, the report called for building member commitment to and participation in the union, and efforts to strengthen the Guild's union and community alliances though unity councils and more systematic efforts at promoting interunion cooperation. (37)

10. Its Canadian contingent broke away peacefully in the early 1970s to create the Communications Workers of Canada. After that, the CWA had no presence in Canada until the ITU joined it, bringing along its Canadian locals. As we will see in the next chapter, a number of Canadian ITU locals chose to break away and join CEP.

11. Foley became president of the union in 1995.

12. See the CWA fact sheet, "Facts at a Glance," 1998.

13. CWA/TNG merger resolution, printed in *Guild Reporter*, 18 November 1994, 1.

14. Text of CWA/TNG merger agreement, printed in *Guild Reporter*, 11 August 1995, 1.

15. "The Information Superhighway: What It Means to Working Families," CWA/TNG research report, July 1995.

16. "Changing Information Services: Strategies for Workers and Consumers," CWA research report, December 1995.

6

Answering the Canadian Question

The labor movements in Canada and the United States are intertwined at many levels. Among industrialized economies, only in Ireland and Britain are the union structures linked to the degree they are in Canada and the United States (Murray 1995, 176). In large part, this is the result of geographical proximity, history, and political economy. English-speaking Canada and the United States share a common language and, though there are national variations, a common culture. Both countries have democratic political systems. And their economies exhibit a significant degree of integration, propelled in recent years by a set of free trade agreements. At the same time, though, the sheer size of the U.S. economy means that what happens south of the border generally has more influence on Canada than the other way around.

The basic structure of Canadian labor law owes a great deal to laws enacted in the United States—especially to the Wagner Act of 1935, which recognized the rights of workers to organize and bargain collectively and created a National Labor Relations Board to administer federal labor law. In Canada, responsibility for labor is divided among the federal government and the provinces. While each province's labor law contains unique features, the provincial and federal laws draw on the Wagner model, recognizing the right of workers to organize and relying on a labor relations board to resolve jurisdictional disputes and administer the certification system (Carter 1995, 62). Canada's labor movement has been influenced by its British and French connections,[1] but the structure and operating principles of Canadian unions owe far more to the union movement in the United States than to Europe. The two major phases of union development in North America, craft unionism and industrial unionism, spilled over from the United States into Canada. In addition, the unions that were busy organizing workers south of the Canada–U.S. border in the nineteenth and twentieth centuries saw the similar work force north of the border as candidates for organizing too. It is no surprise, therefore, that for many years U.S.-based "international" unions dominated the Canadian labor movement.

In newspapers, for example, North American printers believed their monopoly on craft should take precedence over questions of geography or nationality. Just two years after its founding in 1852, the U.S. National Typographical Union urged locals to look into the interchange of union cards with Canadian printers (Zerker 1982, 71). By 1865, the union claimed "original and exclusive jurisdiction in all matters pertaining to the fellowship of the craft in the United States and the British Provinces" (Article I of NTU Constitution, quoted in Zerker 1982, 75). It changed its name to the International Typographical Union in 1869 to reflect its jurisdiction claim and took as an article of faith that its duty was to organize and represent printers wherever it could find an opening, in Canada or the United States. Later, industrial unions like the American Newspaper Guild treated the international border as no impediment to organizing. Just five years after its founding in 1933, the Guild had fought (and lost) its first organizing drive in Canada (S. Craig 1987, 3). It signed its first contract in Canada in 1949, with the *Toronto Star*.[2] By the time the Guild was twenty-five years old, it represented workers in Toronto, Ottawa, Montreal, Vancouver, and Victoria,[3] and across the country at the CBC (S. Craig 1987, 5).

Newspaper unions are far from unique in having an international profile. Between 1921 and 1970, the percentage of Canadian trade unionists belonging to international unions ranged between 60 and 72 percent (Dawes 1987, 8–9). This number began to drop precipitously in the late 1960s, and by the mid-1970s less than 50 percent of Canadian trade unionists belonged to international unions (17). By the mid-1990s, this was down to less than 30 percent (Murray 1995, 177). The decline in numbers was mirrored by a decline in the directive authority international unions have had over their Canadian sections (Dawes 1987, 2).

Without a doubt, a significant factor in the relative decline of international unions in Canada was the rise of Canadian-based unions, especially within the public service. Between 1970 and 1986, for example, membership in the Canadian Union of Public Employees (CUPE) more than doubled to 304,000 (Dawes 1987, 22). By 2001, CUPE had grown to 485,000 members and was by far the largest union in Canada. Two other public service unions were among the top six: the National Union of Public and General Employees (NUPGE),⁴ with 325,000 members, was the second-largest union in Canada in 2001, and the 145,650-member Public Service Alliance of Canada was sixth. The Canadian Autoworkers Union, which broke away from the United Auto Workers in 1985, was the third-largest union in Canada, with 220,000 members. Only one international union, the United Food and Commercial Workers International Union, with 210,390 Canadian members, was among the top six (Human Resources Development Canada 2001).

Although the growth of public-sector unionism is a key reason for the relative decline of international unions in Canada, it is by no means the only one. Dawes cites a number of factors. These include the relative decline of manufacturing, where international unions are concentrated, and the relative growth of services and public administration, where Canadian unions are concentrated; the failure of international unions to organize the unorganized;⁵ Canadian dissatisfaction with international unionism; the rise of nationalist Canadian trade union leaders; the availability of national union merger partners; and the significance of Canadian sections of international unions with respect to their U.S. parents (1987, 2–3). Looking specifically at the sources of Canadian dissatisfaction with international unions, he argues that this results from concerns about autonomy and sovereignty, the concession bargaining and political-action philosophies of some American unions, international union support for American interests over Canadian ones, the perception that internationals bring fragmentation and disunity to the labor movement and drain money from Canadian members, and the problem of substantial dues increases or corruption in a few international unions (3).

Put simply, the national-versus-international debate raises pragmatic and philosophical questions. In pragmatic terms, it boils down to whether a union based in one country can adequately represent workers in another sovereign state. The more philosophical (and politically charged) question is whether a union based in one country *should* represent workers in the other country. These questions have been the subject of longstanding discussion not just within individual unions like The Newspaper Guild, but within national Canadian labor federations.

Heron notes that the American Federation of Labor treated the Trades and Labour Congress of Canada as "little more than a state federation" (1989, 148). At times, it cracked the whip to keep the Canadians in line with AFL policy. The U.S. Congress of Industrial Organizations had a looser relationship with its Canadian counterpart, the Canadian Congress of Labour, though it too regularly tried to make the Canadian body conform. The merger of the two wings of the labor movements into the AFL-CIO on one side of the border and the Canadian Labour Congress (CLC) on the other "included a clear declaration of independence that American labor leaders agreed to respect" (Heron 1989, 149).[6] Nonetheless, the bulk of CLC members for many years came from Canadian branches of international unions. As a result, these unions were able "to destroy, or at least subdue, nationalist initiatives that came before conventions or the executive" (Dawes 1987, 26).

STANDARDS OF SELF-GOVERNMENT

During the 1960s, the nationalist voice in Canadian labor gained volume and power, and in 1970 the CLC convention adopted a list of "minimum standards of self-government" for Canadian sections of international unions. These included the election of Canadian officers by Canadians, allowing those elected officers and Canadian members to determine policies to deal with national affairs, and giving Canadian elected representatives the authority to speak for the union in Canada. The 1974 convention added other standards: the idea that if an international union was affiliated with an international trade secretariat, the Canadian section of that union should be separately affiliated, and the idea that Canadian members should not be prevented by constitutional requirements or policy decisions from participating in the social, cultural, economic, and political life of Canada (Dawes 1987, 27).

These "minimum standards" were passed as convention resolutions, not as amendments to the CLC constitution. This meant that although they were CLC policy, compliance depended on voluntary action by the individual internationals.[7] In 1973, the CLC surveyed its members to see how many had adopted the Canadian self-government standards. It found that forty-three of its ninety internationals boasted full compliance, twenty-eight had achieved partial compliance, and nineteen had done nothing. This last group included the International Typographical Union (D. Morton 1998, 279).

The Guild addressed the Canadian self-government question at its 1972 convention in Puerto Rico and came up with a number of changes to address the desire for more Canadian autonomy. It gave the Canadian region a second regional vice-presidency; this meant that the union's international executive board would have seven regional and six at-large vice-presidents. It formed a Canadian policy conference. It agreed to appoint a Canadian director on the recommendation of the two Canadian regional vice-presidents, in consultation with the locals and with the consent of the international president. Finally, it decided to change the name of the union from the American Newspaper Guild to The Newspaper Guild (S. Craig 1987, 6).[8]

The question of whether the Canadian director should be appointed or elected was contentious. An appointed director would become part of the union's staff structure, ultimately accountable to the Washington, D.C., headquarters. This meant that although the director would hold a Canadian title, the nature of the job would be to serve as the Guild president's representative in Canada. Advocates of making the office an elected one felt that the Canadian director should be someone who would speak to the union's power structure on behalf of the Canadian locals. They argued that the position should be filled from the bottom up, not from the top down. The question pointed to a conflict between democracy and demographics: the Guild's Canadian membership was concentrated in one Toronto-area local,[9] and that local could, therefore, determine the outcome of any election for a director. For Guild members outside southern Ontario, there was no certainty that an elected director would serve their needs better than a director appointed by the international in consultation with the Western Canadian vice-president. That view won the day, and Bob Rupert, a former Ottawa local president who was then on the Guild's staff, was named the first Canadian director in 1972.[10] In a 1987 interview, Rupert, by then an associate professor in the School of Journalism at Carleton University, said he was disappointed that the job ended up as an appointed position rather than an elected one, but noted it was the choice of the Canadians themselves (S. Craig 1987, 6). He reaffirmed his disappointment in 1999, in an article written for the program of the CWA/TNG sector conference in Ottawa: "I could write a book about these Guild experiences. It could have a chapter about the Guild's too-slow move to grant more autonomy to its Canadian members, about my term as the Guild's first Canadian director: appointed, not elected, as would have been my preference."[11] Once the decision was made that the Canadian directorship would be an appointed position, it was remarkably difficult to change. For almost fifteen years, it remained an appointed job.

In 1985, the Guild took a step toward granting more autonomy for Canadian members by replacing the Canadian policy conference, which began meeting in 1973, with a Canadian District Council. The conference's primary emphasis was on education. While it had served as a vehicle for Canadians to get together and discuss issues, it was, in some respects, a vehicle without wheels: it offered no means for the Canadians to express their views on pressing public issues. The council, by contrast, had the authority to express itself autonomously on Canadian social and legislative issues. It also advised the international executive board and Guild conventions on how internal Guild policies affected Canadian members and locals (*Guild Reporter*, 16 February 1990, 8).

Proponents of Canadian autonomy saw the creation of the district council as an important and progressive step. Nonetheless, some Canadian members of the union, led by the large, active, and independent-minded Southern Ontario Newspaper Guild local (SONG), were increasingly unhappy with their position in the international union. Their discontent stemmed in part from a feeling that the union had not done enough to serve the Canadian minority. In addition, they felt that the differences between the Canadian and American branches of the union were growing, not shrinking.

Gail Lem, a long-time Guild activist and former SONG president who was the chief architect of the local's eventual withdrawal from the international union, recalls vividly the growing frustration of the Canadian autonomy advocates during the 1980s (Lem 1998). Two incidents in particular stood out. One occurred in 1986, after the U.S. Supreme Court handed down a ruling against clauses in union contracts requiring people who had signed up as union members to maintain their membership. (The issue in the case known as *Pattern Makers League v. NLRB* was whether workers could drop their union membership on the eve of a strike.) The ruling in effect outlawed a portion of the Guild constitution in the United States, but not in Canada. Lem, now with the Communications, Energy and Paperworkers union (CEP), says Guild president Charles Perlik came to a Canadian District Council meeting that year and assured the Canadians that their position would be protected. "When we got to the convention we discovered that the international executive board was proposing simply to drop this clause from the Guild constitution," Lem recalls (1998). It took "a huge floor fight" to make sure that Canadian locals were not affected.[12] The experience left some Canadians feeling bitter that their union would consider that Canadian members fell, in effect if not in fact, under the jurisdiction of the U.S. Supreme Court.

The second incident occurred in 1987, as SONG was gearing up for a strike at *Maclean's*, the Canadian weekly news magazine. Perlik, who knew the head of Maclean-Hunter, told the Toronto local to put their strike plans on hold until he could talk to the magazine's management. This infuriated local leaders, who saw it as interference and went ahead with their strike as planned. But for more than a week, Lem says, the Toronto workers didn't know whether they would receive Guild strike pay. That's because under the Guild constitution the international executive board—which Perlik headed—had to sanction strikes, and Perlik had put matters on hold. Eventually, the *Maclean's* strikers got their money. According to the *Guild Reporter*, strike pay was "authorized to the strike's start following clarification of several issues involved in the calling of the strike" (10 April 1987, 4). But anger over the way the international leadership handled the *Maclean's* situation erupted in what Susan Craig described as "a diatribe against Perlik" in the next issue of the local's newsletter, *SONGsheet* (S. Craig 1987, 6). The president wrote back, asking the local to "cancel my subscription to *SONGsheet*." He later apologized for the letter, but not for his attempt to go directly to management. "I was afraid we were going on strike for nothing. . . . If I'd pulled it off I'd be a hero," he said. As things worked out, he conceded, the situation was "custom-made for the nationalists" (quoted in S. Craig 1987, 6).

PRESSING FOR AUTONOMY

In 1988, SONG decided to bring its concerns about American control to the annual Guild convention. But it did not simply put together a list of complaints; it came up with a proposal, endorsed by its executive, which the local felt would solve the problem of Canadian autonomy within the international union.

The twenty-one-page document, "The Guild and Canadian Autonomy: A Blueprint for Change," began by discussing the scope of the problem. It argued that since the rise of Reaganomics starting in 1980, the American and Canadian members of the union had been heading in different directions on a number of fundamentals, such as organizing, bargaining, and political action. The American locals, trying to cope with a series of anti-labor measures adopted in the United States, found themselves "scrambling to collect dues from their members while at the same time trying to co-ordinate fight-back campaigns to protect their collective agreements" (SONG 1988, 2). The Americans were in this position because two things that in Canada were mainly housekeeping matters—dues checkoffs and the modified open shop—had reappeared as organizing issues in the United States.[13] Following the U.S. Supreme Court decision that forced the Guild to revise its constitution, union members in the United States could opt out of their union membership any time. In addition, some employers were pursuing a tactic of breaking off negotiations and then posting conditions that did not include dues collection.

As a result of these developments, "the first priority for organizing in the United States, and therefore for the Union we have been told, is to sign up free riders"—or people who reap the benefits of Guild contracts without contributing to the union (SONG 1988, 2). In Canada, free riders were not an issue. The priority there was on organizing new bargaining units.

As for collective bargaining, the blueprint held, "we in Canada view with some alarm the increasing number of concessions agreed to by American unions over the last few years, the Guild included" (3). In part this reflected the increasingly difficult political climate for American unions, the blueprint acknowledged, but in Canada, "even though we have our share of right wing governments," concession bargaining was far less of a problem. As for political action, the SONG blueprint said, the issues that gripped Canadian Guild members were of considerably less interest to U.S. members. Canadians were consumed with fighting the Canada–U.S. free trade agreement, privatization of government services, and deregulation. In the United States, it said, political activity focused on helping to elect pro-labor candidates for federal office, and lobbying between elections (5). In Canada, by contrast, labor has "a political arm," the New Democratic Party (4).

Given these differences and others, the document argued, Canadians needed more autonomy within their union. But under the existing Guild structure, "no one person can speak for Canadians or be responsible for ensuring that the interests of the entire Canadian membership are looked after at the executive level of our union" (13). The union had two regional vice-presidents on the executive board (one from eastern Canada and one from western Canada), a situation that encouraged regional bickering and rivalry rather than cooperation. The Canadian director, meanwhile, had not become the strong, national Ottawa-based voice the Guild envisioned in its 1972 resolution creating the position. "The reality is that the Canadian Director is an International Representative based in Western Canada," the blueprint said (15). It emphasized that SONG was not blaming the current director, whom it did not name.[14] Rather, the problem lay in the nature of the position: as an appointment, it had no domestic Canadian political base or clout. The holder of the job answered to the American administration rather than to the Canadian membership. As a result, no one in Canada could give members "a strong voice in the Canadian community and within our international union" (14).

The blueprint praised the Guild for creating the Canadian District Council, which it said had become a forum for sharing information, passing resolutions on issues of concern to Canadians, and presenting educational seminars to those who attended. But the council alone was not enough:

> The CDC alone cannot provide the leadership that is needed to unite the Guild across Canada and make it an effective force in Canada. It can't act in any practical way between meetings. It can't implement a program or mobilize the Canadian membership on an issue. That has to be left to each local. Any staff support that is needed must be requested of the administration in Washington. (16)

It concluded with several recommendations that the SONG executive felt would create more Canadian autonomy in the Guild (20–21). The Canadian director, it said, should be elected nationally at the same time as the regional vice-presidents. The director should be the political leader of the Guild in Canada, sitting on the international executive board. The director and vice-presidents should together form a Canadian executive board, which would be responsible to the Canadian membership through the Canadian district council and the locals. This board should take over from the international executive board the responsibility for making decisions on approval of strikes, defense-fund expenditures, and contract settlements. The Canadian director should hire and direct Canadian staff. The budget for the Canadian office should be approved by the convention but controlled by the Canadian director. Finally and perhaps most provocatively, the Guild constitution should be amended to recognize the right of the Canadian membership to merge with another union and to have a separate vote on any international merger proposals: "The Canadian members should have a legal and democratic method to express and act on their desire, should that be the case in the future, to go in a different direction than the rest of the Guild through another union" (21).

SONG delegates took the blueprint to the 1988 Guild convention in Vancouver. There, they suffered what Lem calls "a crushing, humiliating defeat"—largely at the hands of the other Canadian locals (Lem 1998). The SONG proposal went to the constitution committee, which quickly agreed to postpone debate on it indefinitely. Its report to the convention indicated that it did so after the Canadian caucus decided it wanted to examine the document at the next Canadian District Council meeting.[15] SONG's Bill Petrie took the proposal to the floor of the convention as a minority report from the constitution committee, claiming that the committee's decision to postpone consideration of the report and then to cut off debate amounted to "orchestrated procedural moves aimed at the suppression and censorship of the legitimate concerns of the second-largest local of this union" (*Proceedings* 1988, 60). Petrie said that at the 1988 CLC convention, delegates had agreed to incorporate the standards on self-government into the CLC constitution, which meant they would become a constitutional requirement for all CLC-member unions, including the Guild (67). SONG wanted a full and fair hearing on the Canadian autonomy issue at the current Guild convention, he said. He concluded by arguing that the document was not "a declaration of independence, as has been suggested by a number of people. It's a declaration of self-determination" (68).

Under convention rules, speakers addressing a minority report were limited to five minutes each, with the chair keeping time. Petrie was followed to the microphone by two other SONG delegates, then by Jim Smith of Los Angeles, who argued that giving Canadians what they wanted would strengthen the Guild. Then Jan Ravensbergen of the Montreal local asked the convention to defeat the minority report on behalf of the other Canadian locals. He said these locals had only received SONG's report within the last few days.

> Without proper advance notice or consultation and only having just concluded a Canadian District Council meeting this May, we find out that SONG is bringing a brief forward to this international convention that seeks major changes within TNG on a solely Canadian issue. As a Canadian caucus . . . all seven of the other Canadian locals agreed that this subject go to the Canadian District Council meeting in October with no preconditions. . . . We ask that you allow us the opportunity to first discuss this subject in our own house. (70)

Chuck Dale, who was elected president of the union in 1987, was the final speaker. Dale, a former CBC news staffer who became an international representative and eventually a U.S. citizen, stressed that the Guild was "first and foremost an international union," whose members shared common employers and common problems, many of which called for common solutions (73). Where differences existed, he said, the Guild had responded with "tools specifically honed for Canada" (72). Dale spent several minutes summarizing how the Guild had met Canadian concerns in the past, then noticed that he had used up his five minutes. Jerry MacDonald, staff representative with the Canadian Wire Service Guild local representing CBC journalists among others, said he would donate his five minutes to Dale. The president continued, saying that while he was aware the Canadian sections of some international unions "have separated from their parent unions in recent years," he hoped the Guild had been responsive enough to prevent that from happening here.

He concluded with an old-fashioned appeal to solidarity: "United we stand; divided we fall. It's a hallowed motto that has particular validity for the labor movement. All we have, against the bosses' power, the bosses' money, the bosses' hired guns is our unity. Let's not give that up, not a single iota of it!" (72). Dale got a standing ovation. The SONG report was defeated on a voice vote (73), its future left to the Canadian District Council.

TOWARD CANADIAN AUTONOMY

SONG's decision to take the Canadian autonomy blueprint directly to the convention angered some of the other Canadian locals, who felt the Toronto local had tried to circumvent the Canadian District Council. The council had discussed Canadian autonomy on and off for many years, and its other members were not nearly as committed to the idea as SONG was. At the first post-convention council meeting, in October 1988, the other locals reacted with little enthusiasm to the SONG document.[16] The Montreal and Windsor locals went on record as opposed to the report—in Montreal's case, as "unalterably opposed." Ottawa took no position but said the document raised a number of questions. Victoria, Vancouver, and the Canadian Wire Service Guild said there was no strong interest among their members in pressing for more Canadian autonomy. Mike Bocking of the Vancouver local, however, brought his own counterproposal on autonomy to the meeting.[17] SONG offered a four-part motion covering much of the same territory as the recommendations in its blueprint. The council defeated this proposal, then defeated Bocking's alternative plan as well. Without the support of the council, SONG's plan to get the Guild to change its constitution was dead.

But SONG was by no means finished. Between February and June, 1989, it filed complaints with the Canadian Labour Congress, charging the Guild with violating the standards for self-government that were by then part of the CLC constitution, and therefore enforceable. SONG also brought charges under the CLC code of ethical practices and the code of union citizenship (*Guild Reporter*, 14 December 1990, 1). The action again pitted SONG against the rest of the Canadian contingent. A letter to CLC president Shirley Carr from Larry McInnes, head of the Montreal local (28 February 1989), said the other Canadian locals were unanimous in their support of The Newspaper Guild.

In early 1990, while the charges were pending before the CLC, the executive of the Canadian Wire Service Guild voted to withdraw from the Canadian District Council. Local president Dan Oldfield complained in a letter to the council president that the educational role of the council "has been largely replaced by political manoeuvring," blaming SONG for the change. Since 1987, "SONG has used the CDC as a forum for promoting its version of greater Canadian autonomy within TNG," he said. "While being for greater Canadian autonomy within an international union has some emotional appeal, most Canadian locals view SONG's policies as ill-advised" (*Guild Reporter*, 16 February 1990, 8).

The act of filing charges presented the CLC with a problem. The source of the complaint had to be taken seriously: SONG was the largest Canadian local in the union, and it represented the elite of Canadian print newsworkers, including reporters and editors at *The Globe and Mail*, *Toronto Star*, and *Maclean's*. In addition, due in large part to Lem's leadership and talent as an organizer, SONG was an unusually active local, compiling an impressive record in organizing new Guild units even while it was fighting with the international.[18] At the same time, though, the CLC was aware that SONG's views were not shared by the rest of the Guild in Canada. And the Guild was not only a longtime member of the CLC, but a union that had worked hard on Canadian self-government. As for the actual charges, they delved into some fairly murky waters: the standards of self-government called for the election of Canadian officers by Canadians. While it was true that the Guild's Canadian director was appointed, not elected, the Guild did indeed have two elected Canadian vice-presidents.

The CLC, balancing the interests of Canadian union members who wanted more autonomy against the interests of the international unions that belonged to it, decided to appoint a fact finder. The fact finder's report found no evidence that the union violated the self-government standards, "notwithstanding that the Canadian director is not an elected position." It added that making the directorship an elected position "would no doubt ... lessen the tension" between SONG and the international union, noting that this was something the Guild should sort out on its own. SONG's complaint that the Canadian District Council did not have the authority to direct the Canadian district vice-presidents was "once again ... an internal matter that should be resolved by the parties" (*Guild Reporter*, 14 December 1989, 7). SONG had also complained that the international president chose a Canadian representative to go to the International Federation of Journalists convention, saying the Canadian District Council should have made the choice. The report said that while the fact finder "can appreciate that the Canadians would want more say" in selecting the delegate, perhaps this matter could be resolved internally before the next Federation convention. It concluded: "It would appear that the international union is seriously trying to comply with the principles set out" in the CLC code (7). On 27 November 1990, more than eighteen months after SONG filed the initial charges, CLC president Shirley Carr informed SONG that "in the absence of *prima facie* evidence of a violation" of the CLC constitution, "I must dismiss your claim... unless such evidence is forthcoming" (1).

President Dale greeted the report as a vindication of the Guild. SONG president Lem told the *Guild Reporter* she felt the report "doesn't diminish the validity of our complaints." In her view, the fact finder "in essence recommended that TNG talk to us about these issues" of Canadian autonomy (*Guild Reporter*, 14 December 1990, 1). And that, after all, was the dialogue SONG tried to initiate at the 1988 convention.

Lem (1998) says that when she and other activists at SONG began to press for more Canadian autonomy, they were interested in working with other members and the international leadership to develop a stronger Guild. The Southern Ontario local wasn't the only unhappy voice in the union in the late 1980s and early 1990s: two groups were pushing for reforms, and both were critical of the elected leaders of the union, and especially of Chuck Dale. Lem and Juan Gonzalez of the New York local were co-chairs of a group known as Concerned Guild Members, which called for a more progressive, activist leadership. This group felt that the union's leaders were too conservative, too willing to make concessions to employers, and not aggressive enough in organizing or in dealing with employers. In an article in the influential *Columbia Journalism Review*, Stephen Simurda quoted Gonzalez as saying, "It's not that they're evil or corrupt; they're just not very smart or capable" (1993, 26). A second dissident group, the Coalition for Constructive Change, felt that the Guild was spending too much energy responding to crises and too little time developing a coherent organizing strategy. Bruce Meachum, who helped found the group and ran for president against Dale, told Simurda, "You can't go out and organize when you're telling people that all you're doing is putting out fires" (28). He added, "What's missing is a more aggressive stance—more aggressive in dealing with publishers and more aggressive in organizing" (26).

But eventually, Lem came to believe that SONG's future lay outside the Guild, not inside a reformed Guild. In an article headlined "It's time to say 'Goodbye Charlie'" in the December 1990 *SONGsheet* newsletter, she wrote: "as close as some of us may feel to The Newspaper Guild, it appears clear that our legitimate aspirations may not be met in this union.... Do we want to continue being second class members in The Newspaper Guild?" (quoted in *Guild Reporter*, 4 October 1991, 5).

If SONG was to think seriously about leaving, however, it had to tackle some key questions: how to manage an exit from the Guild without losing either its assets or the loyalty of its membership, and where to go from there. SONG began to develop an answer to the first question in late May 1991, by setting up a nonprofit corporation, the Southern Ontario Media Workers' Society. In September, the fifty-five-member local executive committee voted to transfer to this society the local's $1.3 million defense fund and its $200,000 headquarters building. The executive committee's action was approved at an 11 September membership meeting (*Guild Reporter*, 4 October 1991, 5). In essence, it meant that the local had declared financial independence from the Guild, though not political independence.

The move alarmed the leadership of the union. John Bryant, a former member of the SONG executive who was by then the Guild's Canadian director, went to court seeking a temporary injunction against the transfer. When his motion was turned down on 19 September, he filed, unsuccessfully, for a permanent injunction. The *Guild Reporter* noted that an affidavit filed by Lem in opposition to the injunction request argued that it was "quite typical" for Canadian unions to hold buildings in nonprofit corporations, saying this would shield the properties against the possibility of seizure through lawsuits against the unions (4 October 1991, 5). She also said in the affidavit that she knew of no "secession drive" that would take SONG out of the union, and promised the membership in a column in the local newsletter that before taking any steps toward leaving the union, they would have a chance for "full and open discussions" (5).

SONG had set up the corporation through an amendment to its bylaws, but it had not submitted the amendment to the international board for its approval, as required by the Guild constitution. In October 1991, the international executive board ordered the local to repeal the measure and reverse the transfer of funds. The board said the SONG action violated several provisions of the Guild constitution, which prohibited incorporation by locals and required locals that disbanded or had their charters revoked to turn over all books and property to the parent union. The board also expressed concern that transferring funds to a nonprofit organization amounted to transferring control away from the local's membership (*Guild Reporter*, 15 November 1991, 3).

In a 16 September letter to SONG members, president Dale warned that the local risked "rupturing its bonds not only with Guild locals in the United States but throughout Canada." He said the international executive board's effort to overturn the transfer was meant to protect SONG members' control over their funds. "It is *not* a move toward international trusteeship. It *will not* give TNG control of the local's funds. It *will not* interfere in any way with the local's use of those funds for normal Guild purposes" (*Guild Reporter*, 4 October 1991, 5; emphasis in the original).

Here, though, the Guild found itself at a loss. The Ontario judge who threw out the injunction application in September ruled that the local's action did not violate the Guild constitution because the local was not itself a corporation. He also said he was not convinced that the local's assets had been removed from control by the local. The executive of the corporation had exactly the same structure as the executive of the local (*Guild Reporter*, 4 October 1991, 5).

With SONG's assets secured, Lem and other proponents of Canadian independence embarked on a turbulent and intensely political period of activity. This involved, at various times, the Canadian District Council, the union as a whole, other unions representing Canadian media workers, and the Canadian Labour Congress. And while SONG's leaders made plans for life beyond the Guild, they still had to take care of the day-to-day affairs of running a large and busy local: organizing new units, bargaining, providing service to members, and so on.[19]

In terms of Canadian autonomy, two critical developments occurred in the Guild, in 1992 and 1993. In the first, the Guild convention agreed to a constitutional amendment saying that any merger proposal would have to be approved by separate votes in Canada and the United States (*Guild Reporter*, 24 July 1992, 5). This idea, one of the recommendations in SONG's 1988 blueprint for autonomy, was approved at a time when the union did not have a merger partner in sight, much less an agreement on the table. Again, it took a floor fight at the convention to get the change through. The amendment was taken to the convention floor as a minority report after the constitution committee turned it down. During the floor debate, delegates from six Canadian locals—SONG, Vancouver, North Bay, Ottawa, Northern Ontario, and the Canadian Wire Service Guild—spoke in support of the idea. The minority report said that without the support of the majority of Guild members in both the United States and Canada, a merger would not be viable.

> Canadians are asking to be recognized as citizens of a separate country in an international union. Americans at the same time, deserve the right to determine their own future in a merger agreement, regardless of Canadian decisions. A

requirement for a double majority ... provides this recognition and protection to members in both countries.[20]

Opponents of the amendment contended that it amounted to a Canadian veto: if the large U.S. membership endorsed a merger but the smaller Canadian membership did not, the deal would be sunk. Bruce Meachum of Denver argued, however, that this missed the point: a double majority, he said, would be the best mechanism to keep the Guild together in a merger (*Guild Reporter*, 24 July 1992, 5). Earlier in the same session, convention delegates rejected another amendment—this one proposed by the Victoria local—that would have excluded Canadian locals as a group from a merger if a majority of Canadians opposed it, but would have permitted individual Canadian locals to become party to a merger. This plan was seen as potentially too divisive.

The fact that several Canadian locals spoke in favor of the double majority shows that the other Canadian locals were beginning to grapple seriously with the autonomy issues SONG had raised several years earlier. By this point, SONG and many others in the Guild, in Canada and the United States, had come to believe that continued mergers were inevitable—and even, according to Lem (1998), desirable. But they wanted to have a genuine say on whether a possible merger deal was good for the Canadian contingent. By getting the convention to agree to a double majority, they felt more confident that any potential suitor would have to win the Canadian membership's approval in particular, as well as the Guild's approval overall.

Later that year, the Canadian District Council finally reached an agreement on a plan for greater Canadian autonomy within the Guild. Lem, who was by this time the eastern Canada vice-president of the union, and Mike Bocking of Vancouver, the western Canada vice-president, outlined its key elements to the international executive board in April 1993. It called for the election of a Canadian director, the creation of a Canadian executive board, and a separate "global" Canadian budget, to be approved by the convention. In short, the plan contained the key elements of the original SONG blueprint for autonomy, a plan that had been defeated at the convention in 1988 and by the Canadian District Council later that year.

The international executive board did not take up the autonomy document itself at that meeting. Rather, it agreed to continue discussions on the issue (*Guild Reporter*, 30 April 1993, 1). During the meeting, Lem was grilled on whether SONG intended to remain in the Guild regardless of whether that year's convention endorsed the Canadian autonomy plan.

She affirmed that there was strong sentiment among SONG leaders that the local should begin exploratory talks with Canadian unions, but said a membership vote on this had not been taken (*Guild Reporter*, 30 April 1993, 5).

In August 1993, the Canadians who had struggled so hard for so many years to gain more autonomy within the Guild finally got their wish. By unanimous voice vote, delegates to the Guild convention approved amendments to the constitution that would turn the job of Canadian director into an elected position and would make the director the chief spokesperson for the Guild in Canada (*Guild Reporter*, 20 August 1993, 1). The director, to be chosen at a special Canadian convention in the spring of 1994, would join the two Canadian vice-presidents on the international executive board and would be responsible for organizing and collective bargaining in Canada. The director would still have to seek approval from the international executive board on hiring, contract approval, and strike sanction. The Guild's Canadian office would be located in Ottawa (though the director would not be required to move there), and would have a full-time staff person trained in research techniques. The Canadians had won a point some felt should have been won in 1972: the election of the top Guild representative in Canada and the transfer of substantial control over day-to-day affairs from the Guild's Washington-area headquarters to Ottawa.

ONE BIG UNION—CANADIAN-STYLE

The Canadian autonomy plan passed with barely a whisper of debate when it reached the convention floor in Hawaii in 1993 (*Proceedings* 1993, 146–50). But it came too late to stop the departure of SONG. By this time, SONG's leaders and many of the local's members had become convinced that they simply were not getting enough out of their Guild membership. The local did not have control over the dues its members paid; the international did.[21] It also did not have enough control over what it saw as crucial local decisions, like strike votes or bylaw changes.

The big question was where to go from there. Lem says the dream was to create one big media union for Canada, drawing in national media workers' unions and the Canadian locals of international unions. This union would not be limited to newspaper workers, or even to newsworkers. Rather, it would include Canadians who worked in print and broadcasting, in news and entertainment, as professionals and as craft workers. This was not simply Lem's personal dream: in the early 1990s a number of people from a number of unions were interested in exploring the possibility of converging into one new union—or at least, one restructured union. In some ways, the idea of a Canadian media workers' union mirrored Communications Workers of America president Morton Bahr's thinking that, given corporate concentration, they would all end up working for the same employers anyway.

One group interested in exploring the idea came from the former ITU, by then members of the Printing, Publishing, and Media Workers sector of the CWA. Canadian CWA/ITU members had faced even more frustrations than their Guild counterparts in the struggle for Canadian autonomy within their union. At the time the ITU merged with the CWA, it still had no Canadian director, elected or otherwise, and had done very little to comply with the CLC standards of self-government. The Canadians met at conventions in an *ad hoc* caucus, but that was as far as the ITU was willing to go in recognizing them as citizens of a different country. Indeed, one of the main reasons the Canadian ITU contingent supported the CWA merger was that the union promised a better deal for Canadians, says Doug Grey (1999), now with the Communications, Energy and Paperworkers Union.

Grey, who was then with ITU Local 91 in Toronto, says the American ITU leaders tended to treat Canadians as second-class citizens and used their paid staff of international representatives to fend off or break up any attempts by the Canadians to develop solidarity among themselves. "Every time we thought we had a position on something, someone would vote against it. We found out later that they were using the reps to work us against each other—especially to work the large locals against the small ones," he says (1999). Grey and many other Canadian ITU members hoped things would improve after the CWA merger. And in some ways, they did: a Canadian Conference was established in 1987, and in 1991 the union created the elected post of Canadian director. Grey won the job in early 1992.

But neither development lived up to its potential, according to Grey. The Canadian Conference used a different voting system than the union convention—one that allowed the small locals (who according to Grey were more likely to be under the control of the representatives) to dominate.[22] Eventually, under pressure from Grey and the large locals, the voting structure for the Canadian Conference was changed to mirror the standards in the U.S. union. As a result, Grey says, many of the smaller locals stopped coming to Canadian Conference meetings. As for the Canadian directorship, Grey found the job difficult right from the beginning. He says his mandate, duties, and responsibilities were never spelled out clearly. The leadership of the union tended to treat him as a staff representative—in other words, as a subordinate rather than as an equal.[23] And he discovered to his horror that the staff in his own office in Ottawa worked for the president of the Printing, Publishing, and Media Workers sector of the CWA, not for him: "The first time I tried to give an order to the woman who worked in the office, she said no. So I phoned down to Washington and they said, 'Well, she's under the direction of Bill Boarman.' So everything I did had to be approved by Washington" (Grey 1999).

[Margin note: Grey could be a problem giving his version]

Grey used his first convention speech as Canadian director to express concerns about the structure of his job. He said the Canadian contingent saw the director as the spokesman for Canadians on Canadian issues, not as "another representative under the control of Washington."[24] Grey also gave delegates a briefing on what was going on with other Canadian media workers. He noted that SONG was "in a dispute" with the Guild "and they may soon be taking a referendum vote on separating and joining a national Canadian union or forming their own media union" (10). Meanwhile, he said, Guild locals in British Columbia were working closely with CWA/ITU typographers and were interested in joining CWA (10). He also suggested that the Canadian branch of the National Association of Broadcast Employees and Technicians (NABET), which split amicably from its U.S. parent organization in 1974 (A. Craig 1986, 103), might be interested in joining CWA.[25]

> These examples are pointed out to illustrate that some very creative thinking must go into developing a strategy to establish a Canadian structure and bring all the unions together into one printing and communications international union and even to try to interest independent unions in Canada to join. (CWA *Proceedings* 1992, 10)

During the convention, Grey says, he told Bahr and Boarman about a meeting to be held in Toronto with a number of Canadian media unions and locals—among them SONG, several CWA/ITU unions, the Association of Canadian Television and Radio Artists (ACTRA), the Canadian branch of NABET, and the GCIU. Grey says he saw the meeting as a chance to talk about the possibility of the Canadian media unions converging within the CWA. But a few days before the meeting, he says, he got a letter from Washington telling him it was not appropriate for him to attend. "They said, 'Morty Bahr handles all mergers. So you can't go'" (Grey 1999). Grey sat in a restaurant across the street from the meeting, getting reports from members of the ITU locals who attended.

In his report to the next print sector convention, Grey complained bitterly about the decision:

> When the meeting was arranged to meet with all the unions in the media industry in Canada, GCIU, NABET, The Newspaper Guild, [ACTRA], CWA, and just a week prior to the meeting I was ordered not to attend the meeting because one of the leaders of the TNG had been leading her union, SONG, to disaffiliate from TNG and the "call" for the meeting was to establish a Canadian media union. We assured everybody that we were going in there to try to get them to merge with CWA. We believe that CWA lost an opportunity and credibility because the elected autonomous CWA Canadian Director did not attend that meeting. President Bahr in a letter later told Canadians not to talk to other unions about affiliation with CWA. Only the CWA President and the Executive Board had the mandate to do it. So where does that leave us. In the mainstream of labor with all those amalgamations going on in Canada. (CWA *Proceedings* 1993, 10)

Lem and Grey say this meeting was one of several held in the early 1990s to discuss whether unionized Canadian media workers might somehow get together, and if so, how. Some meetings occurred at CLC conventions; others were held separately. Lem confirms that Grey was directed not to talk with the other Canadian unions, and recalls meeting him by chance on an airplane and joking that she guessed he would have to jump off (Lem 1999).

The talk of creating a Canadian media workers' union echoed the "one big union" talks of the early 1960s, in that each group brought a different vision to the table. Grey told his colleagues in CWA that he saw the meetings as leading toward the creation of a strong Canadian media workers' wing within the union. Lem hoped the meetings would create something more ambitious: a new Canadian media workers' union. That hope faded fairly quickly, however. The failure to proceed with a new union was not really anyone's fault, she argued: "No one was a deal-breaker. The fact is that because of the history of the way we had been organized, we weren't at the same stage of development at any given time" (1999). The large ITU locals were farther along the path to independence from their international than any of the others. Among Guild locals, SONG and a few others were thinking seriously about cutting their ties to the Guild, but most were committed to remaining with the international union. ACTRA's participation mattered more to the NABET people, because members of the two unions often worked together, than to the other unions. But NABET, facing a financial crisis, was strongly motivated to find a merger partner, while ACTRA was less interested. And the GCIU's

Canadian leaders were less enthralled by the idea of a Canadian media union than some of the other unions. "It became obvious to some of us that unless the GCIU and ACTRA would come on board, we wouldn't have the numbers to create a Canadian media workers union," Lem says. Without the GCIU, which had 20,000 members in Canada, "it would be hard to realize the economies of scale" (1999). In short, while many of the Canadian union leaders thought the idea was interesting, they were not prepared to pursue it seriously.

MOVING TOWARD CEP

At the CWA/ITU, relations between the large Canadian locals and the Americans were increasingly troubled. Montreal's Local 145, with close to 4,000 members,[26] had decided in 1987 that it wanted to be affiliated directly with the CWA, not with the Printing, Publishing, and Media Workers sector.[27] At the 1990 CWA/ITU sector conference, delegates passed a resolution declaring that the local was delinquent because it had not paid its sector dues, and recommending that it be ejected from the union (CWA *Proceedings* 1990, 14–17). According to Grey, the local was required to be on its own for two years, and then could look for a partner. It settled on the 44,000-member Communications Workers of Canada—the former Canadian arm of the Communications Workers of America that had broken away from the CWA in the early 1970s and represented telephone and telecommunications workers.

At the time Local 145 joined it, CWC was itself on the eve of a major merger with the Paperworkers Union of Canada and the Energy and Chemical Workers. The resulting union, the Communications, Energy and Paperworkers Union of Canada, known as CEP, had 137,000 members and instantly became the fourth-largest private-sector union in Canada (Papp 1992, A21). But while size mattered—articles in the trade press pointed out that the three-way merger gave each of the constituent unions access to a larger strike fund[28]—the merger's significance involved more than sheer numbers. Bringing off a merger of this magnitude required creativity, energy, and flexibility in the union's leadership, attributes many Canadian media unions found appealing. In addition, the new union immediately began presenting itself to its members, and the broader public, as a response to consolidation among the companies that employ union members ("Three-Way Merger" 1993, 7a). Suddenly, it seemed, Canadian labor had a major player in the converging communications industry.

This idea was brought even more sharply into focus in October 1993, when Canadian NABET, representing about 8,000 broadcast production workers, signed an agreement to merge with CEP.[29] With NABET on board, CEP was beginning to look more and more like the Canadian equivalent of the CWA: a large union, composed of highly skilled technical workers in several branches of the communications industry, including telephone workers, broadcast employees, and print-media workers. CEP also represented pulp and paper workers—people who, while not *in* the communications business, produced a product that was essential *to* the communications business. Increasingly, it seemed, CEP was becoming the natural national choice for Canadian workers in the information age.

By 1993, a number of other Canadian ITU locals had come to the end of their patience with their position in the CWA. Grey (1999) says the Canadian sector decided it wanted a free vote on leaving the CWA/ITU and joining a Canadian union—most likely CEP, which would reunite the other Canadian locals with Local 145. Fred Pomeroy, the former president of the CWC and by then a vice-president of CEP,[30] was at the 1993 Canadian conference meeting and was asked to talk with CWA president Morton Bahr about the idea of a separation vote for the Canadians.[31] Grey says Pomeroy reported back to the Canadian locals that Bahr did not believe the majority of Canadian members were unhappy. But at the convention that summer, Bahr announced that he would agree to a free vote of the Canadians.[32]

Bahr told the conference that Grey had briefed the board the previous day. "He was very candid. He expressed his opinion. I suppose his frustrations about his status and that of the Canadian membership within CWA. More importantly he told us of his desire to have our Canadian members vote to decide if they want to continue their membership in CWA" (CWA *Proceedings* 1993, 21). Bahr recalled that a few years earlier, when the sector was developing a structure that would meet Canadian Labour Congress self-government guidelines, he had asked Grey whether there was anything the CWA could do to satisfy him, short of a separation. "He was honest enough to say no and he conceded that when I asked him that question again yesterday before our board" (20). Nonetheless, the executive listened, debated the issue, and decided that the only way the nationalism issue could be resolved was through a vote as soon as possible. "In announcing this," Bahr said,

> let me make it very clear that this is by no means an abandonment by our union of our Canadian members. . . . But it is clear that this issue continues to be a

cancer within the union. It has clearly affected your conference here, the CWA executive board and the CWA convention. . . . Once the referendum is held and the votes counted, CWA will honor the results whichever way it comes out. In the same respect, I hope and trust that if the majority of Canadians vote to stay in CWA, then those who are leading the charge to disaffiliate will be firm in standing with and implementing the majority who wish to stay. This question must be resolved once and for all. And we have now started that process. (20)

The vote, by mail ballot, was set for the fall of 1993. An article in the October 1993, printing and publishing sector newsletter set out two possible outcomes:

A majority "yes" vote would keep the members in CWA and eligible for Sector and CWA representation and programs such as the strike and mortuary funds. . . . A majority "no" vote would divorce the workers from the Sector and CWA and leave them free to handle their own bargaining, representation and legal concerns and to establish their own, new strike and mortuary funds, if they choose to. (*CWA Sector News*, October 1993, 6A)

Nothing this clear-cut emerged, however. In what was by then almost characteristic ITU fashion, the vote was split: 1,626 in favor of leaving CWA, 1,563 in favor of staying—a difference of just sixty-three votes. But when the vote was broken down by local, a distinct pattern emerged. A majority of members in the seven large locals wanted to leave, while a majority of members in the twenty-nine small and medium-sized locals wanted to stay (*CWA Sector News*, December 1993, 6A).

The sector newsletter declared the result "a virtual dead heat." Bahr wrote to the Canadian locals in December, saying that those who voted to leave CWA could do so if they wished, as long as they followed proper procedure. He repeated the message on 10 January 1994, when Fred Pomeroy of the CEP and officers of the CWA Canadian conference came to Washington (*CWA Sector News*, February 1994, 6B). This interpretation of the results infuriated Grey and his allies in the large locals, who argued that a majority was a majority and that Bahr was going back on his convention promise to honor the results. A number of the smaller locals, meanwhile, had begun lobbying to stay within CWA. In January, twenty-three local leaders sent a letter to Bahr asking to keep their affiliation, complaining that the Canadian Conference was not representative of the Canadian membership but rather was "in the hands of those who are proponents of disaffiliation." The letter charged that Doug Grey "has not worked on behalf of CWA, but rather the CEP," and asked that he be fired as Canadian director (quoted in *CWA Sector News*, February 1994, 6A).

In January, Canadian Conference leaders invited all Canadian locals to a meeting to get an update on the sector's dealings with the CWA and to meet leaders of the CEP. The locals that sent representatives to the meeting—those that supported a move to the CEP—decided to bar CWA loyalist Dave Esposti, a representative from Sault Ste. Marie, from attending (*CWA Sector News*, February 1994, 6B). Shortly thereafter, Grey says (1999), he was dismissed as Canadian director.

In March 1994, nine Canadian locals voted by referendum to move to CEP. While Grey was happy with the move, he still smarts over the fact that the Canadian district of the union ended up divided between CWA and CEP. He blames CWA for changing the rules on the Canadian district after the vote was taken. But he also blames CEP for not going after the CWA more aggressively.

> Fifty percent plus one is a victory, right? That's democracy, right? . . . But the Americans didn't understand what democracy means. They changed their position. . . . They violated the CWA constitution. If we had taken legal action against them we would have won. But that was the failing of the CEP to follow through with that. (1999)

SONG MOVES ON

While the Canadian ITU locals sorted themselves out, SONG was moving inevitably toward its own departure from The Newspaper Guild. By early 1994, the parent union had undergone some significant changes. It now had an elected Canadian director, Mike Bocking of Vancouver, acclaimed at a special convention in Victoria, British Columbia (*Guild Reporter*, 25 March 1994, 1). It had also picked up a large new group of members at the CBC, as a result of a consolidation vote ordered by the Canada Labour Relations Board.[33] These workers swelled the membership of the Canadian Wire Service Guild fivefold, to 3,500. This local, soon to be renamed the Canadian Media Guild, surpassed SONG as the largest Canadian local and was the second-largest local in the union (*Guild Reporter*, 18 February 1994, 4). By May 1994, The Newspaper Guild was actively in the market for a merger partner, and the CWA had emerged as a main contender (*Guild Reporter*, 20 May 1994, 1).

In an attempt to ensure the continued support of its Canadian membership, the union was drafting plans for the creation of something known as TNG Canada, an autonomous Canadian section within the Guild—wherever the Guild might end up. The plan called for shifting responsibility for day-to-day affairs of the Guild in Canada to a Canadian national committee. TNG Canada would have its own budget and would service its own locals. Guild officials estimated in June 1994 that about $1 million of the $1.5 million in dues collected from Canadians each year would stay in Canada. The Canadian director would sign off on contract settlements, in consultation with the international executive board. Use of the strike fund in Canada would be governed by resolutions established for all locals by the union's executive and conventions (*Guild Reporter*, 24 June 1994, 1).

None of this stopped the SONG secession drive. While Gail Lem and her colleagues had fought hard for more Canadian autonomy within the union, by 1994 that was yesterday's story. They were fed up with belonging to a union headquartered in another country. The arrival of the CWA as a merger partner did nothing to change their view that SONG should move to a Canadian union. Indeed, if anything it reinforced their concerns about belonging to a minority rump in the union. SONG had closely followed the CWA's dealings with the Canadian ITU locals, and viewed the departure of Grey's locals as the only reasonable course of action for them. As for a possible merger between the Guild and the CWA, "We thought the CWA was a good partner for the Americans, but not for us," Lem says (1998).

In March 1994, SONG members voted overwhelmingly to authorize their leaders to pursue affiliation talks with a Canadian union (*Guild Reporter*, 20 May 1994, 1). Lem says SONG held exploratory talks with three unions: the Canadian Auto Workers union (CAW), the Canadian Union of Public Employees (CUPE), and CEP. Her personal preference was the CAW, which had managed a difficult but successful divorce from the United Auto Workers union in 1985. But the CAW wasn't interested. A statement to the membership from SONG's Canadian autonomy committee reported that the CAW "decided against providing a new home for us" (20 October 1994). It explained that CAW president Buzz Hargrove felt that CEP "was developing into the Canadian national media-workers union that so many of us had so long sought. [Hargrove] felt our interests could best be met by being in the same union as most other newspaper and broadcast industry workers in the country." Talks with CUPE did not go much further. Lem (1998) said her local felt that union was "too public-sector-oriented." That left CEP.

SONG made its move in June 1994, asking the Guild's international executive board for permission to leave. The board turned down the request (*Guild Reporter*, 23 September 1994, 1). This raised the prospect of a bitter legal battle between the local and the parent union, in which SONG's assets might become contested terrain. In August, SONG sent a letter to the Canadian Labour Congress asking for a ruling that the local had "justification" for leaving the Guild and joining another union. In her letter, Lem said the Guild "may or may not be technically in violation of the Constitution of the Canadian Labour Congress at this point in time" (see *Guild Reporter*, 23 September 1994, 7). In any event, she said, SONG was convinced that belonging to the Guild was not in the best interests of its members. She complained that the Guild was too small to provide for the minimum service needs of the large local (7). The last time the local approached the CLC with a complaint against the Guild, in 1990, it had been rebuffed. This time, after a hearing in September, the CLC's executive committee ruled in SONG's favor. It invoked a rarely used section of the CLC constitution to grant the local's request for a finding of justification.[34] This was not simply a symbolic victory for the local: the federation directed the Guild to assist in the local's efforts to disaffiliate. If the Guild tried to fight SONG's departure, it might find itself facing sanctions from the CLC (7).

The CLC did not say why it ruled as it did. An aide to CLC President Bob White told the *Guild Reporter* that CLC policy forbade explaining executive decisions (23 September 1994, 1). But it seems likely that the growing power of Canadian unions in the upper echelons of the federation was a factor. Indeed, the CLC president was the man who led the secession of the Canadian Auto Workers from the United Auto Workers. White was seen by Lem and others as likely to be sympathetic on questions about national identity.

The Guild learned about the CLC decision when a press release from SONG announcing the result was posted on the Guild's computer bulletin board by the administrative officer of the Los Angeles Guild. President Dale and Canadian director Bocking responded by publishing a joint statement in the *Guild Reporter* that castigated Lem personally.

> In petitioning the CLC's executive committee and in a press release announcing the CLC decision, SONG President Gail Lem repeated a falsehood she has used in various other forums for several years, to wit: that TNG does not provide for its Canadian members even the bare minimum of services that a local should be able to reasonably expect from a parent union. We categorically reject claims of inadequate service.... (*Guild Reporter*, 23 September 1994, 7)

The next few weeks were fraught with tension. At the time the secession drive reached its climax, SONG was in negotiations with *The Globe and Mail*, the leading Canadian daily newspaper. Workers there took a strike vote on 24 September, though according to Dale, SONG's leadership had not consulted with the international when it set a strike deadline (*Guild Reporter*, 21 October 1994, 7). On 28 September, SONG leaders proposed to affiliate with CEP, and made plans for a referendum to ratify the agreement. On 29 September, the Guild's international executive board decided in a conference call to revoke SONG's charter (*Guild Reporter*, 21 October 1994, 1). This action cast SONG free while it was in the final hours of negotiations with *The Globe and Mail* and before it had its merger with CEP fully in place. Lem (1998) blames Dale personally for the decision and believes there was more than a hint of malice in the action.

The *Guild Reporter* account of the meeting shows that Dale took the hardest line against the renegade Toronto local, but was by no means alone in making the decision to revoke the local's charter. Canadian director Bocking told the board he had advised the leaders of other Canadian Guild locals that his recommendation would be to allow SONG to depart. But Bocking's approach was decidedly more gentle than Dale's. In a press release issued after the vote, Bocking said the board took the decision with "regret and reluctance." He wrote, "The Toronto local has been a strong part of the Guild for decades and has served its members there well. We wish them every success in their future endeavours in their new home" (*Guild Reporter*, 21 October 1994, 1).

Dale was less gracious. In a fax to Lem after the vote he wrote, "It is regrettable that SONG has precipitated and compelled this course of action. We hope that the members of your local will benefit as much from their new affiliation as they have throughout their long and successful relationship with TNG" (*Guild Reporter*, 21 October 1994, 1). Pat Bell of the Ottawa local, who was then the union's eastern Canada vice-president, expressed concerns about what the decision would mean to *The Globe and Mail* workers. Dale replied, "The strike deadline is SONG's issue," essentially washing his hands of the matter (1). As it turned out, the local reached an agreement with the newspaper early on 30 September, averting a strike. Lem (1998) says CEP was prepared to support a SONG strike, even though the merger had not yet been ratified. An undated document in the SONG archives indicates that when the ratification vote came later that fall, the results were overwhelmingly in favor of the merger. The tally was 1,300 to 50, or 96 percent, in favor of the merger.

In October 1994 Dale sent a letter to the CLC complaining about its handling of the SONG request for justification. "The short shrift given to TNG's presentation and examination of material left for you suggests strongly that this long-time affiliate of the Congress was denied the due process it deserved," he wrote (*Guild Reporter*, 21 October 1994, 7). He also claimed there had been "a distortion of the facts," and said the CLC executive should review its decision. And he suggested that the CLC would eventually regret the move, saying it "will create a disastrous precedent for other international unions which hope to continue to function in Canada" (7). But none of this mattered: SONG was long gone.

DEPARTURES AND REALIGNMENTS

Most of the Guild's attention in 1994 was focused on finding a merger partner. By the end of the year, CWA was it. Because of the constitutional change approved in 1992, however, any merger had to be ratified by both the Canadian contingent and the American majority in the union. While the international leaders were negotiating a deal with the CWA, the Canadians struck their own "futures committee" in the fall of 1994 to study merger options for Canadian Guild members (*Guild Reporter*, 20 January 1995, 2).

In early 1995, the CWA and Guild negotiators came up with an idea they thought might be enticing for all concerned: the possibility of a "reverse merger" in which the remaining former ITU members in Canada would move to TNG Canada, the evolving autonomous Canadian branch of the union (*Guild Reporter*, 17 February 1995, 6). This would expand the Guild's reach in Canada, giving it a presence at newspapers in the Maritimes, for example, where the Guild had no members. It would also add 1,500 new members to the 6,000 remaining Guild members in Canada. And it would serve as an example of convergence in action, putting workers from two different CWA sectors into the same Canadian home. Ironically, this would create in Canada the kind of organic Guild–ITU merger that had died at the international level in the 1980s. For the CWA/ITU print sector, which was responsible for servicing a large number of small locals scattered across a wide terrain, the idea also made sense. After a meeting with Boarman and Bocking, the conference of Canadian CWA locals expressed interest in the idea (6).

Although the merger negotiations at the international level proceeded very quickly, the Canadians took their time in deciding what to do. First, they figured out whether it was in their interest to try to go it alone. The futures committee solved that one easily: at a meeting in January, they agreed that with just 6,000 members, the Canadian branch of the union was simply too small to survive as a freestanding union (*Guild Reporter*, 20 January 1995, 2). But rather than rushing to embrace the CWA, they decided to study a range of merger alternatives. They invited three unions—the CWA, CEP, and the Canadian Auto Workers—to make presentations at a meeting in March. Anyone who hoped this would settle things was to be disappointed. After hearing from all three, the committee members felt that they still needed more information. Said Bocking, "The group had a long discussion on Saturday afternoon. At the end, the group was not able to make a recommendation that would represent a consensus of the people there" (*Guild Reporter*, 24 March 1995, 2). Some wanted to know more about CEP. Others had questions about the structure of the proposed TNG Canada. The large Canadian Media Guild brought to the meeting a number of ideas about how to grant even more autonomy to TNG Canada, including the radical notion that locals should be able to opt out of their per-capita payments to the international and instead reimburse the international only for services rendered (2). The other locals objected to that plan, feeling it would weaken both the locals and the union itself. But clearly, the Canadians were still divided on what kind of deal they felt would serve their interests in a CWA–Guild merger.

By late March 1995, however, the Canadians had agreed on a plan for TNG Canada and approved a proposal for its structure. It was adopted almost immediately, and unanimously, by the Guild's international executive board. The plan was approved by the Guild convention on 19 June on a voice vote, "with several audible 'nos'" (*Guild Reporter*, 11 August 1995, 1). TNG Canada was created as an autonomous body within the Guild, with constitutional jurisdiction in Canada and an affiliation agreement with CWA/TNG. It would be governed by an elected representative council, chaired by an elected Canadian director. TNG Canada would send per-capita dues payments to the Guild headquarters in Washington, at a rate to be negotiated. The parent union would return a portion of that to Canada, and the Canadians would be in charge of deciding how to spend this money (1–4).

While the outlines of TNG Canada were clear, there were a lot of blanks to be filled in, especially regarding money. But in an apparent reflection of the divided feelings among the Canadian locals, the longest and most detailed section of the plan dealt not with how to put TNG Canada together, but how locals could opt out of it:

Whereas several Canadian locals have expressed concerns about merging with a large international union, and have shown a preference for joining a national [Canadian] union,

Be it resolved that should any Canadian local decide by a membership referendum, conducted using the international's voting rules, to join a Canadian

union, that the international shall facilitate this process by the following means:
a) Allowing locals to retain current assets.
b) Refrain from raiding charges, trusteeship or other legal challenges etc.
(*Guild Reporter*, 11 August 1995, 1)

This amounted to an escape clause for Canadian locals who weren't sure the merger with CWA was a good idea for them.

The CWA–Guild merger and the proposal to create TNG Canada were approved by the Guild convention in June 1995, and a membership referendum was set for September. Over the summer, however, two Canadian locals—the large Vancouver local representing workers at Pacific Press and a smaller local in Windsor, Ontario, representing workers at the *Windsor Star*—decided the time had come to go elsewhere. For the Vancouver local, there was only one real choice, says Jan O'Brien (1997), who was then president of the local. Local members had become increasingly convinced that they should belong not just to a Canadian union but to a Canadian media workers' union, she says. With NABET, the typographers (including those at Pacific Press), and SONG already on board, that union was CEP. Ironically, Mike Bocking of the Vancouver local was the Guild's Canadian director during the very time his local was considering leaving the Guild to join CEP. Bocking stepped down from the Canadian directorship and returned to his job as a reporter (*Guild Reporter*, 29 September 1995, 7). CBC television producer Arnold Amber, from the Canadian Media Guild, replaced Bocking as the union's top official in Canada and became the head of the newly formed TNG Canada. For the Windsor local, the calculation was a bit different. Windsor is auto country, and for unionized workers the major union in town was the Canadian Auto Workers union. While this union had been reluctant to take in SONG, suggesting it look for a home in CEP, it showed no such reluctance to accept the hometown workers at the *Windsor Star*.

Windsor and Vancouver were still officially part of the Guild when the referendum on the CWA merger took place in September 1995, but neither participated. The remaining Canadian locals approved the merger by a vote of 677 to 83. In every local except North Bay, where the vote was close, the result was strongly in favor of the merger and the creation of TNG Canada.

UNITED, DIVIDED

The Canadian question has been a recurring theme for newspaper unions for more than three decades, and especially for The Newspaper Guild.

The ITU chose largely to ignore the issue of Canadian autonomy until joining the CWA in the 1980s, and then handled the matter with a lack of tact. By contrast, the Guild took steps as early as 1972 to comply with the spirit of the new CLC principles on self-government. It created an appointed Canadian directorship and two elected Canadian vice-presidencies, and followed up with a number of refinements over the next several years. It finally made the top Canadian spot an elected position in the 1990s.

But resolving the concerns about autonomy and representation requires more than constitutional refinements. Not surprisingly, the pragmatic issues raised by the CLC principles are relatively easy to resolve. Those dealing with more politically charged areas like identity and nationalism are much more difficult to answer. Over the last twenty-five years or so, the "hot button" issues surrounding Canadian content in the union movement have varied. In the early 1970s, the debate at the CLC and within individual unions centered on how to improve Canadian representation in the international unions. At The Newspaper Guild, this meant figuring out the appropriate role for the Canadian director—especially whether this individual should serve as a top-down leader, appointed by the international to run the Canadian sector, or as a bottom-up leader elected by the Canadian membership. These were essentially practical questions, and were (or at least could have been) relatively easy to solve.

By the time SONG came up with its "Blueprint for Canadian Autonomy" in 1988, the concerns of at least some Canadians in the Guild had gone well beyond pragmatic matters like the job description of the Canadian director, and into the more difficult terrain of philosophy and national sovereignty. SONG's blueprint was not so much a declaration of independence, or even a complaint against the Guild, as it was an uneasy recognition of what that local was beginning to see as irreconcilable national differences. In the late 1980s, SONG's leaders came to feel that despite decades of close cooperation, the labor movements in the two countries were growing further and further apart. After eight years of Reaganomics and union-bashing by Republican lawmakers, American unions were struggling once again with issues like the security of the bargaining unit, which simply were not relevant to Canada. The proportion of unionized workers in the United States was in rapid decline: from almost 28 percent of paid workers in 1976, it had dropped to 17 percent by 1986. In Canada, by contrast, the proportion of unionized workers was stable: indeed, between 1976 and 1986 it had actually inched up, by just under one percentage point, to 37.7 percent (Murray 1995, 164). The

Canadians, meanwhile, had their own political and economic concerns—free trade and the privatization of previously public institutions and services, for example—which were of less gripping interest to the Americans. The kinds of questions the SONG document raised did not lend themselves to simple, pragmatic fixes. But the local nevertheless tried to come up with an answer, proposing the creation of an essentially autonomous Canadian branch of the Guild. This answer was shouted down at convention, and ironically the loudest voices were those of the other Canadian locals. In 1988 the Canadian locals were not prepared as a group to confront the issues SONG raised, and they were angry that SONG chose to bring these issues up at the convention, rather than within the Canadian District Council.

Over the next six years, as SONG slowly cut its ties with the international, the local's leaders argued for Canadian autonomy on both pragmatic and philosophical grounds. In pragmatic terms, they focused on issues like whether the Guild was providing adequate servicing to its Canadian locals, or whether American leaders should have the final say on a strike call by a Canadian local, or who should appoint Canadian delegates to the International Federation of Journalists meetings. Led by Gail Lem, they were also thinking about larger questions, such as whether the time might be right for Canadian workers from previously discrete parts of the communications business (newspapers and broadcast outlets; telecommunications and magazines) who did substantially different types of work (reporters and entertainers; technicians and professionals) to create a Canadian media workers' union. They also questioned the role Canadians might play when the Guild merged with CWA. While Lem was out front on most of these questions, and often took the blame from the American leadership and even from her Canadian colleagues, the other Canadian locals eventually began asking the same kinds of questions.

SONG and some other Canadian Guild and CWA/ITU locals worked their way through most of the items Dawes identifies as sources of Canadian dissatisfaction with international unions: questions of autonomy; the concession bargaining and political-action philosophies of some American unions; international union support for American interests over Canadian ones; the perception that internationals fragment Canadian labor and drain money from the country; and the problem of substantial dues increases or corruption in some international unions (Dawes 1987, 3). With the exception of corruption, all the factors Dawes identifies were irritants or sore spots at one point or another within the Canadian contingent of the Guild in the 1980s and 1990s. The Canadian members of the former ITU felt the same irritants and more; not only did they have to confront the autonomy question, they had to do so amid the tumultuous years in which their union sought partner after partner before settling into a happy union with the CWA.

In the end, Canadian media workers in the Guild and elsewhere came up with two very different answers to the so-called Canadian question—answers that resulted in a dramatic restructuring of the media unions in Canada. Convergence was a key consideration in both answers.

One group ended up as part of the American-based CWA union, a union that sees itself, according to its president, as the leader in the rapidly converging "TIME" industries—telecommunications, information, media, and entertainment. Under the merger agreement with CWA, The Newspaper Guild agreed to set up the autonomous branch TNG Canada. In a so-called reverse merger, this branch acquired former Canadian members of the ITU, which had itself merged with CWA. As a result, TNG Canada is a living example of labor convergence in the communications sector: it draws together newspaper editorial and business office workers in Ontario, Quebec, British Columbia, Saskatchewan, Alberta, and the Maritimes; national, regional, and local broadcast workers within the CBC; producers and reporters at TVO, the Ontario public broadcaster; wire-service reporters and editors across the country with The Canadian Press and Reuters; and former typographical union members at small newspapers nationwide. Indeed, TNG Canada represents a considerably more thorough merger than the one at the international level. In the United States, the former ITU and Guild have their own separate sectors within CWA; in TNG Canada, they are breaking new ground together, on everything from housekeeping matters to organizing strategy.

For Canadian Guild members, the establishment of TNG Canada offered attractions on two seemingly contradictory fronts. On the one hand, it gave Canadian workers the chance to belong to an international union of 600,000—a union that was bigger and more powerful than the very biggest Canadian unions, and was delighted to regain a foothold in Canada through the Guild and ITU mergers. TNG Canada was set up as an autonomous sector of a bigger sector of the CWA. In other words, although TNG Canada belongs to the CWA, its Canadian locals have more independence than Guild members of the early 1970s ever dreamed possible. At the same time, though, TNG Canada is a relatively small organization: its membership of roughly 8,500 amounts to little more than 1 percent of total CWA membership. In addition, despite efforts to consolidate some smaller locals, the membership is unbalanced: the

Canadian Media Guild local alone accounts for more than half the total membership.

The other answer to the Canadian question was the clustering of media workers' unions within a converged Canadian union—CEP.[35] Through its own series of mergers, CEP has picked up the formerly free-standing broadcast technicians' union, two large former Newspaper Guild locals, and the biggest of the former ITU locals in Canada. CEP's power, like CWA's, rests on representing workers in telecommunications and the media. The former Guild and ITU locals do not have the same kind of sector-based autonomy within CEP as their one-time parent unions have in CWA. Instead, they are all members of a shared media workers' sector. In this respect, though, they are much like their counterparts in TNG Canada. Within CEP, however, the media workers are more of a force to be reckoned with than their Canadian counterparts in CWA: about one in seven CEP members comes from the former Guild, ITU, or NABET.

A key indicator of a labor union's success is whether it is able to organize new groups of workers. Both TNG Canada and CEP have had some successes in this area. TNG Canada won the right to be the bargaining agent for newsroom workers at the *Regina Leader-Post* in late 1998, after being defeated in an earlier organizing drive. Negotiations for a first contract were long and slow, and in the end the Saskatchewan Labour Relations Board imposed one.[36] Through one of its former ITU locals, TNG Canada organized the newsroom at the independent *Halifax Chronicle-Herald*.[37] In early 2000, a small union of background performers in Canadian-made movies and television shows voted to join the Canadian Media Guild local of TNG Canada (*The Globe and Mail*, 11 January 2000, R3). In 2002 it organized editorial workers at the Aboriginal Peoples Television Network.[38] These organizing drives have expanded Guild jurisdiction into new territory, enhancing the Guild's position as a national union. The Saskatchewan drive was particularly satisfying: though it took two tries, the union succeeded in getting in at a paper that suffered badly after being bought by Hollinger.[39]

CEP has also been active in organizing. New members include newspaper carriers in Winnipeg and Toronto and newsroom workers at the Chinese-language *Sing Tao Daily* (*SONGsheet*, November 2001). Its most spectacular organizing success—becoming the bargaining agent for reporters and editors at the *Calgary Herald* newspaper—turned out in the end, however, to be a spectacular defeat. In Calgary, CEP penetrated distinctly hostile territory: not just a Hollinger newspaper but a newspaper in Alberta, a province where private-sector unions are rare indeed and where, unlike Saskatchewn, there is no first-contract arbitration. Negotiations between the union and *Herald* management dragged on for almost a year. The union went on strike in 1999. In June 2000, the newspaper offered CEP members a buyout package, conditional on decertification of the union. Though Calgary was a failure, the Toronto and Winnipeg campaigns added new types of workers to the fold. And in British Columbia, a single CEP local has become the most powerful media union in the province.

Each group of Canadian Guild members, those who went to CEP and those who went to CWA, felt it had the best answer to the Canadian question. And while there is some bitterness about the division of the Canadian branch of the Guild, there is also a degree of mutual respect,[40] and a realization that though they came to different solutions, they all struggled with the same kinds of questions.

In fact, the Canadian question has resurfaced recently, this time at the Canadian Broadcasting Corporation. Following a wave of cutbacks in the 1990s, the CUPE bargaining unit moved into TNG Canada's Canadian Media Guild local. In 1999, the local submitted a proposal to the Canada Industrial Relations Board to merge the two bargaining units. The CBC responded by proposing that its two Guild units and its CEP unit, which represents former members of NABET, should all be combined into one. TNG Canada supports a single union, arguing that "The pace of change and the technological revolution in the industry, change which has been accelerated at the CBC because of budget cuts, make the old jurisdictional lines obsolete."[41] CEP argues that consolidation is unnecessary, as the current structure is only a few years old and there is no reason, either in terms of law or labor practice, to alter it.

The board was expected to rule on the consolidation sometime in 2002. If the decision favors the CBC and Guild, unionized workers at the CBC might be asked to vote on which union to represent them. Given the numbers—TNG Canada represents roughly twice as many CBC employees as CEP—the contest would seem to favor TNG Canada. But for CEP especially, nationalism is already a key factor in the case. Peter Murdoch, vice-president for media of the CEP, says, "We would certainly be dismayed to have Canada's national public broadcaster represented by an American-based union" (Murdoch 2001).

Murdoch and Arnold Amber, head of TNG Canada, staked out their positions in an exchange published in the online journal *Straight Goods*, during and after a three-week CBC lockout of CEP technicians late in 2001. Amber, responding to an article on the lockout by Murdoch, accused the CEP leader of attempting "to demonize the Canadian Media Guild because it is part of the Communication Workers of America." He added, "We like the strength we have in being part of the CWA family and love the autonomy we have here in Canada over our policies and action" (Amber 2001). Murdoch shot back, saying CEP members "are proud to be in a Canadian Union, one which represents the vast majority of Canadian media workers in both broadcasting and print." He said that if CWA should win the vote, "the CBC would become the only national public broadcaster in the world represented by a union with a home base outside its national borders" (Murdoch 2002).

Three decades of work on two different fronts—uniting previously separate unions, and ensuring adequate Canadian representation—have resulted in a distinctly Canadian brew of separation and unity. Many members of CEP and CWA would prefer to see only one Canadian media workers' union. But there is no agreement on which one.

NOTES

1. For more on this see D. Morton 1998; Heron 1989, 1996.
2. See "Guild Milestones," in The Newspaper Guild Constitution, adopted at the sixtieth annual convention, 1993.
3. The Vancouver and Victoria locals both began in the 1940s as independent unions under direct charter from the Trades and Labour Congress. They affiliated with the Guild in the mid-1950s (S. Craig 1987, 3).
4. Unlike other large public-service unions that provide service directly to members, NUPGE is a federation of autonomous provincial unions (Murray 1995, 176).
5. This is seen most dramatically in the growing discrepancy between the two countries in the proportion of unionized workers. While the number has been relatively stable in Canada, the proportion of unionized workers in the United States has been in sharp decline (Murray 1995, 164).
6. Indeed, Alton Craig contends that the labor federation mergers are another example of how actions taken by the U.S. labor movement influence Canadian labor: "it is undoubtedly true that [the creation of the CLC] would not have taken place in Canada (at least not as early as 1956) if the AFL-CIO merger had not taken place in the United States" (1986, 73).
7. D. Morton notes that these standards did little to appease the nationalists in the CLC (1998, 279–82). At the same time, they enraged some of the international unions, especially those in the building trades. A number of these unions withheld their affiliation checks in protest. The president of the CLC went to Washington to discuss the issue with the international and the checks resumed. Eventually the construction unions withdrew from the CLC and formed the Canadian Federation of Labour in 1982.
8. President Charles Perlik explained later that the union decided against changing "American" to "international" because Canadians thought the word "interna-

tional" in the name of a union was synonymous with "American." Instead, it chose a title that neatly avoided the question of nationality (S. Craig 1987, 6).

9. This local eventually became the Southern Ontario Newspaper Guild (SONG).

10. Rupert left the post of Canadian director after less than two years, taking a job with the Guild as an organizer in California. He was replaced as Canadian director by Bill McLeman, who held the job from 1974 to 1988. The last nonelected Canadian director was John Bryant, who held the post from 1988 until the early 1990s.

11. Bob Rupert, "No Life Like a Life in the Guild," program for CWA/TNG sector conference, 29 April–2 May 1999, in Ottawa, 9).

12. Convention proceedings show that the debate took up much of an afternoon. But the convention moved into executive session twice and approved a motion to suspend the rules. The reason, according to Jerry MacDonald, a staff representative with the Canadian Wire Service Guild local who proposed it, was "for the purpose of expunging the record" (*Proceedings of The Newspaper Guild Annual Convention*, 1986, [n.p.,] 81). Ultimately, the convention approved a clause in the constitution stipulating, "In Canadian Locals only, no resignation or withdrawal may be accepted during a strike or lockout, or at a time when a strike or lockout appears imminent" (Article X, Section 13[c] of TNG Constitution). Section 15 then set out the resignation rules in each country. These changes represented a significant bifurcation of the constitution, since it meant some sections applied in one country but not the other.

13. In Canada, contracts tend to follow the so-called Rand formula, named after Ontario Justice Ivan Rand, the arbitrator in a major 1945 Ford strike. Rand ruled that the employer would deduct union dues from all members of the bargaining unit and remit the money to the union. But while everyone would be required to pay union dues, no one would actually be forced to join the union (D. Morton 1998, 186).

14. That individual was Bill McLeman, who was about to leave the Canadian directorship for a new post within the union.

15. *Proceedings of The Newspaper Guild Annual Convention*, 1988, [n.p.,] 60. Hereafter *"Proceedings."*

16. See minutes of the Canadian District Council meeting, 29–30 October 1988. The minutes are held in the SONG archives in Toronto.

17. Bocking's counterproposal called for retaining the Canadian directorship as an appointed position, but elevating the chair of the Canadian District Council to chief spokesperson for the Guild in Canada (minutes of CDC meeting, 29–30 October, 1988.

18. The union's organizing summary for 1989 shows that SONG gained representation for more employees than any other local in the Guild that year. These gains included newsroom employees at the *London Free Press*, the Brabant weeklies in Ontario, and the Polish Alliance in Toronto (*Guild Reporter*, 5 January 1990, 1).

19. Indeed, that November SONG began two strikes, one of which would last five months (*Guild Reporter*, 13 March 1992, 1; and 24 April 1992, 1). In the spring of 1992, its biggest unit, representing 1,300 people at the *Toronto Star*, waged a thirty-one-day strike (*Guild Reporter*, 24 July 1992, 1).

20. Minority report of constitution committee, TNG annual convention, 1992; quoted in *Guild Reporter*, 24 July 1992, 5.

21. Between 1991 and 1994, SONG sent $1.2 million in per capita payments to the

international, or about one-third of what it collected from its members. President Dale contended that it got that much back in organizing subsidies, reimbursements for organizing expenses, legal fees, and strike benefits (*Guild Reporter*, 21 October 1994, 7).

22. Grey explains that the ITU constitution was based on "one member, one vote." The Canadian conference, by contrast, was based on "one delegate, one vote." This meant that although six large locals contained the bulk of the union's Canadian membership, they could easily be outvoted by the thirty or so small locals who could send delegates to the conference.

23. At a sector convention shortly after he was elected, Grey recalls (1999), he was shocked to learn that he had been named a sergeant-at-arms. This was a low-level convention job carried out by the paid staff but not by the elected leadership. He says he and the Canadian contingent took this as an insult and fought it. The head of the sector told him he either had to serve as a sergeant-at-arms or not appear on the convention floor at all. Grey pressed the point and won. The next year, however, he was given the same order. This time, he put on the armband of a sergeant-at-arms.

24. *Proceedings of CWA Printing, Publishing, and Media Workers Sector Conference*, 1992, [n.p.,] 11. Hereafter "CWA *Proceedings*."

25. The American branch of NABET was also exploring a merger with the CWA. It became the union's Broadcast and Cable Television Workers sector in 1994. See the CWA fact sheet, "Facts at a Glance," 1998.

26. This local had begun as a traditional typographical workers' union but had taken seriously the idea that the ITU should be an industrial union, not one limited to workers in a particular trade. Its membership includes a broad range of non-newspaper workers (Lem 1998).

27. The local had been engaged in a dispute with the ITU over strike pay and decided that while it no longer wanted to be affiliated with the ITU's sector inside CWA, it would be willing to be affiliated directly with the CWA. It remained so until being expelled in 1990.

28. See, for example, "Three-Way Merger" 1993, 7A; and Cagampan-Stoute 1993, 76.

29. See text of merger agreement between Canadian NABET and CEP, 28 October 1993, in CEP national office, Ottawa.

30. Pomeroy became president of CEP in 1995 (Van Alpen 1995, D18).

31. Bahr and Pomeroy had a history of working together. In 1989 Pomeroy joined CWA leaders at the bargaining table to show support for CWA members who were on strike against Northern Telecom plants in the United States. A CWA press release issued at the time (21 August 1989) said it was the first time Canadian and U.S. unions had joined together in this manner to put pressure on an employer.

32. Grey (1999) says the Canadian locals had brought to the convention a resolution condemning the actions of a CWA/ITU representative in dealing with a strike in Nova Scotia. The resolution would have embarrassed the leadership of the union. In return for the promise of a free vote, the Canadians agreed to withdraw the resolution. The proceedings of the conference show that the resolution died in committee. Bill Boarman, head of the sector, told delegates that the faction in favor of Canadian independence tried to use the Nova Scotia incident to embarrass the union and promote their agenda of separation (CWA *Proceedings* 1993, 27–28).

33. The CBC had been fighting since the early 1990s for a realignment of its unions. In 1991 the Guild and two other independent producers' unions at the CBC combined to form the Canadian Council of Broadcast Unions, which they hoped would serve as a joint bargaining council at the CBC. The federal labor board rejected that idea, ordering a consolidation vote in the summer of 1993. The Guild polled 56 percent of the ballots, beating out ACTRA, which won 25 percent, and CUPE, which picked up 19 percent. This meant that the Guild was the sole bargaining agent for CBC employees who write, edit, and produce CBC news programs (*Guild Reporter*, 14 July 1993, 1). In 1998, CUPE-affiliated workers voted to merge with the Guild. This added 750 members to the local, now known as the Canadian Media Guild, making it the largest local in the Guild (*Guild Reporter*, 18 June 1998, 1).

34. The CLC ruling cited three sections of its constitution that it said were relevant to the case, but it did not specifically find the Guild in violation of the CLC constitution (*Guild Reporter*, 23 September 1994, 1).

35. The Windsor local's move to the CAW is most properly seen as a local solution. Even so, the CAW holds many of the same attractions as CEP. It is a large union, a Canadian union, and a union that is diversifying the kinds of workers its represents.

36. TNG Canada newsletter, March/April 2001, at www.tngcanada.org (accessed 18 June 2001).

37. TNG Canada newsletter, May 1999, at www.tngcanada.org (accessed 20 February 2000).

38. News release, 28 March 2002, at www.cmg.org (accessed 10 April 2002).

39. Within days of buying the *Saskatoon StarPhoenix* and *Regina Leader-Post* in 1996, Hollinger fired 27 percent of the work force at the two dailies. The firings occurred *en masse* on a day critics and union activists call Black Saturday (Miller 1998, 94).

40. For example, TNG Canada and CEP both participated in meetings of the Inter-Union Newspaper Council, set up in the 1990s to encourage cooperation among organizations representing Canadian newspaper workers.

41. "'One Big Union' at CBC: What Is It, Where's the Process At?" 5 July 2001, at www.cmg.ca (accessed 21 September 2002).

7

Convergence on Command

Earlier chapters have examined how labor unions representing newspaper workers have converged into unions that represent workers across the communications sector. These mergers at the national or international level have occurred largely in response to corporate and technological convergence. They represent a recognition by the unions that new circumstances require new approaches, and that unity offers the hope of strength. So far, however, the union mergers have had relatively little impact on the day-to-day work life of members. Employees pay their dues and do their jobs; their bargaining agents negotiate contracts and handle grievances or arbitrations. And while the Communications Workers of America (CWA) and the Communications, Energy and Paperworkers Union of Canada (CEP) encourage mergers at the local level as part of the larger merger process, for the most part they do not require them to do so, and few locals do.

Things are dramatically different, however, at the Pacific Newspaper Group in Vancouver, British Columbia. There, seven different bargaining units, including those represented by CWA and CEP, have been rolled into one. This labor convergence began at the instigation of the employer, then known as Pacific Press, which successfully petitioned the British Columbia Labour Relations Board for an order to consolidate all its unions into a single bargaining unit. Its case rested on the idea that technological convergence had eliminated the boundaries between previously separate forms of work, and that therefore the jurisdictional boundaries of the various bargaining units no longer applied. The unions fought the consolidation, and fought hard. In the end, however, they came to see consolidation as an opportunity to undertake further convergences of their own—a chance to strengthen their position not just at Pacific Press but across British Columbia.

The Pacific Press consolidation is unique among North American media unions. It occurred in a province where the labor laws encourage consolidation of bargaining units, and in a company with an unusual corporate history, an unusually strong and diverse set of unions, and a lengthy record of joint council bargaining. Nevertheless, the case offers insights into how the forces of convergence may play out at the shop-floor level.

BACKGROUND TO CONSOLIDATION

With union density of 38.7 percent,[1] British Columbia is one of the most strongly unionized provinces in Canada. In addition, unions in British Columbia have been among the most successful in Canada in organizing workers in two areas of strong employment growth: trade and services (Murray 1995, 168). Not surprisingly, labor relations are serious business in the province, and nowhere are they taken more seriously than at Pacific Press, which produces the *Vancouver Sun* and the *Vancouver Province* daily newspapers. Workers at Pacific Press have been unionized for a long time.[2] As workers at the biggest dailies in the biggest city of the province, their contracts have been a bellwether for industrial relations in the rest of the province.[3]

Vancouver was one of six cities chosen for study by labor relations researchers for the Royal Commission on Newspapers (Hébert et al. 1981).[4] Under the revealing title "Vancouver: A History of Conflict," researchers described labor activism in the province as "perhaps the most militant in Canada" and said labor relations at Pacific Press included "all the elements found in many historic struggles: genuine mistrust between the parties; changing technology affecting time-honoured tradition; and conflict between unions over jurisdiction" (Fraser and Angel 1981, 24).

At the time of the Royal Commission study, Pacific Press had an unusual corporate structure, and an equally unusual collective-bargaining structure. The company was the product of a 1957 joint agreement between Southam, which owned the *Province*, and Sun Publishing, which owned the *Sun*. Control of the *Sun* was sold to FP Publications in 1964, then to Thomson Newspapers in 1980 and later that same year to Southam (Hébert et al. 1981, 30). This meant that between 1957 and 1980,

Southam and FP/Thomson, the leading newspaper chains in Canada and companies that were fierce competitors elsewhere, operated as partners in Vancouver.[5] On the labor side, the unions began bargaining as a joint council a few years after the formation of the company (Fraser and Angel 1981, 28).[6] Joint councils are rare in Canadian industry (Chaykowski 1995, 232), but the longevity of the council at Pacific Press suggested a degree of stability. At the time of the Royal Commission study, the council included six of the eight groups of unionized workers at Pacific Press. The largest was a local of The Newspaper Guild. The others were the mailers and compositors, represented by two different locals of the International Typographical Union; the pressmen and company truck drivers, represented by one local of the International Printing and Graphic Communications Union but with two certifications; and the engravers, part of the Graphic Arts International Union. The electricians and machinists, representing eight workers each, were not part of the council (Fraser and Angel 1981, 25).

The council, which had no constitution and no bylaws, evolved out of the practice of unions sending observers to each other's contract negotiations. Between negotiations, the council met on an irregular basis to discuss issues, such as jurisdictional problems or disputes with management over clauses common to all contracts. Bargaining issues at Pacific Press fell into two categories: "commons," or matters affecting all the unions, and "peculiars," which were specific to a particular union. The chairs of the council of unions negotiated the "commons" with the company. The individual unions all turned in their "peculiars" at the same time, but negotiated them individually (Fraser and Angel 1981, 29). In general, the "peculiars" were settled first. Sometimes, however, a particularly difficult "peculiar" showed up on the "commons" table.

The Royal Commission labor researchers looked at negotiations between 1970 and 1980 and found a decade of "almost continuous conflict" (Fraser and Angel 1981, 32), much of it resulting from technological change. There were three strikes/lockouts, the most serious one lasting from November 1978 to June 1979. Writing not long after that bitter dispute, Fraser and Angel noted a significant level of union mistrust of management, a tendency to use third parties (mediators and arbitrators) to resolve disputes, and a lack of consensus within the informal joint council on the one hand and the company on the other. Fraser and Angel took the company to task for spending a minimum amount of time or effort on improving labor relations, and for its traditional pattern of seeing bargaining as a matter of enforcing, or trying to enforce, strict legal rights. (That pattern was starting to change, they added.) They also observed that the turmoil within the newspapers was related to the culture of work and the particular workplace: "Management has guaranteed that no one will lose employment as a result of technological change. But the unions fear a loss of pride, skills, and tradition, among other things. Management appears not to have recognized that there is more to working than having a guaranteed job" (47).[7] The study concluded that Southam's purchase of Thomson's half-ownership in Pacific Press in August 1980 would likely have beneficial effects on labor relations: "It will be easier for management to reach and implement decisions than it was when two companies shared control" (Hébert et al. 1981, 172).

Fifteen years later, labor relations were still difficult. According to the company, the source of the problem was a labor relations structure that was frozen in the precomputer age. In 1995, the company proposed a solution: a radical restructuring of its unions. It asked the B.C. Labour Relations Board for an order to consolidate its seven bargaining units, representing 1,400 workers, into the Vancouver Newspaper Guild. This local of The Newspaper Guild already represented about 800 workers,[8] or more than half the staff at Pacific Press. Three other bargaining units had substantial memberships: the Graphic Communications International Union Local 25-C represented 192 pressroom workers; CWA Local 14003 represented 201 mailers; and CEP Local 226 represented 126 compositors.[9] In addition, there were three smaller groups: an engravers' unit, part of GCIU Local 525-M, had thirty-two members; an electricians' unit, part of the International Brotherhood of Electrical Workers Local 213, had eighteen members; and a machinists' unit, part of the International Association of Machinists and Aerospace Workers, Vancouver Lodge 692, also had eighteen members.

Pacific Press argued that in a time of technological convergence, when computerization has resulted in a highly integrated workplace, the existing collective bargaining structure was not just out of date but dysfunctional. And as the company pursued plans for a major investment in new production facilities, it saw no signs that things would improve.

WHY CONSOLIDATION?

The company began work on a consolidation application in 1993, after the provincial labor relations board handed down a landmark decision setting out its policy on what constitutes an appropriate bargaining unit (*Island Medical Laboratories Ltd.*, BCLRB No. B308/93). Pacific Press saw this ruling as evidence that the board would take a "more contemporary stance towards rationalizing bargaining structures," in line with recent amendments to the province's labor legislation (Pacific Press application, 10). Jan O'Brien, then president of the Guild local, recalls that during the late stages of collective bargaining in 1993–1994, she was visited at home by company officials. They showed her a draft of the consolidation application, which sought to have the Guild designated the sole bargaining agent (O'Brien 1997). O'Brien said she was stunned by the move. "My response was, 'Holy shit! If you want to prolong bargaining, that's how to do it!'" O'Brien let other union leaders know about the plan. The company waited until after negotiations ended before filing its application.

The application drew heavily on the *Island Medical Laboratories* decision, which set out three factors to examine in such cases: whether one or more of the existing bargaining units are no longer appropriate; what constitutes an appropriate bargaining unit for workers with a given employer; and whether there is evidence of actual or potential industrial-relations instability. In determining what would be an appropriate bargaining unit, the board would take into account a number of factors: similarity of skills, interests, duties, and working conditions; the structure of the employer; the degree of functional integration of workers; geography; the current collective-bargaining scheme; and the practice of collective bargaining in the industry (Pacific Press application, 9).

Pacific Press argued that the roots of the collective-bargaining structure lay "in turn-of-the-century divisions based on the skills, trades, and crafts that were necessary to operate the hot metal-based technology of that era" (1). But in recent decades, "more efficient processes" began to transform the newspaper and the work of newsworkers: "Computerization and automation diminished the need for craft skills. The skills needed in many areas of the operation converged and met on the computer" (27). Pacific Press had become a workplace where operations were functionally integrated and interdependent, where traditional distinctions between the bargaining units had been eliminated "in fact and in practice," and where employees "increasingly use the same or similar skills or interdependent skills when using computers" (25). This "departs radically" from the pre-1960s newspaper on which the bargaining unit structure was based (13).

But while the labor process in the newspaper had been transformed, the application said, the collective bargaining structure had not.

> The current jurisdictional boundaries between unions are arbitrary and artificial. Work that historically required a high degree of skill and training has been

modified or eliminated. The jurisdictional boundaries that separate the bargaining units cannot be justified when the units use similar or identical skills, technology is shared across jurisdictions and production is computer-driven and highly integrated. (12)

The company said the unions' response to technological change was to negotiate protection for their members and to "compete over jurisdictional claims to the changed work" (32). The result has been "industrial instability which is not likely to change unless the bargaining structure is rationalized" (32).

The Pacific Press application set out a chronology of technological change at the newspapers and described, department by department, how employees from the various bargaining units had become, in the company's view, functionally integrated. The description amounts to a vivid and detailed account of how computerization had changed the labor process as of mid-1995.

In the advertising department, Guild sales staff and Guild graphic artists worked with customers to design ads (Pacific Press application 14–16). Members of the compositors' unit stationed in the advertising department set the text of these ads in type, while members of the engravers' unit scanned in the graphics. Guild artists and compositors both used computers linked by an Ethernet network to put together display ads. Guild advertising assistants delivered ad components between the engraving and composing departments. Some ads came into the advertising department ready for publication. Guild staff in the advertising department received these ads, flagged them with notes on where and when they should run, and sent them to the compositors, who pasted them up. Classified ads came in by telephone, fax, or mail, or over the counter. Guild ad-takers handled ads sold by telephone or over the counter, typing the ad into the computer system. Compositors handled ads that arrived by mail or fax. Once an ad was in the computer, compositors or Guild ad-takers could call up the copy and make corrections. Guild computer operators in the data processing department "paginated" the classified ads, sending full and complete pages to the composing room electronically. In a separate area of the advertising department known as the makeup section, Guild staff slotted the display and classified ads into a "dummy," which directed the layout of the next edition of the newspaper. Once the dummy was made, pages were sent electronically to the editorial department. Pacific Press added that Guild makeup staff were in daily contact with the pressmen to discuss the laydown of the newspaper and to coordinate the location of color ads with the configuration of the press.

The two Pacific Press newspapers, the *Sun* and *Province*, shared business office and production functions, but each had its own newsroom. The company application noted that Guild members did most of the work in both editorial departments, though each newsroom had up to two compositors permanently on staff (16-17). Reporters and columnists typed their own stories into the computers, or filed their copy from another location by modem. If a writer had to phone a story in, a compositor typed it into the computer. The compositors also set in type letters to the editor or other bits of text that arrived on hard copy. Once in the computer, articles were transmitted to editors electronically, over an Ethernet link. The editors prepared the copy for publication, using software that showed the editor exactly what the page would look like in print. Photographs supplied by wire services came in electronically and were placed on the dummy electronically. Local photographs, taken by Guild photographers, were developed in a Guild photolab. Guild editors selected the pictures they wanted to use and worked with members of the engravers' unit on the sizing and quality of pictures. Guild clerical staff and photo technicians delivered pictures to the engravers, who used electronic scanners to properly size the photos.

Though compositors did a range of tasks at Pacific Press, their work centered on two primary functions: typing text into the computers and pasting up newspaper pages. According to the application (17-18), they interacted with a number of people from other bargaining units. These included Guild reporters, editors, and advertising and promotions staff. Guild production clerks coordinated the production of display ads by compositors. The secretary in the composing room was a Guild member, reporting to the general foreman, who was part of the compositors' bargaining unit. Compositors also worked closely with the engravers about corrections, type, color, and quality of images on pages. The engravers produced screened half-tone images, transforming photographs into a form that could be reproduced on the press. Compositors aligned the half-tones on the page form, pasted in display advertisements, and integrated color pictures with text in preparation for the production of printing plates.

The engravers, who processed images rather than text, created the plates used to print the newspapers and worked on the creation of display ads containing graphics and pictures. This meant they worked closely with members of the Guild, and the compositors' and pressmen's bargaining units (18-20). They received photographs from Guild photolab staff, consulted with Guild editors about photographs, and sent them low-resolution pictures for pagination. They worked in the same area with Guild ad production workers, and communicated with compositors about the content and production quality of ads. They delivered halftone images to the compositors for paste-up. The engravers also had ongoing interaction with the pressmen about the quality, delivery, and replacement of printing plates. The engravers received completed, pasted-up pages from the compositors. They used a photographic process to create a negative of the page and transfer it to a plastic printing plate.

The pressmen operated and did some maintenance on the printing presses. According to the application (20–21), they had ongoing contact with engravers, Guild members, mailers, machinists, and electricians. They received printing plates from the engraving department and often consulted with engravers about missing plates or plates whose quality was poor. They followed instructions from Guild makeup staff about the laydown for that day's newspaper. They also worked regularly with other Guild staff in the maintenance department and some business departments. The pressmen kept in constant touch with the mailers about the quality and flow of the production, letting them know whether the presses must be slowed or stopped. Finally, they worked extensively with the machinists and electricians. The former installed, maintained, and repaired equipment; the latter were in charge of work on electrical or computer equipment.

In the mailroom, mailers loaded and operated machines called inserters that put flyers and supplements into the newspapers as they arrived by conveyor belt from the pressroom. They also operated stacking machines that counted, stacked, and wrapped bundles of newspapers, preparing them for loading onto delivery trucks. In addition to working closely with pressmen on the flow of newspapers from the press, mailers worked with Guild maintenance staff, Guild business office staff, and Guild data processing staff, who produced labels for the bundles. They also worked with machinists and electricians (21–22).

The reader sales and service department, more commonly known as the circulation department, was staffed by Guild members who generated lists, counts, and other information to create the bundles and to set the waybills of delivery truck drivers. Pacific Press contracted out its trucking to other companies. Home delivery was also contracted out (22). The maintenance department employed machinists and electricians, as well as Guild janitors, painters, carpenters, and air conditioning workers (22–23). At the Vancouver plant, the machine shop was next to the pressroom. The company estimated that machinists spent 50 to 60 percent of their time in the pressroom. The electricians also had a shop next to the pressroom, though they worked in all areas except the composing room, where the compositors had jurisdiction over maintenance work. Finally, most workers in the business departments (human resources, accounting, information systems, editorial services, security, and promotions) belonged to the Guild (23–25). The data center was staffed by Guild members, compositors, and mailers. In almost every one of these departments, Guild members interacted with workers from another bargaining unit.

This portrait of the workplace differs substantially from descriptions of newspapers in the precomputer age, when news and advertisements moved, almost in lockstep, from one department (and one group of unionized workers) to the next, and when each unit used its own specialized tools and relied on its own mastery of craft knowledge to do its part in transferring ideas to ink on newsprint. At Pacific Press, new technology had broken up the production chain, collapsing stages into each other. Almost everyone used a common tool—a computer terminal networked to other computer terminals—and everyone interacted, in greater or lesser degrees and in person or over the Ethernet, with other groups of workers.

The company concluded that while the functions of the bargaining units were substantially integrated, the fact that the units themselves were not had resulted in a significant degree of industrial instability. The application expressed frustration over how long it took to negotiate collective agreements, especially in 1993–1994, when the company was putting together plans for a $200 million investment in a new downtown office building and a new printing plant in suburban Surrey that would print both newspapers.[10] The company originally proposed that the unions negotiate a two-year extension of their existing contracts. That failed. The company proposed the use of a facilitator to help in the negotiations. That eventually failed too. In May 1994, the company met with the council of unions to discuss its long-term goals. The company announced that it needed the stability of long-term contracts to get through the major rebuilding of the plant. In June and July, while the joint council continued to bargain "common" issues, a number of unions brought forward their "peculiars." In July, the company offered buyouts to engravers and compositors, whose work would be further eroded by the next stage of pagination. By October, three unions had indicated they were willing to strike over "peculiars." By the end of that month, all the unions had taken strike votes. The pressmen, who had said they were willing to strike over manning issues for the new presses, walked out on 1 November for a "study session." A ten-day strike/lockout ensued.

Eventually, the company and the unions reached agreement on five-year contracts (Pacific Press application, 64–69).

In addition to difficult collective bargaining, Pacific Press complained about lengthy jurisdictional disputes or skirmishes over which union was responsible for a particular task. In the pressroom, three such disputes were unresolved at the time of the application. Perhaps the most significant—and certainly the nastiest—dealt with who could push the button to start or stop the presses during repair and maintenance work. The pressmen claimed that starting and stopping the presses was solely in their jurisdiction, and that no one else could push the button. The electricians argued that they had the right to start and stop the machinery to test for safety. The employer sided with the electricians, saying this was a safety issue and that the Electrical Code of Canada and workers' compensation board regulations should prevail. The dispute played out in months of stress and tension in the pressroom. The electricians and machinists (who did maintenance work) complained that the pressmen physically intimidated them while they were working in the pressroom. They feared the situation might escalate to violence (50). The dispute peaked in an ugly shoving match in April 1995, in which a pressman threw a rag and a magazine at the company's labor relations manager, then pushed him and the foreman (50–51).

In the 1970s, as the actual and potential impact of computer technology began to be seen, the unions and the company had worked out a mechanism for resolving jurisdictional disputes. By the 1990s, the company argued, this mechanism was out of date. Indeed, it had resulted in artificial jurisdictional boundaries that bore a diminishing relationship to the traditional boundaries based on craft expertise.

> As the work has become less distinct, less skilled and more homogeneous, it has become increasingly obvious that the problem is no longer one of parsing increasingly similar work amongst the existing bargaining units. . . . Multiple bargaining units now represent employees performing the same or similar work in a functionally integrated operation. They compete for the same technologically changed work. Their differences inevitably boil into jurisdictional and collective bargaining disputes. (55)

The company concluded that the existing bargaining structure "is dysfunctional and urgently requires rationalization" (102). It had impaired Pacific Press's ability to compete in the marketplace, and to respond to technological and organizational change in the industry. For Pacific Press, the solution was straightforward: the unions had to be consolidated, and they had to be consolidated under the umbrella of the industrial union that represented the largest group of Pacific Press workers, the Guild.

THE UNIONS' RESPONSE

The unions had known since the contract negotiations of 1993–1994 that the company was working on a plan to consolidate them. When the company filed its application in 1995, they quickly came up with a strategy on how to respond. They decided to ask the B.C. Labour Relations Board to divide the case into two distinct phases. The first would address the question of whether the existing structure was, as the company contended, dysfunctional. If the board sided with the unions and determined that it was not, that would be that. If the board sided with the employer, then the case would move into a second phase, to decide on an appropriate bargaining structure for Pacific Press. The board agreed to this two-step process.

The unions also decided to argue the case on two levels, as a joint council and as individual units. Interestingly, this tactic echoed their approach at collective-bargaining time, with the joint council handling the "commons" and the individual unions responsible for the "peculiars." Behind the show of unity, however, some union leaders felt they were fighting a losing cause.[11] In addition, defending the status quo meant putting the best face on a labor relations picture that the unions also knew had been contentious. Nonetheless, the union leaders firmly believed that the company, in proposing consolidation, was really seeking a collective-bargaining advantage. The best way to fight it, separately and collectively, was to argue that while bargaining at Pacific Press had its rough spots, the system worked.

The joint council's formal response to the application conceded that there was a "superficial, first-impression appeal" to the consolidation plan (Joint council response, 1). But it argued that what the employer saw as a sign of failure—the collective bargaining record—was actually a sign of success. The council said a dysfunctional structure would be characterized by a number of things: rogue units with noticeably richer collective agreements; a mishmash of expiry dates; short duration contracts; and the absence of a jurisdictional dispute resolution mechanism.

> How do the collective agreements at Pacific Press stack up? Do the contracts reflect these telltale signs of bargaining structure instability? The answer is, no. The wages, benefits and job security provisions in all contracts are essentially

the same. . . . All contracts have a common expiry date. . . . All contracts have the identical provision for resolution of jurisdictional disputes. Do the collective agreements at Pacific Press reflect instability? Quite the contrary, these agreements represent a strong, stable collective bargaining regime. (4)

As for the company complaint that it took more than a year to negotiate the five-year contracts reached in 1993–1994, the joint council response was brusque: "So what[?]" (4). That round of bargaining dealt with some particularly hard issues. Just before talks began, the company contracted out delivery and laid off more than 100 drivers who had been represented by the GCIU, the same local that represented the pressmen. "Understandably, the pressmen wanted to try to do something for the drivers in collective bargaining; understandably, protection against contracting out of jobs became a prime concern for all employees and their unions" (4–5). Pacific Press then opened collective bargaining by announcing it planned to eliminate at least 200 jobs. It demanded long-term contracts in a workplace where one- or two-year contracts had been the norm, and it "took its traditional run at the pressmen and mailers' job security provisions"(5).[12] Finally, the council argued that much of the delay in negotiations was a result of the employer's uncertainty over plans for the Surrey production plant.

> These are extremely difficult bargaining issues. Moreover, all the contentious issues were created by employer bargaining demands or issues. Under the circumstances, can the employer complain that negotiations took a long time? That new five-year collective agreements were achieved with only a ten-day strike must be considered a remarkable collective bargaining success. (5)

Because the bargaining structure had been able to produce a fair and workable contract, the joint council argued, the employer had to have another reason for applying for consolidation: "to try to shift the balance of bargaining power in its favour with the ultimate goal of negotiating lower cost labour contracts" (6). The council said that consolidating the work force into the Guild would destroy the craft unions, the ones that traditionally had "bargaining muscle" because publishers could not put out a newspaper without them (8). Pacific Press had been campaigning for years to break these unions, it charged, and had used new technology as a tool in this campaign. On almost every major change in technology, the company had assigned remaining work to the Guild rather than to a craft union (8). As a result, Guild membership rose from 650 in 1978 to 800 in 1995, while membership in the compositors' union dropped from 319 to 114.

The council also rejected the employer's contention that it wanted to be freed of the jurisdictional barriers so it could retrain and move employees around to make best use of the new technology. "The employer has used the new technology to eliminate the trades, not upgrade them. All initiatives for combined skills and combined work groups have come from the unions. The employer has consistently killed these initiatives" (10). Similarly, the council disputed the claim that new technology had created an integrated work force. Although there had been "some mixing of skills at the interface," the vast bulk of Pacific Press employees worked in clearly distinct jobs. "An ad sales person is never going to run the press; a mailer is unlikely to be sent to photograph a fire" (14). Finally, it rejected out of hand the idea that the employer should tell workers which union to join.

> On this application, the company names the Guild as its choice of bargaining agent. Needless to say, the choice of bargaining agent is for the employees, not the company. The company's purpose in naming the Guild as the successor bargaining agent is first and foremost an attempt to stir up trouble, to split the united front of the joint council. (9)

It argued that consolidation would force skilled tradespeople to give up their union, the body that certified their skills. This in turn would cost them their mobility rights—the so-called travel cards that allow craft workers to change jobs yet retain their craft status. In addition, they would lose their ability to take a stand on issues that mattered deeply to one group but less so to others.

> Collective bargaining with this employer is bare knuckles reality. All the employer needs to break the pressmen is the ability to contract out the press work. The employer is betting that the necessary contracting out provision can be pushed through the majority. In the amended bargaining structure, the pressmen lose the ability to say, "no." Now they can shut the place down. In an all-employee unit, the pressmen have only the power of reason and moral suasion. How far does that get you in the crunch of collective bargaining? (13)

The council noted that consolidation was part of the newspaper environment in Canada. On the employer side, concentration of ownership was intensifying. "In response, the unions have restructured" (15), through the creation of fewer but larger unions, and through new arrangements at individual workplaces.[13] The labor board, it said, should allow the Pacific Press bargaining structure to continue to evolve on its own. "No matter how painful, sometimes torturous, the route, evolution finds the better path" (15). The joint council position offered a show of solidarity among unions with a long record of working together successfully. Nonetheless, it offered glimpses into the tensions that existed between the more militant craft unions, like the pressmen, and the Guild. These tensions would grow as the case proceeded, eventually derailing the effort to prevent consolidation.

Each union supplemented the joint council response with a response of its own. Many of these struck similar themes to those in the joint council submission. But they also expressed the specific interests of the individual unions, along with their own interpretation of what the consolidation application meant.

The Guild rejected as "ludicrous" the employer's contention that industrial strife has worsened at Pacific Press since the settlement of 1993–1994. It added that Pacific Press's chronology of that round of negotiations was "extremely one-sided," arguing that the employer's conduct "was a cause of industrial unrest, delay and frustration of collective bargaining. The employer's bargaining goals zig-zagged all over the map. This was one of the major reasons for protracted bargaining."[14] The Guild added that despite all the difficulties, the joint council had maintained a united front in 1993–1994 (5) and that a deal was reached through direct bargaining, with the help of a mediator. "What we have in the Pacific Press application is an employer complaining that bargaining has been tough and that the unions have exercised their legal right to strike," the Guild argued. But consolidation won't necessarily prevent strikes in the future: "No matter what the bargaining structure there will still be common concerns of job security, technological change, wages and benefits that have led to strikes and lockouts in the past" (6–7).

The Guild submission also said that merging all the unions into one would not be an easy task. The Guild constituency alone represented more than 225 job classifications, covering a broad range of administrative, editorial, and advertising employees whose working conditions were markedly different from those in the craft unions. The craft unions played a role in apprenticeship training and operated hiring halls; the Guild did neither. In addition, the Guild argued that the fact the members of the various bargaining units interacted with each other did not constitute functional integration (8–9). It also rejected as "laughable" the idea that workers using the same tools, such as printers connected to computers, shared a job duty: "The work outputted will vary dramatically. It could be anything from an accounting report to a news story. All employees may use the telephones but that does not mean their job duties are shared" (10).

The submission from the compositors questioned Pacific Press's sincerity in arguing that consolidation would allow the company more flexibility in retraining and reassigning workers whose jobs were eroded by new technology. It said the history of how its members fared after negotiating job guarantees in the 1970s showed otherwise. The compositors originally expected that job guarantees would encourage retraining. That did not happen: "The employer has steadfastly refused to retrain and redeploy the printers. . . . Cynically, the employer has turned the job guarantee into a weapon: you are redundant; there is nothing for you to do; don't you feel useless; wouldn't you rather go elsewhere; how about a buyout?"[15]

The compositors' submission acknowledged that most jurisdictional disputes at Pacific Press had been between members of its union and the Guild, and that the compositors had consistently lost. Nonetheless, the compositors lived with the joint council and with the disputes resolution mechanism. The only exception was the "spec ads" dispute, over the company's decision to use Guild graphic artists to put together ads "on spec" for sales representatives to show prospective advertisers. If the advertiser liked the idea, the "spec ad" would become the real ad. The compositors' refusal to handle these ads in 1993 "is properly viewed as an aberration," the union said (3).[16] The response added that this assignment of what had traditionally been compositor work to graphic artists had nothing to do with new technology, and therefore did not fall within the jurisdictional dispute resolution mechanism of the collective agreement. The compositors concluded by pointing out that consolidation at Pacific Press would have ramifications beyond Vancouver. For the union's local, it would mean the immediate loss of more than 100 of its 1,400 members, and the loss of the standard-bearing contracts at Pacific Press. "If [CEP Local] 226 is developing as a potential vehicle for broader-based representation in the newspaper industry, the Board's intervention on this application may very well kill that potential, scattering the experience acquired to date," the response argued (6).

In the shortest individual response, the engravers union noted that since 1984, Pacific Press had lost only eleven days to collective bargaining disputes; "We submit that eleven days lost in eleven years is not evidence of an unstable collective bargaining history."[17] It argued that the company got much of what it wanted in the 1993–1994 round of bargaining: "a five-year contract, buyout provisions coupled with reduced manning and a number of its other demands" (1). The jurisdictional disputes mechanism, meanwhile, "has not inhibited the company's introduction of extensive and virtually continuous technological change." In short, the union argued, "this is not a situation calling for the labour relations board to alter the current bargaining structure" (2).

The electricians argued that unlike other trades, their job at Pacific Press had not changed with the move from hot metal to cold type.[18] But another form of convergence—between the electrical and electronics industries—had affected the work of electricians. The union said it had responded to this convergence by providing training in computer maintenance, installation, and repair (1). But instead of capitalizing on the reskilling one of its unions had undertaken on its own, Pacific Press "has made every effort to maximize contracting out of electronic and computer work." The submission argued that this experience with the employer shows it has little interest in retraining or reassigning workers. "It is hard for this union to imagine this employer going out of its way to crosstrain workers to safeguard employment" (2). The submission also accused the employer of trying to provoke jurisdictional disputes, including the so-called button dispute; of misleading the unions about their plans for new presses; and of refusing to grant the electricians established "commons" provisions for years after they joined the joint council of unions (5–8). It argued that a one-day strike by the electricians in 1991 was the result of company provocation: Pacific Press sought one-sided concessions from the electricians, who refused to make them. The union characterized the strike as "a wakeup call" that convinced the company to refer the question to arbitration, concluding, "It is unacceptable for the company to paint itself as the trapped victim of a dysfunctional system. . . . It is difficult to reconcile the employer's stated desire for common contract terms with their continuing behaviour at the bargaining table" (8).

The machinists argued that each bargaining unit had a separate community of interest that had "survived the technological revolution."[19] The jurisdictional boundary of the machinists' union was largely defined by the nature of the work, which was unlike that of any other unit. Though the crafts worked alongside each other, each performed separate and distinct duties. In addition, the machinists expressed concern that consolidation would mean the absorption of the machinists by an all-employee union, severing their links with their craft and their union, which had certified their status as craft workers.

While the other unions took some pains to avoid criticizing each other in their submissions to the board, the pressmen were less temperate. After expressing support for the joint council submission, their submission continued:

The pressmen take the position that their unit is a craft unit and therefore is an appropriate unit even if other units at Pacific Press are inappropriate. There is no basis to destroy a viable, functioning bargaining unit because another unit in the workplace is inappropriate. Such action amounts to throwing a baby out with the bath water.[20]

The submission accused Pacific Press of seeking to be "delivered to a corporate utopia" (1). It took issue with the assertion that the unions were the reason for the delay in bargaining in 1993–1994, saying that Pacific Press's uncertainty over which presses it would buy meant that manning had to be negotiated three times (2). The submission also rejected the idea that the "button" dispute was a jurisdictional issue, saying that giving electricians the right to start and stop the press contravened the collective agreement. The pressmen's chief argument, however, rejected the idea that technology had blurred craft work. The pressmen contended there was little or no functional integration between them and the other employees, and no overlap of duties (4). Pressmen worked in a separate area of the building, with its own showers and washrooms, and ate in a section of the cafeteria reserved specifically for them (9). Despite technological change, the submission argued, some aspects of press work had not changed in seventy-five years (3). The chief difference between the work in the 1990s and in the hot-metal days was that modern printing plates were lighter (5). "The distinct skills of the pressmen's craft remains as vibrant and distinguishable today as they were centuries ago," it maintained, adding that the pressmen were "a true craft union" and one that was critical to the success of the newspaper business (4, 8).

> It is the pressmen who, through the union-administered apprenticeship program, provide the continuity of skilled trades for the industry in general and Pacific Press in particular.... There is no basis to believe that the Newspaper Guild or CEP would be able to provide the teaching skills and expertise that is currently being provided by the GCIU in order to preserve the continuity of supply of skilled tradesmen. (11)

Finally, the mailers' union, after arguing that there was no evidence of bargaining structure instability in the mailroom,[21] contended that in its area of jurisdiction, the company's real goal in seeking consolidation was to allow for contracting out. It noted that in the 1970s the company took on more flyer work and hired more mailers.

> Having sought and received the union's co-operation in expanding and upgrading the mailroom work force, the company changed direction. Suddenly, jour-

neymen mailers were too expensive. Southam set up a new company, Flyer Force, to take over the flyer business across Canada. In Vancouver, the union organized the Flyer Force employees. The Flyer Force closed. (3)

At the beginning of 1995, the submission noted, Pacific Press cut flyer work and laid off forty-four mailers (5). It argued that Pacific Press was out to break the union and that the union had to fight hard for contract restrictions against contracting out mailroom work: "The company's new scheme is straightforward. The company has set up distributorships, pulling work out of the Guild. The Guild had challenged the company's action. If the company is successful in setting up the distributorships, the next step is to contract out the mailroom work to these distributorships" (4). The mailers said Pacific Press needed the labor board's help, through the consolidation application, to break the ban on contracting out: "From the mailers' point of view, the company's application has nothing to do with the bargaining structure; everything to do with bargaining strength, the employer's drive to eliminate proper mailroom jobs at Pacific Press" (4).

In their individual statements, the unions voiced more than simply their opposition to the consolidation application. They also catalogued a range of fears and frustrations over the meltdown and reconstitution of the labor process in the digital age. The statements from the compositors, pressmen, and mailers are especially interesting in this regard, since all three deal with the question of technology and skill. The compositors, who had been deskilled by the introduction of computerized typesetting in the 1970s, were still angry twenty years later that their hard-won job guarantees had not translated into meaningful work at Pacific Press. But the compositors seemed, overall, resigned to their changed situation, and willing to embrace the idea that their best hope for survival was to move beyond a rigid adherence to craft. Their own local, they pointed out, was an industrial union at smaller papers. Indeed, their statement presented compositors as not really a trade at all, but rather as "the link between the front end and the back end of the newspaper, between editorial and sales and the trades that produce the paper."[22]

The pressmen, by contrast, clung ferociously to the notion of craft integrity and insisted that new technology had had virtually no impact on the pressroom. This denial of the impact of technological change was remarkable, given that manning in the pressroom was such a significant issue in the 1993–1994 negotiations, and that GCIU was in the process of compiling a series of studies on the impact of changing technology in the pressroom.[23] In addition, unions and management both knew that the new presses Pacific Press had purchased included software that automatically set ink and water levels, one of the more skilled aspects of the pressman's job (Pacific Press application, 45). The pressmen's statement was almost arrogant in its insistence that it was viable as a stand-alone union, even if others at Pacific Press were not. Indeed, it was eerily reminiscent of the kind of statements made by some ITU leaders in the 1960s and 1970s: claiming strength and appealing to the tradition of craft integrity even as new technology rendered much of their work obsolete.

The mailers' statement suggested this group was considerably less confident than the pressmen about the integrity of their skill, and less confident than the compositors about the centrality of their work to the newspaper production process. Their fear was that as the final group of unionized workers to handle the newspapers, they were the most vulnerable of all to contracting out. Indeed, they had some grounds for this fear: until the early 1990s, truck drivers had been the final group of unionized workers in the production chain at Pacific Press. A few years before filing the application, the company decided to contract out delivery and began cutting back on flyer work handled by the mailers. With the possibility of transmitting circulation data electronically—to anywhere, not just to the mailroom—and with the increasing depth, flexibility, and sophistication of those data, the mailers were concerned that automation and the company's desire for cost savings meant that their future was on the line. As the workers closest to the street, they feared their next step would be out the door.

DEFINING WHAT IS APPROPRIATE

The company and the unions hashed out the nuances of their arguments during several days of hearings spread out over many months in 1995 and 1996. Not surprisingly, one of the touchiest issues had to do with the status of pressroom work. The employer contended that pressroom work had become deskilled, and that pressmen, rather than being skilled craft workers, had become operators. Bob Osipa, head of the pressmen's local, reacted with anger to this claim. "We are crafts, in my mind, and very talented and skilled crafts."[24] The company eventually withdrew that argument.

On 2 May 1996, the B.C. Labour Relations Board ruled in favor of the company, finding that the existing collective bargaining structure was inappropriate for Pacific Press.[25] The board said the key factor was the notion of industrial instability, on two fronts. The first had to do with the administration of collective agreements, including jurisdictional disputes and what it characterized as "inflexibility" in adapting to continuous technological change. The second related to the collective bargaining process itself, including "the potential for industrial instability through whipsawing, as well as the history of strikes at Pacific Press."[26] It said that the frequent and protracted jurisdictional disputes at Pacific Press arose "directly from the multiple bargaining unit structure" (22). For example, the "spec ad" dispute had been going on for more than three years, it said, and the "button" dispute in the pressroom had resulted in potentially unsafe tensions in the workplace. Further developments in technology would only make the situation worse:

> Historically, the changing technology in the production of newspapers has cut across craft lines and telescoped functions and skills. We are satisfied that will continue with the move to full "pagination" and the new, computer-driven technology of the new presses. As a result, we do not see any lessening of the jurisdictional disputes on the horizon. Quite to the contrary, the employees and the Unions themselves (who likely know best) are engaged in a competitive "grab for the grey" or staking out their "turf" to secure and protect their respective jurisdictions in the face of the new technology. (25)

Jurisdictional divisions have stood in the way of the retraining and reassignment of workers, it said (26). The board praised an effort by the Guild and the employer to retrain Guild employees whose jobs had disappeared or been eroded by technological change. "Although not a 'love-in' . . . the committee has been successful. . . . That success, however, was again only within the Guild's unit. That limitation, of course, is the crux of the issue before us" (26).

In collective bargaining, the "peculiars/commons" structure had been problematic. The board noted, for example, that when the employer agreed to a Guild "peculiar" on same-sex benefits, the same issue then showed up as a "commons" demand; when it agreed to a "peculiar" with the machinists on resoling workboots, the mailers' unit then put forward resoling as a "peculiar" of its own (27). The board ruled that the voluntary nature of the joint council and the lack of formal rules governing it had aggravated the potential for whipsawing. The board said it was satisfied that the employer was not seeking a collective bargaining advantage. It also dismissed the unions' emphasis on the distinctive nature of their particular crafts: "Where industrial instability arises out of a multiple bargaining unit structure, as it has in the present case, the unique craft skills of the separate bargaining units will not preclude the Board from finding the bargaining unit structure to no longer be appropriate" (29).

The ruling put an end to decades of collective bargaining history at Pacific Press. By determining that the collective bargaining structure was inappropriate, the board had given Pacific Press half of what it wanted: an end to what it saw as a dysfunctional multiunion structure held over from an earlier era. For the unions, the decision was a stinging defeat, though not an entirely unexpected one. They had based their argument on the idea that despite occasional difficulties, the multiunit structure and the joint council of unions worked well enough. When the board ruled against them, they were left with a choice: they could try to come up with a new structure of their own, or they could give in to the employer and agree to be rolled into the Guild. Given their conviction that the employer's true agenda was to achieve a collective bargaining advantage, they rejected the second option. But what kind of new structure could they develop? That question consumed the attention of the unions, separately and jointly, in May and June 1996.

Five unions agreed that the best way to protect their diverse interests was to formalize the joint council. They began meeting to draw up a constitution for this council, which they believed should have a simple and straightforward structure and should operate on majoritarian principles. But these unions were unable to convince the other two—the pressmen and the mailers—to sign on. Those two unions had come to a different conclusion about how future collective bargaining at Pacific Press should be shaped. The company's restructuring plan would result in Pacific Press running two plants in two distinct places and with two distinct functions. Editorial, advertising, and administrative work would stay in downtown Vancouver, and the presses and distribution system would be in suburban Surrey. The mailers and pressmen argued that the most sensible approach, therefore, was to have two unions: the Guild representing what they called "pre-press" workers in Vancouver, and another union, selected by a vote of production workers, representing people at the Surrey plant. In an 11 June submission to the labor board, the pressmen argued that there was no "community of interest" between the two groups of workers. "The interests of the pre-press employees compared to those of the production employees are completely different," it said.[27] The letter noted that several other Canadian dailies—the *Toronto Star*, *Edmonton Journal*, and *Ottawa Citizen* among them—operated with a similar division of labor. This approach was the most appropriate structure because it would take into account a number of so-called community of interest factors identified in the original *Island Medical Laboratories* decision: "similarities in skills, interests, duties and working conditions; physical and administrative structure of the employer; functional integration; and geography" (8). It concluded by restating its objection to joining the Guild: "The pressmen submit that a single, all-employee unit represented by the Guild is not appropriate. Such a single, all-employee unit would have a devastating effect on, and cause irreparable damage to, the rights and interests of employees currently represented by the pressmen and other unions" (5).

Jan O'Brien, who was president of the Guild local during the consolidation debate, said later that most of the other unions thought the two-union scheme was unworkable and would hurt all the unions in the long run (O'Brien 1997). Representatives of the Guild and the other four unions, still hoping to get the pressmen and mailers to change their minds, applied to the B.C. labor minister on 5 June 1996, asking that the labor relations board consider whether a council of trade unions would be an appropriate bargaining agent for Pacific Press. The letter from the unions suggested that a formal joint council would accomplish a number of things: ensure stable, orderly, and simplified collective bargaining; avoid unfair bargaining advantage by either side; protect the employer from jurisdictional wrangling; maintain the mobility of specialized craft workers throughout the larger newspaper industry; maintain the democratically chosen union ties of the workers; promote a cooperative and harmonious climate among workers; allow for cooperative approaches to lateral mobility and retraining with the company; accommodate future voluntary mergers of unions; and fit the current policy trend favoring larger and all-employee unions.[28]

The letter acknowledged that the pressmen and mailers had decided not to go along with the formal joint council idea. It said that if the board determined that the joint council was the appropriate choice, then those two unions should be given a choice: to join the council, "or, in the alternative, to put their locals forward as alternatives to the council in a vote of the entire combined bargaining unit to determine which of the three bargaining agents will represent the all employee bargaining unit" (5). If the council won such a vote, as it almost certainly would, given that the Guild vastly outnumbered the combined membership of the pressmen and mailers, "it is the position of the applicants that the current membership of these two local unions should be administered by one of the member unions in the council" (4).

The board rolled that application into the existing proceeding. During the weeks between the first decision and the start of the second stage of the proceeding later that spring, the unions and management engaged in a series of alternative dispute resolution meetings, aided by a board mediator. The goal was to allow all sides to air their concerns and work out a satisfactory arrangement.

One of the key issues in the joint-council idea was how to work out a formula for strike votes and contract ratifications that would be based on majoritarian principles but would at the same time respect the individuality of the various unions. The five unions came up with a number of variations, but ultimately were unable to satisfy the pressmen and mailers. The board noted later that, "after engaging in what must have been difficult, heartfelt discussions with the assistance of a board mediator, the unions found that they could not agree upon a proposal to put to us for a council of trade unions."[29]

O'Brien (1997) says the stumbling block was that the pressmen and mailers would not go along with any plan based on majority rule. "They would not concede that a joint council had to be based on numbers. They wanted a veto." Submissions to the labor relations board from the pressmen and mailers show that the two dissident unions ranked the two-union idea as the best option, and a formal joint council as a second choice. Any such council, however, should be based on a "one union, one vote" principle.[30] This structure would continue past practice, in which a single union could force a walkout of them all.

The pressmen also reacted with anger to the section of the joint council application dealing with what to do if the pressmen and mailers did not want to join the council. The other five had suggested that these unions would have to put themselves forward as alternatives to the council in a vote open to all employees. If they lost, their membership would be administered by another local.

> To advance such an alternative would not only destroy the pressmen as an entity with significant and distinct characteristics, but also inevitably lead to constant strife between employees of the employer. . . . Further, to force a large number of employees against their wishes, to become members of another trade union, which is not their freely chosen representative, can only lead to further disharmony amongst members of the entire bargaining unit. For these reasons, the pressmen strongly oppose a council of trade unions which could contemplate such alternatives.[31]

The employer, meanwhile, remained steadfast in arguing that the Guild was the appropriate choice. Again drawing on a technological argument, it rejected the two-union proposal of the pressmen and mailers: "We remind the panel that the mailers and pressmen seek to divide the work force along geographic lines. Pacific Press geographically is truly located on the information highway."[32] As for the formal joint council proposed by the other five unions, the employer found it significant that two unions had refused to sign on: "The unions themselves have proven incapable of a viable relationship in the past and where now a significant portion of the unionized work force rejects the workability of a joint council, the board ought to reject imposing a process so lacking in support and evidence of possible success" (15). Pacific Press also felt the council had a "fundamental" flaw: it would not prevent jurisdictional disputes and therefore would "perpetuate, not eliminate, a fundamental source of industrial instability" (15). During the alternative dispute resolution process, however, the employer made one important concession: it agreed that the 1,400 employees could vote to choose which union would represent them.[33] Given the numbers, it was likely that management's choice, the 800-member Guild, would win anyway.

Once it became clear during June 1996 that there was no way the unions would agree to either a seven-member joint council or a two-union split based on geography, and that the employer would in any case not support either idea, the unions all had to move to their fallback positions. For the five unions advocating the joint council, that position was a single bargaining agent, to be chosen in a referendum of all union members. The pressmen and mailers again staked out a different position: they decided that a joint council was the way to go after all, but it should be a joint council of three unions, not seven. They proposed that the Guild be given 50 percent of the employees, and that the compositors should be among that group. The remaining 50 percent would be divided between two other unions, chosen in a run-off vote among the pressmen, the mailers, the engravers, the electricians, and the machinists (8). Given the numbers, the pressmen and mailers would probably win this election—and would each end up with roughly twice their existing membership. The mailers argued that the other, smaller unions were moribund and not viable (27), and therefore should be rolled into viable unions. The five unions opposed this plan as well. By the time the hearings began in late June, they had withdrawn their support for the idea of a joint council.

The failure to devise a plan for a new joint council defined and deepened the cracks in the solidarity of the Pacific Press unions. The five unions that had advocated a new council ended up siding with the employer, agreeing that if a joint council was not in the cards, then a single union was the only viable option. Opposing them were the pressmen and mailers, who feared that the council would cost them the ability to control their own destinies, and that a single union for the plant would be even worse. But these two were unwilling to make the kinds of compromises that would have retained much of what they liked about the old joint council. Instead, they dug in their heels, stubbornly insisting on standing their ground even as it eroded from beneath their feet.

When the second round of hearings began in late June, two ideas were on the table: the employer's original proposal for a single unit, amended to allow for employees to choose their bargaining agent in a company-wide vote; and the pressmen and mailers' proposal for a three-party joint council, which none of the other parties would endorse. The labor board ruled that a joint council of unions was not appropriate, in large part because of "fundamental, major disagreement among the unions as to the advisability and workability of such a joint council" (33). It added that it was "not a stretch" to suggest that the unions' inability to agree on the structure of such a council reflected the kind of divisions that led to the industrial instability identified in the first decision (3). As for the three-union idea of the mailers and pressmen, the board said that the strong opposition of the other five unions meant that the council would probably be unable to resolve jurisdictional problems, and that "technology has, and will continue to, cut across craft lines. There will thus be a continuing need to overcome the jurisdictional orientations and accommodate retraining and relocation throughout the workforce" (33–34). The work processes of the newspaper were increasingly functionally integrated, it said, and this reinforced the principle set out in the *Island Medical Laboratories* case against multiplying the number of bargaining units.

The board concluded that a single bargaining unit, chosen by referendum, was the appropriate structure for Pacific Press. It gave the unions two weeks to decide whether they wanted to put their names on the ballot. In the meantime, it would accept submissions on how to work out the voting procedure.

THE CAMPAIGN

The night the second labor board decision came down, the pressroom on Granville Street in downtown Vancouver that printed the *Sun* was an unhappy place. The pressmen learned, through reading an article being printed in the newspaper that night, that the board had decided in favor of consolidation. This meant that, in effect, they had lost their union. That night, the presses had twenty-four web breaks, or ruptures in the paper loaded on the press. The company foreman felt this was an "extremely high" number.[34] Over the next two weeks, the number of web breaks averaged 8.73 a day, compared with 4.07 a day between 15 June and 3 July.

The company complained that the web breaks and a rash of minor incidents of vandalism amounted to an illegal strike and filed a complaint with the B.C. Labour Relations Board.[35] It argued that the union was attempting to exert retribution and that the web breaks were "concerted acts of mischief" (6). In testimony before the board, the pressmen's union leader, Bob Osipa, and John Savage, the local's secretary treasurer, rejected that idea. In fact, they said, the union had told the pressmen to remain calm.[36] The board's decision on the complaint said "both admitted that during collective bargaining disputes in the past the union had deliberately disrupted production, however, they have not encouraged that type of action now" (5). Mark J. Brown of the labor board, who heard the case, found that some of the incidents the company complained about had no impact on production, and were therefore disciplinary matters. He wrote, "It is not surprising that the union members were upset with the decision," noting that the pressmen's union leaders had testified that members were "unhappy, disappointed and frustrated" (8). He concluded that the web breaks were caused by operator error, "either by inadvertent poor work performance caused by poor morale or by deliberate error of some individuals" (8). But this did not constitute the concerted activity that would define a strike.

The complaint offers insight into the state of affairs at Pacific Press in the weeks before the consolidation vote. The pressroom workers were unhappy and angry—some of them angry enough to commit minor acts of sabotage. Many members of other unions were also unhappy: they had lost their second consecutive decision before the board and were now entering uncharted territory. A consolidated union was a new and unfamiliar idea. No one knew for sure whether it would work, or how. The company, meanwhile, was apparently in an intolerant mood, unwilling to put up with any mischief and quick to see signs of discontent as an illegal strike.

It was in this tense atmosphere that the leaders of the Pacific Press unions had to make a crucial decision: whether to put their names on the ballot. Only four unions represented significant numbers of workers at Pacific Press: the Guild local, which by this time had moved to CEP; the GCIU pressmen; the CWA mailers; and the CEP compositors. The compositors were, however, a relatively small unit in a large local, CEP Local 226-M, which represented 1,400 newsroom and production workers throughout the province. Harold Funk, who was president of the local at the time, says local leaders gave serious thought to putting CEP

226 on the ballot: "We thought that if we could take all the non-Guild members and some Guild members, 226 could prevail" (Funk 1997). But they knew this would be a long shot, and it would mean drawing people away from another CEP local. Instead, they decided to throw their support behind the Guild/CEP local.

The Guild local had known all along that its name would be on the ballot. The mailers—who, like the compositors, were once members of the ITU but stayed with CWA rather than moving to CEP—decided to run, too. So did the pressmen. The vote was set for 31 October and 1 November. The campaign the unions waged in September and October developed into a hard-fought though ultimately uneven contest between the Guild local and the mailers' union. This made it a contest between Canada's CEP union and the international CWA.

The Guild local's campaign, outlined in a large, glossy edition of its *Inside Story* newsletter (October 1996), was based on the idea that the local was "the logical choice" to represent everyone at Pacific Press. The newsletter's main story drew on workers from a number of departments who explained why they felt the Guild local was the best choice:

> For many, it stems from the Guild/CEP 115-M intervening in their personal dispute with the company. For others it comes from looking at larger issues such as combatting technological change or corporate concentration of the media. And some find they support the Guild/CEP 115-M for a combination of personal and political reasons. (2)

One of the workers quoted was reader sales and service representative Jim Lepper, the brother of John Lepper, who was head of the rival mailers' union.[37] Lepper said the Guild supported him in 1993, when the company wanted to lay him off. The Guild took the case to the labor board and won. "I never missed a day of work. That's one reason I will support the Guild," Lepper was quoted as saying (2). Another story included statements of support from leaders of the machinists', electricians', engravers', and compositors' unions. It quoted electrician Al Sear as saying, "[The Guild is] the only union on the ballot qualified to represent Pacific Press employees. Today, labor relations battles call for far more than just workplace disruption. The Guild/CEP 115-M has shown it's effective in handling the challenges union members face in these times" (*Inside Story*, October 1996, 3). Compositor Lewis Hansen said the Guild local was in the best position to weather technological change, and predicted that "the mailers and the pressmen will be further reduced by attrition" (3). In an editorial headlined, "Let's Show PacPress We Stand

Strong," local president O'Brien made a plea for unity and solidarity: "A strong vote for the Guild will send the company the message that we're united—that we are ready to stand up for every employee no matter what job they do or which department they work in" (*Inside Story*, October 1996, 4). The newsletter also included an interview with Brian Payne, CEP's chief officer in Western Canada. He was quoted as saying that media corporations have learned that CEP can solve problems and finish a deal. They have also learned that CEP can take on a company in a labor dispute and in a public campaign (4).[38]

The mailers' campaign drew heavily on the unit's connection to the CWA and through it to the former Newspaper Guild, the old ITU, and the fledgling TNG Canada. It argued that by choosing the CWA local, Pacific Press workers would end up in a union that would be, according to the headline of one of its campaign bulletins, "better than the joint council": "CWA/TNG is going to take the model of the Joint Council and make it even better. Your new bargaining team will have representation from every area of the workplace to ensure the interests of one department are not sacrificed for another," it promised.[39]

During the campaign, the mailers distributed a flyer headlined, "Ottawa Guild Members Reject CEP."[40] It reported on the results of the referendum at the *Ottawa Citizen*, in which members of the Ottawa Newspaper Guild local decided to stay with the international rather than switch to the CEP. The bulletin quoted Arnold Amber, head of TNG Canada, as saying, "It was a great victory because for the first time the Guild took the opportunity to properly debate the merit of the Guild versus CEP. With that, the members chose the Guild. This will help CWA/TNG Canada get even stronger across the country." Some in Vancouver interpreted the comment as a barb directed against the Guild/CEP local. By contending that the Ottawa vote was the "first time" the Guild had "properly" debated the relative merits of the CWA and the CEP, the letter implied that something was amiss in the Vancouver local's move to CEP.

The mailers followed this up with an open letter from Amber dated 29 October,[41] describing the consolidation vote as "an opportunity for journalists at the *Sun* and the *Province* to resume their ties with their counterparts in newsrooms, news agencies and broadcast outlets in Canada and indeed throughout the world." Amber listed a number of benefits of CWA membership, including lower dues, better strike benefits, and access to the CWA's defense fund, which was ten times the size of CEP's. "And working with the CWA we are now better able than ever to take on international media companies such as Conrad Black's Hollinger."

Amber's letter echoed some of the same themes as a 5 October open letter from Bill Boarman, head of the CWA's Printing, Publishing, and Media Workers sector—the former ITU. Boarman wrote that TNG Canada's autonomous governing structure allowed Canadian publishing and media workers to make decisions without the intervention of union leaders who were more concerned about chemical plants and pulp mills than newspapers and computers. (This was seen in Vancouver as a slap at CEP, whose membership included pulp and paper, chemical, energy, and communications workers.) Boarman also said that TNG Canada combined the traditions and expertise of two of the oldest and most successful unions at Pacific Press, the Guild and the ITU.

The mailers campaign angered some leaders of the CEP locals, who felt that the mailers were not only trying to usurp the Guild/CEP local's position in Vancouver but were portraying themselves inappropriately as a Canadian union, and as the Guild. In terms of national identity, CEP felt it had the stronger claim. The Guild/CEP local circulated a newsletter dated 15 October with a question-and-answer section addressing the matter directly:

Q. Why is another union calling itself the Guild?

A. The mailers are a local of the CWA. So now the mailers are using a merger of two American unions to try to use our name and reputation to confuse voters. Make no mistake, the Vancouver Newspaper Guild is CEP 115 on the ballot.

William Saunders, secretary treasurer of CEP Local 226-M, circulated a letter dated 8 October with the heading: "Can the CWA be trusted to live up to its promises? Look at their record!" It said his local's experience with CWA "reveals a very different union from the one presented in the literature CWA is circulating seeking to represent all employees at Pacific Press." He reminded employees that the CWA president had reneged on his promise to respect the results of the close 1995 referendum on Canadian sovereignty. This not only broke a promise to Canadian workers, he wrote, but violated CWA's own constitution. When the compositors' local voted to join CEP, he added, CWA put it under trusteeship and applied unsuccessfully to the labor relations board for control of more than $300,000 in assets. "CWA consistently broke promises to our local and to their Canadian membership," he wrote.

In the end, the CWA campaign made some headway, though not

enough to be decisive. When the votes were counted, the Guild/CEP local received 631 votes (*Guild Reporter*, 18 November 1996, 1). This was a majority of the 1,133 ballots cast, but about 200 fewer than its membership at Pacific Press. The mailers' local, whose membership was about 190, got 306 votes. This meant that more than 100 members of other locals voted in favor of the CWA affiliate. The pressmen's union got 196 votes, apparently sweeping the pressroom but making no progress elsewhere. The *Guild Reporter* wrote, somewhat ungraciously, that CEP "barely received enough support to claim a majority" (*Guild Reporter*, 15 November 1996, 1).[42] It also quoted Amber's complaint that the CEP local continued to refer to itself as "the Guild" when it no longer belonged to the former Newspaper Guild (4).

MOVING BEYOND CONSOLIDATION

From Pacific Press's point of view, the outcome of the vote was perhaps the best of all possible worlds. The company ended up with exactly what it sought in its application to the labor board: a consolidation of its seven bargaining units into the Guild local. Interviewed a year after the vote, Andy Smith, the head of human resources at Pacific Press and the chief advocate of consolidation, said he was happy with the outcome. The transition from seven unions to one had gone "very smoothly—more smoothly than we thought it would" (Andy Smith 1997). Jurisdictional wrangling had come to an end. There were no disputes over work assignments. The compositors had moved into the advertising department, where they were indistinguishable from other workers. "Under the old regime we'd still be in hearings as to whether it was engraver work or compositor work," he said. Smith also said that Pacific Press workers' convergence in one big union did not worry management. "The bigger union may not be the stronger union on specific issues," he explained. In the past, each union could call a strike over its own special concerns, and the other unions would refuse to cross the line. This meant that a tiny unit could, in effect, shut down the plant: "With a big union you've got to have the entire bargaining unit buy in. For example, if you have a manning issue in the mail room, they've got to be able to convince an ad taker that it's important enough to go on strike for."

If Smith was upbeat about how smoothly the transition had occurred, members of the consolidated local were less enthusiastic. Jan O'Brien, who as Guild local president became president of the consolidated local, said in a December 1997 interview, "it's been a very difficult transition."

O'Brien and her staff faced the task of integrating the old and proud (if slightly battered) craft units into a local that was vastly different from what they were used to. The craft unions had to give up elements of their craft culture, something they did with reluctance. In addition, they had to adjust to being in a local with a significant number of women—a common feature of Guild locals but not of mailers' or pressmen's locals.[43]

John Lepper, head of the mailers' local, agreed that the transition had been tough. "You're ripping apart something like fifty years of history," he said (1997). But while he blamed the company for putting the unions in this position, he also had some harsh words for CEP. Lepper felt the national leaders of CEP should have called a meeting after the vote to discuss how to proceed. Instead, he said, they left it to the local to handle the transition. "I was told to come to the CEP (local) office and turn over everything to them." That was far from easy, especially since relations between the CWA mailers and the CEP Guild had been strained over the campaign for the consolidation vote. Lepper said that for the first year, the CEP local was "a fractured union," and some of the craft workers who now belonged to it felt they were not represented "properly or fairly—or at least not as they traditionally were."

But a number of developments beginning shortly after the consolidation vote started to turn things around. In late 1996, Mike Bocking, a long-time Guild activist locally, nationally, and internationally, went out for a beer with the leaders of the craft side to talk about how to build the consolidated union. O'Brien had decided she would not seek reelection as local president after her term expired in late 1997. Over the next several months, Bocking and the craft workers' representatives met several times to plan for the local elections and to discuss improvements in the staffing and administration of the local office. They eventually drew up a "unity slate" of candidates that included people from all the previous members of the joint council. The slate, headed by Bocking, swept the election. The local also made some changes to its staff, including hiring pressman Osipa to work with production workers at the new printing plant (Bocking 1998a). By the end of 1997, a number of Pacific Press union leaders who originally saw consolidation as a devastating defeat had decided it could be turned to their advantage. For example, John Lepper of the former mailers' unit said he was delighted with the outcome of the local election: "We have a unified group of people on council, from virtually every area of the company. I believe we have a group of officers who won't make Andy Smith happy at all. The people he sees as most troublesome are in charge of the large union" (Lepper 1997). Lepper also said he believed that in the long run, the consolidation would turn out to be a better choice than the two-union setup his union and the pressmen had proposed. "Ironically, today I think the union would have been weaker had that happened," he said. Osipa was equally enthusiastic about the consolidation a year after it occurred: "People are getting comfortable with consolidation. People are united. We look at it as a situation where the company may have made a mistake" (Osipa 1998).

By early 1998, the Pacific Press local had not only adapted to the idea that consolidation was a positive development, it had decided to undertake a further consolidation, this time with CEP Local 226. This local had represented *Sun* and *Province* compositors but its real power was outside Vancouver, where it represented editorial and production workers at a number of smaller newspapers. The Pacific Press consolidation had posed an additional challenge to Local 226: its leaders, people like Bill Saunders and Harold Funk, would end up in the same union, but in a different local. For the short term, the two locals worked out an arrangement that allowed Funk and others to belong to both CEP locals. (Other former Pacific Press locals had made similar arrangements with their own unions, aimed at letting craft workers maintain their craft status.) But Local 226 also began thinking about the longer term. At a weekend strategy seminar in 1997, the possibility of a merger with CEP Local 115 was the main item on the agenda. By early 1998 the two locals had come up with a merger agreement (Bocking 1998b). It was ratified easily by the memberships of both locals in the spring and summer of 1998. The merged local chose a new name and an optimistic number: Local 2000, the Media Union of British Columbia. Suddenly, Pacific Press workers were part of a 2,500-member local representing workers all over the B.C. mainland.[44]

For any local, the biggest test is whether it can succeed in negotiating a contract with the employer. The consolidated local at Pacific Press took on that test in late 1998, as the five-year contracts negotiated in 1993–1994 expired. As had long been the pattern at Pacific Press, the negotiations were time-consuming and difficult. The union served seventy-two-hour strike notice in late June 1999, after winning a strike mandate by an overwhelming 93.5 percent (*The Globe and Mail*, 28 June 1999, A5). It eventually set a strike deadline of noon on 7 July. At precisely that time, the employees walked out and set up picket lines outside the downtown headquarters and the Surrey plant. But just two hours later, the strike ended with a tentative agreement providing wage increases of 3, 2, and 3 percent over three years (*The Globe and Mail*, 8 July 1999, A3). The newspapers did not lose a single day of production.

The strength of the strike mandate was indicative of how well the consolidated local had been able to build solidarity. The fact that the local won a contract without a production shutdown is also noteworthy in a company with a long history of labor unrest. The cover story of the next issue of the local's newsletter *Insider* said that the most significant achievement of the bargaining was "the unity achieved by members of Local 2000" (August 1999, 1–3). The newsletter quoted Osipa, by then a Local 2000 vice-president, as saying, "They threw seven unions together and instead of going for each other's throats we showed unity and cohesiveness. . . . I've never worked with a better committee" (3). Bocking added that other media unions could learn from Local 2000's experience: "I personally believe we need one union in media in Canada. Although the consolidation was forced upon us, in retrospect I believe it is a good thing" (3).

FROM COERCION TO CONVERGENCE

In arguing for consolidation of its unions, Pacific Press successfully presented a case to the British Columbia Labour Relations Board that computer technology has eroded skills, blurred jurisdictional lines in the printing crafts, and turned newspapers into workplaces where skills "converged and met on the computer" (Pacific Press application, 27). Although the merger was a "shotgun wedding," the consolidated local has emerged in better shape than many of its members expected. The fights over jurisdiction that the company and the board saw as signs of a dysfunctional relationship have ended—an outcome all sides, including the local, see as a positive development. The local has a united leadership and a first contract, two things many leaders of the former units doubted would ever be achieved. And it has undertaken a strategy of growth, joining with newsworkers across the province.

What started as an act of coercion, therefore, appears to have become a case of convergence: an effort by the unions themselves to transcend craft lines and old divisions to create a new organization that is well positioned to represent media workers of all kinds. The long and bitter fight by the unions against consolidation shows, however, that convergence at Pacific Press was by no means an easy accomplishment. Indeed, when asked whether the unions would ever have done this on their own, many leaders of the former Pacific Press locals were doubtful. Jan O'Brien of the Guild said that given the changes in the industry, a merger of the unions would have eventually occurred, but it would have taken a much longer time (O'Brien 1997). Harold Funk of the compositors unit said a merger at the local level would have occurred only if the Canadian branch of the GCIU decided to move to CEP (Funk 1997). Mailer John Lepper said pressman Bob Osipa once approached him and asked him to merge his CWA mailers into the GCIU pressmen (Lepper 1997). His response was to invite Osipa to merge his pressmen into the mailers. "Could we have ever gotten over our egos? I'm not so sure," he said. But he quickly added that reluctance to merge was not simply a matter of ego:

> We all did business in a certain way and we all thought we did it in the best way for our members. Could I have been convinced that Mr. Osipa would do a better job of representing the mailers than I could? I doubt it. Would he have been convinced I would represent the pressmen as well as he could? Again, I doubt it. (Lapper 1997)

By forcing a consolidation of its locals, Pacific Press forced the unions to reexamine their position within the company and their role within the industry. And while their initial response was to defend their turf, the consolidation process allowed the unions to see the possibilities inherent in creating a new structure. Indeed, painful though it was, the Vancouver convergence may offer a template for how the mergers at the national and international level can filter down to the level of the workplace.

NOTES

1. Density is calculated on the basis of union membership and the number of paid workers, excluding pensioners and the unemployed. British Columbia ranks third in Canada, behind Newfoundland (53.3 percent) and Quebec (40.6 percent). Neighboring Alberta, by contrast, has the lowest density at 26.4 percent (Corporations and Labour Union Returns Act data, 1993, reprinted in Murray 1995, 193).

2. Records kept by the former International Typographical Union (now the Printing, Publishing, and Media Workers sector of the CWA) show that the Vancouver Typographical Union was chartered in 1887.

3. Pacific Press joint council of unions, response to application by Pacific Press Inc. to B.C. Labour Relations Board (BCLRB) for consolidation of bargaining units, 6 September 1995, 27. Hereafter "Joint council response."

4. The goal of the research was to determine whether there was a correlation among concentration of ownership, newspaper closings, and labor–management relations. The study used an industrial-relations model that saw technology, along with the legal framework and the product market, as forming the context in which negotiations occur. It concluded that labor relations "interact with other factors affecting the fortunes of newspapers, and have been of major consequence in many cases" (Hébert et al. 1981, 177). Vancouver was not, however, one of those cases (176).

Convergence on Command 181

5. Conrad Black's Hollinger Inc. took control of Pacific Press in 1996, through its controlling share of Southam. In July 2000, CanWest Global bought most of Hollinger's Southam newspaper assets, including the Vancouver dailies. Pacific Press's name was changed to Pacific Newspaper Group shortly thereafter.

6. The company pinpoints the formation of the joint council in 1967, when five of the nine unions then at the plant began bargaining together. See Pacific Press Inc., application for consolidation of bargaining units to BCLRB, 12 June 1995, 27; hereafter "Pacific Press application."

7. Pacific Press and its joint council of unions negotiated the job guarantees in 1972, see Pacific Press application, 34.

8. Partway though the Pacific Press consolidation case, the Vancouver local left The Newspaper Guild (which was then merging with the CWA) and joined CEP, changing its name to CEP Local 115-M. For the sake of simplicity, it will be referred to here as the Guild, the name by which it was known to both the employer and the other unions during the consolidation case.

9. The mailers' and compositors' units were originally in the ITU, which merged with the CWA in the 1980s. Following the split result of the referendum on Canadian autonomy, the mailers stayed with the CWA and the compositors joined CEP.

10. At the time of the application, Pacific Press printed the *Sun* at its Vancouver headquarters and the *Province* in a plant it opened in Surrey in 1991; see Pacific Press application, 41.

11. Harold Funk of the compositors' local says that before the hearings began, his local had legal advice that the company would prevail. Bob Jennings of the engravers' union says he had the same view (Funk 1997, Jennings 1997).

12. The submission noted that shortly after signing the contract, the company reduced the flyer business and laid off forty-four mailers (5).

13. The joint council's response referred to the merger of the former ITU with CWA or CEP, and to the merger with CEP being undertaken by the Guild local. At smaller papers, it said, "the trend is toward representation by one or two unions" (15).

14. Local 115, TNG, response to Pacific Press application, September 1995, 4-5; parenthetical page references to this document follow in the text. TNG Local 115 became CEP Local 115-M while the case was under consideration by the BCLRB.

15. Local 226, CEP (compositors' unit), response to Pacific Press application, September 1995, 2. Parenthetical page references follow in the text.

16. The submission noted that this dispute was exacerbated by internal union politics over whether to move to CEP or to stay with the rest of the ITU in the CWA. Resolution of the union's successor rights took "considerable time and several board decisions." As a result, the arbitration of the spec ads dispute was delayed and simmering frustrations boiled over (3).

17. Local 525-M, GCIU (engravers' unit), response to Pacific Press application, September 1995, 1. Parenthetical page references follow in the text.

18. Local 213, IBEW (electricians' unit), response to Pacific Press application, September 1995, 1. Parenthetical page references follow in the text.

19. Lodge 692, IAMAW (machinists' unit), response to Pacific Press application, September 1995, 1.

20. Local 25-C, GCIU (pressmen's unit), response to Pacific Press application, September 1995, 1; parenthetical page references follow in the text. The statement did not specify which other unit or units the pressmen saw as inappropriate.

21. Local 14003, CWA (mailers' unit), response to Pacific Press application, September 1995, 1. Parenthetical page references follow in the text.

22. Local 226, CEP, response to Pacific Press application, 5.

23. The GCIU published three such studies, written by Karen Hadley, in 1995.

24. Bob Osipa, testimony before BCLRB, 2 February 1996, 108. Osipa charged that the consolidation application was really an attempt to break his union: "And once they've got their ducks in order . . . and they are successful at consolidation, they've got now a situation where they will have a major proportion of the number of votes in the Guild unit, which aren't all craft-rated, and they threaten [, . . . '] accept what we tell you or we're going to take you down. We're going to scab you. We're going to run.'" If that happened, he added, the pressmen's and mailers' wages would be up for grabs (108–09).

25. BCLRB No. B146/96, decision, 2 May 1996. Parenthetical page references follow in the text.

26. BCLRB No. B146/96, 21. Whipsawing refers to the practice of one union demanding concessions equal to or greater than concessions gained by another union.

27. Local 25-C, GCIU, submission to BCLRB, 11 June 1996, 4. Parenthetical page references follow in the text.

28. Local 213, IBEW (on behalf of CEP locals 225-M and 226, GCIU 525-M, and IAM Lodge 692), letter to Penny Priddy (B.C. labor minister), 5 June 1996, 2. Parenthetical page references follow in the text.

29. BCLRB No. B292/96, decision, 30 August 1996, 5.

30. Local 14003, CWA, submissions to BCLRB, 19 June 1996, 1; and 19 June 1996, 2.

31. Local 25-C, GCIU, submission to BCLRB, 19 June 1996, 2.

32. Pacific Press Inc., submission to BCLRB, 19 June 1996, 7.

33. BCLRB No. B292/96, 6. Parenthetical page references follow in the text.

34. See BCLRB B320/96, 30 September 1996. The company's general foreman explained that web breaks can be caused by a fault in the newsprint, a mechanical problem, or operator error. A number of the breaks were noted in pressroom records as "running breaks," a term meaning that there was no particular reason for the break (3).

35. The allegations by Pacific Press included a metal ring found in the press blanket, which caused damage that required four hours and $150 to repair; vandalism of new markup sticks designed to help standardize the splicing of newsprint reels; damage to a pane of glass in the pressroom's "quiet room"; and hot water left on in the showers (BCLRB B320/96, 30 September 1996, 4–5).

36. Osipa testified that he told members at an 8 September meeting that the union was appealing the decision. He advised the workers not to panic or disrupt production, but warned that they might have to live with the result of the decision (BCLRB B320/96, 30 September 1996, 4).

37. The newsletter noted that Jim Lepper started at Pacific Press out of high

school in 1976, had been a shop steward for ten years, and was then in his second year on the local executive; "He developed his union roots from his father, Stan, who was a long-time president of the Mailers' Union" (2). The newsletter did not mention his brother John.

38. CEP was "standing up to Conrad Black" by sponsoring a court challenge to Black's acquisition of Southam, Payne said (4).

39. CWA Local 14003, special election bulletin, no. 9, 30 October 1996.

40. CWA Local 14003, bargaining unit consolidation campaign brochure, 25 October 1996.

41. Amber said later that he felt it was important to get involved in the campaign. He had been unhappy that the Guild international let the Vancouver local go without a fight in 1995. The consolidation campaign offered an opportunity for genuine debate. He added, however, that he had not expected to win the vote (Amber 1998).

42. The same story reported on the outcome of the vote at the *Ottawa Citizen*, where members of the Ottawa Newspaper Guild decided to stay with the CWA. It was a squeaker: the final tally was 133 to 125 (*Guild Reporter*, 18 November 1996, 1).

43. O'Brien and CEP staff representative Joie Warnock described two connected disputes concerning chapel rooms as an example of how difficult it was to bridge the cultural divide. Chapel rooms are where chapel chairmen and other union officials organize the schedules and work assignments of their members. For some time, the pressmen's chapel room in Vancouver had been decorated with photos of sexy women, which prompted complaints from some women on staff. The Guild local president asked the pressmen's leader, Bob Osipa, to take down the pictures. He refused. At about the same time, the company announced that there would be no chapel rooms in the new production building. The company argued that chapel rooms were a remnant of the old craft structure, and since the production workers were now part of the CEP Guild unit, which had never had chapel rooms, there was no need for chapel rooms in the new facility. The local took up the case and succeeded at arbitration in winning the right to chapel rooms in the new facility. But O'Brien (1997) said she was deeply aware of the irony of her situation: "While we're fighting with the company to keep the chapel rooms, we're also having an internal fight over girlie pictures in the chapel room." Eventually, a Guild staffer went into the Vancouver chapel room and took down the pictures (Osipa 1998). No one put them back up.

44. CEP 2000 has contracts with a diverse range of newspapers throughout the province, including Campbell River, Cranbrook, Duncan, Kamloops, Kelowna, Nanaimo, Nelson, Penticton, Print Rupert, Surrey, Trail, and Victoria. Most of these cover printers. It also has a master collective agreement with the Trinity Group of Newspapers (now called Metro Valley Newspaper Groups), covering production and editorial workers. See CEP 2000 Web site at www.mediaunion.bc.ca (accessed 6 July 2001); updated by Harold Funk, 14 August 2001.

8

Convergence and Beyond

In the early 1960s, a number of leaders in North American printing unions came up with a remarkably accurate diagnosis of their situation, and an even more remarkable prescription for curing their ills. Elmer Brown, who as head of the ITU led the oldest and most powerful of the North American printing unions, put it most succinctly in a speech to the 1960 Newspaper Guild convention. Due to the "growing power" of the publishers, he said, the labor unions "are down to the alternative of amalgamation or annihilation" (*Guild Reporter*, 15 July 1960, 3).

Those were—or should have been—good times for North American newspaper unions. The economy was on a long trajectory of postwar growth. Wages were increasing. Wall Street was beginning to discover that newspapers could earn astounding profits (Bagdikian 1990, 12–13). Though there was labor strife, union membership in general was on the rise,[1] as was membership in the American Newspaper Guild. The International Typographical Union had recently been described as "one of the most powerful unions for its size in the nation" (Lipset et al. 1956, 23).

But the pattern that worried Brown and other labor leaders in the 1960s was the leading edge of what would turn out to be an unrelenting series of consolidations within and across media, and within and across international borders, that would shake the unions to their very roots over the coming decades. By the 1970s, these changes had attracted some concern from groups other than the unions. In Canada, a Senate committee and a Royal Commission both called on governments to do something about concentration of newspaper ownership, in hopes of preserving the newspaper's traditional role within the local community. In the United

States, The Newspaper Guild and other groups—including scholars, commentators, and some public officials—expressed similar concerns. By the 1980s, the pattern of concentration was developing in a new direction, toward expansion of company holdings across the media spectrum. At the same time, governments in Canada and the United States were embracing the idea of deregulation, which created a climate for further corporate growth, and for growth into areas that had previously been closed off by limits on cross-media ownership. In the 1990s, corporate convergence accelerated, fed by (and feeding into) the convergence of technologies around a common digital language. By the dawn of the new millennium, the notion of the North American newspaper as an independent, local enterprise sounded almost as quaint as the clank of the linotype machines that had revolutionized newspaper production a century earlier. In place of locally owned newspapers were giant enterprises, with stakes in broadcasting, telecommunication, and entertainment as well as the daily press, and an interest in trying to exploit whatever synergies might be found within and across their holdings.

If what Brown saw in the 1960s scared him, it should come as no surprise that almost forty years later, the head of the CWA/TNG sector would see concentration of ownership as the "number one worry" for her union. According to Linda Foley (1998), "it's happening so rapidly and on such a large scale, it's like ten freight trains coming at you. There's no way you'll stop it. What we have to figure out is how can we maintain a voice, how we can maintain power within the context of what's happening."

Though Brown did not offer a particularly close analysis of what constituted the "growing power of the owners"—he was mainly concerned about publishers acting in concert to thwart the efforts of unionized workers—it soon became clear that publisher power was a double-edged sword threatening the unions. Corporate power occupied one side of the blade; technological power, the other.

In the early 1960s, the unions called the technological threat "automation," and some made efforts to understand it, track it, and, occasionally, resist it. But the word "automation" hardly begins to describe the scale of the changes they were about to encounter. Previous innovations in the technology of printing had concentrated, to a high degree, on replacing muscle power with mechanical might. The digital technology that began appearing in newspapers was of a different order. It sought not just to automate in mechanical terms but to transfer to computers a range of functions that previously required the judgment of skilled workers. From computerized spell-check programs to computerized line-justification, headline-counting, and typesetting devices, from electronic sensors that could read and adjust ink levels on the printing press to database management programs that could direct the stacking and delivery of newspapers, the technological changes of recent decades have offered management the potential for "labor savings" on both a new level and an unprecedented scale.

The leaders of the newspaper unions in the 1960s had only the roughest ideas of how ownership changes and technological innovation would change their members' workplaces. They could only guess at how technological advances would fuel consolidation, and vice versa. They had no way of knowing for certain that over the next forty years the pace of change in the newspaper, in terms of both ownership and technology, would be relentless.[2] Nonetheless, some among them knew that if the unions could somehow come together, they would be stronger.

Coming up with a prescription for unity took a leap of the imagination. Filling that prescription was another matter altogether. The consolidation of separate unions into one big union in printing and publishing is still a work in progress, and one that may never be completed. There have, however, been some remarkable achievements, chief among them the transformation of the Communications Workers of America and the Communications, Energy and Paperworkers Union of Canada from (primarily) telephone workers' unions into organizations that can make a firm claim to being the dominant media workers' unions in their respective countries. CEP now represents 150,000 members; CWA's membership is 740,000. And there is support for further mergers among newspaper workers. A 1996 report and action plan by two Toronto-area locals of CEP and the Graphic Communications International Union found that the "overwhelming majority" of participants at two interunion conferences thought more mergers were needed: "They identified the existence of multiple units, locals and unions as a major barrier to developing appropriate union responses to industry changes. They believe a single union would be stronger" (CTAC 1996, 2). But as the action plan concedes, "The reality . . . is that there are multiple units, locals and unions in the industry" (2).

PROBLEMS OF MERGING

The record of the last forty years shows that it is far easier for capital to consolidate than for labor. Friendly corporate mergers—seen by both parties as ways to increase profit, boost share prices, exploit new markets, or create wealth—have rapidly turned communications companies into the multimedia giants that dominate the industry today (see Bagdikian 1997; Roberts, Kunkel, and Layton 2001).

For labor unions, mergers are a much more complicated process. North American labor unions are democratic institutions, with their own governing structures, dues structures, traditions, areas of expertise, and voting systems—and their own bureaucracies. As a rule, the staff of a labor union have a high level of job security—far higher, in many cases, than the members of the union. Unlike corporate mergers, labor union mergers require the approval of the whole range of players: the elected leadership of both unions, the governing structure of each, the staff representatives who have day-to-day contact with the membership, and the rank-and-file members of both unions.

Union mergers are, therefore, more like the unification of rival states than they are like corporate mergers. Divisions within a union's governing structure over a merger proposal, as happened in the ITU–Guild talks of the 1970s and early 1980s, can be fatal.[3] The majority of the ITU's leadership supported the Guild merger and, in the absence of an active opposition, they could probably have convinced the membership to go along with the deal. But a dissident group was able to undermine it, not just once but at many levels: at the negotiating table, where the ITU secretary-treasurer, who opposed the deal, provided conflicting figures on projected members of the merged union (*Guild Reporter*, 20 December 1982, 1); during the day-to-day operations, when opponents courted a rival suitor, the International Brotherhood of Teamsters; in the pages of the in-house *Typographical Journal*, where the faction of the leadership opposed to the deal wrote increasingly hostile columns throughout the fall of 1982; and eventually on the floor of the ITU convention, where the carefully orchestrated ratification vote ended in disarray. A similar pattern of dissent appeared during the ITU's attempt to merge with the Graphic Communications International Union a few years later, though in that case it was the GCIU that pulled out at the last minute, not the ITU. Dissent is, of course, part of the political process—and the politics of trade unions can be as complex and, at times, as nasty as the politics of any other institution. But it is clear that some opponents of the ITU–Guild and ITU–GCIU merger plans went beyond merely voicing dissent; they made mischief. In the end, the failure of these mergers shows just how difficult it is to bring off a successful labor union merger, and how easily a deal can be derailed even though most people in both unions support it.

A second difficulty for the unions as they sought merger partners in the 1960s, 1970s, and 1980s was a shared history of competition and conflict as well as cooperation. Most printing trades unions trace their parentage to the ITU, and their birth to a declaration of independence from the ITU. The modernization of printing in the late nineteenth century had encouraged these divisions. So did the American Federation of Labor's principle of exclusive jurisdiction with specific job boundaries, a principle that some unions clung to long after it had been undermined (Chitayat 1979). By the 1970s, the printing trades unions were facing modernization of a different order, and their tradition of fiercely asserting, and protecting, their jurisdiction was a source of tension not just in the workplace but in dealing with other unions. Almost every print union, at one point or another in the last four decades, has accused another of raiding its members, or undermining its attempts to negotiate a contract, or breaking its strikes, or trying to infringe on its areas of jurisdiction, or trying to reap easy gains from another union's strike.

Although the unions knew they could mount an effective campaign against an employer, they also were keenly aware that, as Susan Craig (1987) put it, "solidarity is a sometimes thing."[4] The interests of various groups of workers in a plant do not always coincide. For example, the printers' so-called reproduction clauses and the pressmen's struggles over manning have been vital to those unions at various points over the last forty years,[5] but such issues are unlikely to win friends in a Guild editorial unit. Similarly, issues of critical importance in the newsroom do not always resonate well in other areas of the newspaper enterprise.

Joe Matyas of the Southern Ontario Newspaper Guild recalls that when the local organized his own newsroom at the *London Free Press*,[6] journalistic standards were the central issue (Matyas 1998). The newspaper was undergoing a major makeover from a traditional Ontario broadsheet daily that ran long local features into the so-called McPaper format of *USA Today*. The newsroom was very concerned about what the change meant to the editorial quality of the *Free Press*, and issues of ethics and professional practice loomed large in both the certification drive and at the bargaining table. "To a craft union, this sounds ludicrous, but it was critically important to the Guild," Matyas says. In that kind of situation, an employer might be able to exploit the fact that what is vital to one union is of little interest to another, by encouraging the second union to pressure the first into dropping the issue or resolving it elsewhere. This helps explain, perhaps, why so few unions have been able to maintain joint bargaining successfully over the long haul. As Arnold Amber, head of TNG Canada, puts it, "One lousy joint bargaining makes it very difficult to do it again" (Amber 1998).

In addition, it is important to note that at the very time the unions were considering merger partners, their own positions (and in some cases their memberships) were being eroded by the introduction of new technology. The ITU, which successfully controlled the introduction of the linotype in the nineteenth century, had no such luck with electronic typesetting devices in the twentieth century. Where the linotype was a single-purpose machine aimed at mechanizing one aspect of printing, the computer had the potential to affect all aspects of work. Successive waves of computer-driven technology not only sped up separate stages of production but began to collapse one stage into another. Despite the high hopes of its leadership (see Kelber and Schlesinger 1967), the strategy the ITU came up with to slow the pace of computerization—the union called it "controlled automation"—was certain to fail. It did, in the early 1970s, in exchange for the promise of lifetime jobs for existing members (Sleigh 1998, 93).[7]

In practical terms, not only was the area of jurisdiction claimed by a craft or mechanical union eaten away by technology during those years, so was the membership. Job guarantees protected existing members, but both unions and management in workplaces with job guarantees understood that employers were simply waiting until the workers quit or retired. This in turn hampered a union's ability to find a merger partner, especially if the potential partner was facing, or was likely to face, the same kind of erosion. With each passing year of unsuccessful negotiations with the Guild during the 1970s and early 1980s, for example, the ITU grew weaker and weaker. By the time the Communications Workers of America took it into its fold, the ITU was largely a spent force.

The trajectory for newspaper production workers from the 1960s on has been toward not just deskilling but what we might even think of as "decrafting," or the elimination of a stage of publishing and the craft union jurisdiction that went along with it. But while The Newspaper Guild is aware of the impact of new technology on its members, it has never found itself in the same desperate straits as the craft unions. As an industrial union almost from its inception, it represents workers who hold a range of jobs, some of which (clerical workers, photo technicians) have been more susceptible to deskilling than others, and some of which (reporters, layout editors) have been reskilled or upskilled. The skills of Guild editorial workers, who dominate the culture of the union, require a significant degree of independent thought and action. Their job is not just to make newspapers but, to paraphrase Golding and Elliott (1979), to make news. The commodity that they produce—journalists call it news, while scholars have called it everything from ideology (Knight

1982) to the reproduction of social order (Hall et al. 1978; GMG 1976, 1982) to a "free lunch" paid for by advertisers (Smythe 1981)—is malleable and fleeting, but nonetheless powerful. And it does not lend itself easily to automation, electronic or otherwise.

As a result, the Guild could afford to be much more strategic in deciding how to reposition itself in the changed media industry of the 1990s. Its 1993 strategic plan set the union on a new course: it would become a union for workers in the "evolving news and information industries in the U.S. and Canada" (Work Directions Inc. 1993, 35). Within a very few years, it found in the CWA a partner that shared its view of convergence—not just as a way of understanding changes within the employers, but as a strategy for planning its own future.

Once a merger occurs, though, it takes much more work to meld two unions into one. At both CWA and CEP, integration at the level of the leadership has been fairly simple and speedy. Integration at the local level is another matter. Foley (1998) explains that for a merger to gain the support of the membership, people at the local level have to feel comfortable with the new union. That is one of the main reasons the Guild wanted its own sector within CWA. At the same time, though,

> we also need to be involved and be part of the CWA enough so that it makes sense that we merged. In other words, if we just kept everything we had, what would be the point of joining CWA? So we have to figure out how to get the synergy out of the merger and at the same time preserve what we said we were going to preserve. (Foley 1998)

Since the Guild–CWA merger, there have been some mergers of locals within CWA, mainly between former Guild and ITU units. CWA has also been able to take advantage of labor convergence in organizing: at the *Halifax Chronicle-Herald*, the newsroom was organized by a TNG Canada local that previously was limited to the back shop. So far, though, Guild and CWA telecommunications locals have remained separate.[8]

At CEP, media workers have their own sector within the union, and their own vice-president, but the sector does not have the same degree of autonomy as the Guild has within CWA. Nonetheless, the premerger configuration of most media workers locals in CEP has remained largely intact. A striking exception is CEP Local 2000, which leads the way in North America in terms of labor convergence of print media units. It must be noted, however, that the consolidation that eventually helped create Local 2000 began at the behest of an employer. Though the previously separate locals eventually came to see the consolidation as a positive development, they fought it tooth and nail.

PROSPECTS FOR CONVERGED UNIONS

Despite the challenges and difficulties that sometimes bedevil union consolidation, there are clear advantages and opportunities inherent in labor union convergence.

Within the CWA, the Guild is carving out territory that ranges well beyond the newspaper business. In doing so, it is following the pattern set by CWA. That union's traditional membership comprised skilled telephone and telecommunication workers, but the union has taken an interest in organizing professional workers, too—nurses, for example.[9] Foley and CWA President Morton Bahr both see the Guild as the sector that can best serve as the link to the professionals in the labor movement (Foley 2001, Bahr 2001).

According to Foley, the Guild has been successful at bringing Web workers at Guild newspapers into the Guild fold—sometimes through convincing employers to extend existing contract coverage to Web workers, other times through side agreements, and in the harder cases through arbitration. The Guild's model contract describes Guild jurisdiction as covering work that is similar in skill and function to work normally performed by Guild members, and the union actively seeks to extend its reach to nontraditional newsworkers. Getting online editorial workers into the Guild fold is especially critical in light of the recent movement toward "converged" newsrooms, which bring together print, broadcast, and online workers.

It is also important in extending the union's reach to non-newspaper Internet workers, and to professionals in other areas. "We've carved a niche with a connection to high-tech," Foley says (2001). The CWA has put its high-technology organizing arm, known as Wash Tech, into the TNG sector. The idea is that white-collar, educated, high-technology workers might find it more appealing to deal with the white-collar, educated media workers in the Guild sector than with a union they perceive as representing technicians or craft workers. Foley says the high-tech focus has attracted the attention of other professional workers. Recently organized Guild members include translators and interpreters. On the surface, their work would seem to have little to do with the Guild's traditional work of writing and editing. But as Foley (2001) says, "They work with words, we work with words, and it seemed like a good fit." The Guild represented 600 court interpreters in California in 2001, and TNG Canada organized 150 interpreters in British Columbia. The union hopes to add more interpreters in California and in Cook County, Illinois.

Through its connections with the interpreters, the Guild has been making inroads in other nontraditional areas. In 2001 it organized a Chinese-language daily in Los Angeles, and was working on others in San Francisco and New York City. Foley says the union also had a "spectacular success" in New York, organizing workers with the Hudson News chain of Manhattan newsstands. Most of the workers were recent immigrants from Asia, whose only connection to the newspaper business was that they sell newspapers at their stands. "This was a group of workers we wouldn't have looked at" in the pre-CWA days, Foley says. It took two organization drives, but the Guild eventually won the right to represent the workers and negotiated a first contract. "Their lives have really improved dramatically as a result," she says.

The Guild sector has been working closely with the CWA in areas of shared interest. One is a campaign to reach out to nonunionized workers in public broadcasting. CWA has put together a mailout brochure emphasizing the breadth of its membership among broadcast workers in Canada and the United States, and its belief in the value of public broadcasting. "The public airwaves in the U.S. and Canada are a precious resource that belong to all of us," the brochure says. It also points out CWA's connections to groups that seek to preserve public broadcasting, like the Friends of Canadian Broadcasting, the U.S.-based Citizens for Independent Public Broadcasting, and the International Federation of Journalists. It concludes by pledging CWA support for public broadcasting funding: "Through CWA we are working to ensure that our industry receives full government funding. This is essential to guaranteeing that public broadcasting continues to serve the interests of the public." Foley says the campaign, coordinated by the CWA organizing department and drawing on the Guild and former NABET sectors of the union, is in the early stages. But the union hopes it will result in organizing more public broadcasting workers (Foley 2001).

In 2000, the union reached out to a different group of professionals, the American Association of University Professors. The two organizations held a joint conference that June dealing with intellectual workers, academic freedom, and freedom of the press. They noted that a "profit-at-all-costs atmosphere . . . pervades campuses and newsrooms alike," and must be resisted to protect the "dignity, freedom and independence of our professions."[10]

Canada's CEP union has been pursuing similar strategies, in terms of organizing new units,[11] extending contract coverage to online workers,[12] building links with other unions,[13] and taking a public stand on issues. Dating back to its earliest days, the Guild has seen itself as the voice of working journalists on a range of public issues, and a defender of the professional practice of journalism. TNG Canada has continued that work. In 2001, for example, its large Canadian Media Guild local made a presentation to a public policy forum on federal access to information policy, prepared a brief for the House of Commons on public broadcasting, and organized a three-day forum on the future of public broadcasting in Canada.[14] But if TNG Canada sees itself as speaking for Canadian media workers, so does CEP. Vice-president Peter Murdoch, who was part of the Southern Ontario Newspaper Guild contingent that left the Guild for CEP in the 1990s, says that as Canada's national media union, CEP needs to take a public stance on behalf of Canadian journalists and other media workers on issues ranging from freedom of expression to journalism's role in the modern democratic state.

Murdoch envisions his union as functioning for media workers in a similar way as Canadian teachers' and nurses' unions operate for their members: as defenders of the profession and the values it embodies, as critics of government, and as advocates for a better society, not just as bargaining agents. "I don't think journalists generally have had much of a voice in decisions on professional standards, ethics, integrity and maintenance of the craft," he says (Murdoch 2001). Since becoming vice-president in the fall of 2000,[15] Murdoch has released a series of statements on media issues that emphasizes the professional concerns of journalists and their role in the discourse of democracy. These statements include a call for the Canadian Radio-television and Telecommunications Commission (CRTC) to force private broadcaster CTV to rescind layoffs in the fall of 2001, arguing that the network is breaking its commitment to local programming; calls for regulation of cross-media ownership; a statement welcoming the appointment of a committee to study media concentration; and a plea to the CRTC to reject CTV and CanWest Global's plans to converge some newsroom operations.[16] That statement said, "Allowing convergence of news in an arena of such enormous concentrated media ownership is, in democratic terms, the equivalent of allowing automakers the opportunity to lower safety standards when sales aren't going well."[17] In August 2001, following the CRTC's decision to renew the licences of CTV and CanWest, he released a statement promising a new spirit of militance on the part of journalists. "This union will immediately be reviewing with its leadership and membership actions to bring to the attention of the public the inherent dangers in this decision," he wrote.

> Under the immense concentration of ownership journalists have witnessed devastating cuts to their staff, increased corporatism in their newsrooms and now

this eradication of competition and diversity of voice under the guise of convergence. I am putting the employers on notice, they are going to see a stronger and more militant voice speaking up and taking action to protect the craft of journalism in this country. We have learned from our friends in education and healthcare that apparently strong protest is the only thing which attracts attention.[18]

In an attempt to push for a stronger union voice in the face of media convergence, CEP applied to the Canada Industrial Relations Board in May 2001 for a consolidation of twelve bargaining units representing 1,000 employees at Global television stations across the country. "It is time we recognized the reality that these members are working for the same employer, not individual stations," Murdoch said in announcing the move.[19] While the announcement expressed the hope that consolidation would make for better working relationships with the company, Murdoch stressed the political purpose behind it: "As these multinational corporate giants grow larger, it should come as no surprise that many workers are returning to the foundations of their own history by locking arms to protect their interests against such immense wealth and power."

THE LIMITS OF CONVERGENCE

In many ways, the CEP–CanWest labor consolidation application exemplifies both the potential benefits of labor consolidation and its limits. The CEP locals are former NABET units, and their membership is composed mainly of technicians who, at present, bargain station by station. A consolidated local would not only be larger; it could be more effective at the bargaining table, representing the interests of the workers at all the stations thoroughly and thoughtfully in a single round of collective bargaining. In addition, the fact that the consolidated local would be a member of a union that already represents a full range of media workers at other CanWest Global holdings, including newspapers, presents the tantalizing prospect of further organizing opportunities—at newspapers and other CanWest holdings, as well as at television outlets. In other words, consolidation could lead to further labor convergence and, the union hopes, increased labor power. In addition, the CanWest application offers CEP the chance to confront head-on the argument that consolidation of capital through the creation of media empires should have nothing to do with conditions on the shop floor. As Murdoch contends, it is time that everyone—labor organizations, corporations, and the state—recognized the new reality of the media business. So regardless of whether the Canada Industrial Relations Board approves the consolidation, the application lets CEP make a point about the need for a rethinking of labor–management relations in an age of multimedia empires.

At the same time, though, broadcast technicians are a group facing deskilling pressures of their own, through the spread of nonlinear digital editing programs and digital cameras. And there is nothing to suggest that employers will not continue their strategy of using technological innovation to extract the maximum return from the minimum number of workers. Indeed, as the North American economy weakened in 2001, the trend in media employment was toward contraction, not expansion.[20] And as Sleigh notes, although unions may try to negotiate or work with management on the introduction of new technology, "the basic premise remains that management decides on issues of new technology, and industrial relations therefore is relegated to dealing with the effects of those decisions." For the most part, he adds, "decisions concerning new technology remain sealed off from workers and their representatives" (1998, 26). Finally, even if the industrial relations board should approve the consolidation, it would represent merely a tiny readjustment in the tremendously unequal balance of power between North American unions and the companies that employ their workers.

There was a time when strikes routinely shut down newspapers, and kept them shut for a long time.[21] As consultant John Morton writes in the *American Journalism Review*, that is no longer the case: "the technological revolution that swept through the daily newspaper industry in the 1970s made it impossible in most instances for unions to shut down newspapers with a strike" (2001). Though there have been some successful strikes in recent years, there have been some disasters, too. In Detroit, for example, the Newspaper Guild local and five others went on strike against the Gannett-owned *Detroit News* and Knight-Ridder's *Detroit Free Press* in July 1995. The newspapers decided to publish anyway, immediately bringing in what Franklin (1995) called "corporate loaners"—editors and reporters from other newspapers in the chain—and hiring permanent replacement workers. The strike dragged on for more than five agonizing years. A post-strike analysis in the activist magazine *Labor Notes* criticizes the unions for what it calls "business-as-usual unionism," but acknowledges that no matter what the unions did, it would have been a tough strike to win. "The *Detroit News* and *Detroit Free Press* are only small pieces of two corporate empires, Gannett and Knight-Ridder, that are largely nonunion. If this had been a purely local struggle, the unions' impressive circulation and advertising boycotts would have brought the papers to the table. But both parent companies were willing to sustain big losses in order to bust unions in Detroit—once considered labor's stronghold—while remaining profitable elsewhere" (Slaughter 2001). In Calgary, a CEP strike for a first contract that began in November 1999 collapsed after a long, cold winter on the picket line.[22] The damage caused by losses like these extends far beyond the locals on strike. A failed strike erodes the confidence of members of other locals. It may encourage other owners to try to break or decertify their own unions. It drains defense funds. It raises questions about the union's leadership. And it makes organizing more difficult.

By comparison to the outcome in Detroit and Calgary, the seven-week Pacific Northwest Newspaper Guild local strike against the *Seattle Times* and *Seattle Post-Intelligencer* at the end of 2000 has to be considered a labor success. The strike was the first in forty-seven years by a local considered even by its own members to be far from militant. According to a report posted on the union's strike Web site, "When the strike began, workers at *The Times* and the *P-I* considered it a fight largely over wages, which they said had not kept up with the area's cost of living. In time the walkout became a fight by the union to keep its traditionally weak membership together..." (Robin and Kaiman 2001). But the strike held, even after *The Times* began hiring permanent replacement workers. In the end, the contract was only marginally better than the company's last prestrike offer. Nonetheless, the fact that the two sides reached a negotiated agreement is significant. In her column in the *Guild Reporter* (19 January 2001, 7), Foley says the Seattle strikers proved "they could do it all: run a successful strike, produce a professional strike newspaper, bargain a better contract than the companies' take-it-or-leave-it final offer and build a real union." Foley calls it a "no brainer" to conclude that the Guild won the strike.[23]

It is clear, however, that the decision to go on strike, in Seattle or elsewhere, is a risky business these days. Given the relative ease with which newspapers can continue to publish through a strike—by bringing in staff from other holdings owned by the same corporation, by hiring permanent replacement workers, or by taking advantage of computers and telecommunications to deliver news by computer rather than on paper—it is much harder than it used to be for a newspaper union to win a strike. But as CWA President Morton Bahr writes, "We do not have to prove how militant we are by calling a strike.... There are many powerful alternatives to strikes and we need to work them into our strategic planning" (Bahr 1998, 265). These include the idea of "wall-to-wall" organizing of all workers with a single employer;[24] working cooperatively with other unions locally, nationally, and internationally; and bargaining with an eye to future organizing opportunities. The alternatives also include political action, such as working for changes in labor law, and community activism. Techniques like these in turn promote further organizing and bargaining. For unions like CWA and CEP, strategic planning also means deepening the connections within the union. CEP vice-president Murdoch, for example, says he hopes to work with the union's telecommunications workers on finding common ground for dealing with the Bell Globemedia empire, which includes the Bell Canada telephone system, the CTV network, and the *Globe and Mail* newspaper (Murdoch 2001).

In debating a strategy of labor convergence, The Newspaper Guild has found itself having to choose between clinging to its traditional strengths in the printing industry or joining a union—be it CWA *or* CEP—that was staking a claim as its country's premier communications workers' union. Neither the Guild itself nor the Canadian locals that broke away to join a national union made their choice quickly or carelessly. They knew it was a gamble, and that at stake was the future of a union with a proud and honorable history of representing workers who were anything but typical union members. The leaders and ordinary members who decided to take that risk felt that in an age when corporate and technological convergence were rewriting the ground rules for workers, labor convergence was the wisest choice. If their decision helps journalists and other communication workers weather the turmoil of their industry in the coming years, their gamble will have paid off.

NOTES

1. Membership in trade unions in Canada rose from 1.35 million in 1956 to 1.44 million in 1961 and 1.74 million in 1966. In the United States, trade union membership declined between 1956 and 1961, from 16.44 million to 15.4 million, but by 1966 it had recovered lost ground and grown to 19.9 million (Murray 195, 164). Union density, meanwhile, hovered at just over 30 percent in Canada and just under 30 percent in the United States.

2. The *Vancouver Sun*, for example, was owned by three generations of the Cromie family from its founding in 1924 until 1963, when it was purchased by FP Publications, at the time Canada's largest newspaper chain (Kesterton 1967, 77). In 1980, Thomson Newspapers gained control of the *Sun* through its purchase of FP Publications. Thomson sold the *Sun* to the Southam corporation that same year (Fraser and Angel 1981, 30). In the 1990s, Hollinger Corp. took control of the Southam group. In 2000, it sold most of its Southam holdings to CanWest Global, including the Vancouver newspaper. Whereas the *Sun*'s first forty years featured stable, one-family owner-

ship, its most recent forty years have featured ownership or control by five companies, each one of them the dominant player in the Canadian newspaper business in its day.

3. Chaison (1986) identifies internal opposition as one of the key barriers to any trade union merger, and suggests that the higher up in the hierarchy the opposition, the more successful it is likely to be in blocking a deal.

4. Sleigh's account of the struggles in the New York newspapers from the 1960s to the 1990s explores many of the fissures between and among unions. He describes the ten unions that made up the Allied Printing Trades Council as "a fractious group with a long history of jockeying for position to set the trend in negotiations, and often, as in the long strike of 1962–1963, developing bitter rivalries between union leaders" (Sleigh 1998, 121). In the 1970s, Guild resentment was directed against Bert Powers, the head of the ITU local, for refusing to honor an agreement on pattern bargaining in 1962 and triggering a 115-day strike (93). In a critical round of bargaining in 1990, cracks began to appear in the union's pledge of solidarity, as the owners of the *Daily News* made a determined effort to break the power of the unions. For example, the ITU announced that in order to protect the lifetime job guarantees of its members, it would not strike even if the other unions did (133). Management negotiated with the two unions it felt were most critical to the paper, the drivers' union and the Guild (137). When a strike eventually began at the *Daily News*, however, the unions managed to put on an impressive display of solidarity. The only break involved 100 Guild members who continued to go to work (155).

5. Reproduction clauses refer to the practice of resetting and disposing of advertising type from outside the newspaper. Manning provisions attempt to assert union control over the staffing levels of the pressroom and may also, in some cases, amount to featherbedding. Sleigh notes that the key issue in the *Washington Post* strike of 1975 was union control over hiring procedures and pressroom work (1998, 92). One by one, the other unions at the paper abandoned the pressmen, effectively breaking the strike.

6. At the time the *London Free Press* certification drive occurred, in 1989, SONG was a local of The Newspaper Guild (*Guild Reporter*, 5 January 1990, 1).

7. See also Pacific Press Inc., application for consolidation of bargaining units to B.C. Labour Relations Board, 12 June 1995, 27.

8. Foley says a CWA–Guild local merger is likely to occur in southern California, where the Guild local was decimated by the 1998 decertification at the *San Diego Union Tribune*. In an interview in the spring of 2001, she said the two locals were close to signing a deal.

9. Morton Bahr says the CWA started organizing nurses in the early 1980s, after he got a call from a nurse in Buffalo asking for a meeting. "They wanted us to organize them. I asked, 'Why?' Here's what they said: 'Your locals in Eastern New York are so active in the community that we just love seeing what they do. You bargain with some of the country's largest and most powerful employers, so you should be able to bargain with Buffalo General. And what you don't know about nursing we'll teach you.'" The union now represents roughly 1,500 nurses (Bahr 2001).

10. TNG-AAUP, "Call to Action" [pamphlet], June 2000.

11. This union has also been organizing workers in the ethnic media, including

Chinese- and Korean-language newspapers in Toronto (*SONGSheet*, May 2001, 1; August 2001, 1). It has also organized newspaper carriers in Toronto and Winnipeg, though its hard work in Toronto unraveled when the *Toronto Star* decided to contract out delivery; see *SONGSheet*, August 2001.

12. CEP has managed to extend its newsroom coverage to workers at in-house Web sites like www.Globeandmail.com with little difficulty, Murdoch says (2001).

13. As a representative with SONG, Murdoch was the driving force behind the creation of an Inter-Union Council on Newspapers, says Joe Matyas (1998).

14. CMG news releases, 6 February, 13 June, and 10 October 2001, at www.cmg.ca (accessed 10 April 2002).

15. Murdoch defeated Gail Lem by a vote of 56 percent to 44 percent in the executive elections of September 2000 (*SONGSheet*, October 2000, 1). Lem took a job on the staff of CEP.

16. See CEP news releases, 13 March, 18 April, 11 May, 31 July, and 18 October 2001, at www.cep.ca (accessed 11 April 2002).

17. CEP news release, 31 July 2001, at www.cep.ca (accessed 11 April 2002).

18. CEP news release, 2 August 2001, at www.cep.ca (accessed 11 April 2002).

19. CEP news release, 4 May 2001, at www.cep.ca (accessed 11 April 2002).

20. An online job board for media workers, Journalismjobs.com, began tracking media layoffs in the fall of 2000. In November 2001 alone, it listed reports of layoffs at Dow Jones, Yahoo, AOL Time Warner, Discovery Communications (owned by Disney), *Condé Nast, Business Week*, PBS, the *Dallas Morning News*, and the British Broadcasting Corporation; see www.journalismjobs.com (accessed 16 November 2001).

21. Sleigh lists several lengthy strikes: a 174-day closure of the newspapers in Wilkes-Barre, Pa., in 1938–1939; a 144-day shutdown in Springfield, Mass., in 1946–1947; a 128-day shutdown in San Jose, Calif., in 1950 (1998, 76). In New York, strikes caused shutdowns of all newspapers in 1953 (eleven days) and 1958 (seventeen days). The 1962–1963 strike led to a news blackout in New York that lasted more than 100 days (86–87). Another lengthy newspaper blackout occurred in New York in 1978 (96–97).

22. As in the *London Free Press* organization drive several years earlier, the critical issue in organizing the Hollinger-owned *Calgary Herald* was editorial integrity.

23. Some critics have argued the opposite. J. Morton (2001), for example, contends that the workers ended up with the same raises they would have received without going on strike, but lost seven weeks of pay.

24. At its 1991 convention, CWA adopted the term "wall-to-wall" to describe its organizing mission (Bahr 1998, 332).

Bibliography

"ACTRA, Extras Dispute Unexpected, Union Says." 2000. *The Globe and Mail*, 11 January, R3.
Adam, G. Stuart. 1993. *Notes toward a Definition of Journalism*. St. Petersburg, Fla.: Poynter Institute for Media Studies.
Adams, Paul. 2001. "CTV, Global Reject Idea of Separated News Units." *The Globe and Mail*, 26 April. Online at www.globeandmail.com. Accessed 26 April 2001.
Adams, Paul, and Catherine McKercher. 1991. "North America." In *Global Journalism: Survey of International Communication*, 2d edition, edited by John C. Merrill, 311–57. New York: Longman.
Amber, Arnold (head of TNG Canada). 1998. Interview by author. March.
———. 2001. "Canadian Media Guild Leader Refutes Charges by CEP Leader." *Straight Goods*, 30 December. Online at www.straightgoods.com. Accessed 21 January 2002.
Anderson, Benedict R. 1991. *Imagined Communities: Reflections on the Origin and Spread of Nationalism*. 2d edition. London: Verso.
Aronowitz, Stanley, and William DiFazio. 1994. *The Jobless Future: Sci-Tech and the Dogma of Work*. Minneapolis: University of Minnesota Press.
Associated Press Managing Editors. 1988. *Media Technology Report*. Boston: n.p.
Associated Press Managing Editors Committee on Technology. 1987. *Meet the Future: A Report on Pagination and Other Mystical Things*. Edited by Gregory E. Favre. Report prepared for APME conference, Boston.
Associated Press Managing Editors Telecommunications and Technology Committee. 1985. *Pagination: An Editor's Guide to Understanding New Technology*. Report prepared for APME conference, San Francisco.
Babe, Robert E. 1990. *Telecommunications in Canada: Technology, Industry, and Government*. Toronto: University of Toronto Press.
———. 1996. "Convergence and the New Technologies." In *The Cultural Industries in Canada: Problems, Policies and Prospects*, edited by Michael Dorland, 283–307. Toronto: Lorimer.

Bagdikian, Ben H. 1983. *The Media Monopoly.* Boston: Beacon. Subsequent editions released 1987, 1990, 1992, 1997.
Bahr, Morton. 1995. Text of speech at CWA/TNG Symposium on Information and Convergence, 8 December, Washington, D.C.
———. 1998. *From the Telegraph to the Internet.* Washington, D.C.: National Press Books.
——— (president, CWA). 2001. Interview by author. May.
Baker, Elizabeth Faulkner. 1974. *Printers and Technology: A History of the International Printing Pressmen and Assistants' Union.* New York: Columbia University Press, 1957. Reprint, Westport, Conn.: Greenwood Press.
Barlow, Maude, and James Winter. 1997. *The Big Black Book: The Essential Views of Conrad and Barbara Amiel Black.* Toronto: Stoddart.
Barnett, George E. 1926. *Chapters on Machinery and Labor.* Cambridge: Harvard University Press.
Barwis, Gail L. 1981. "The Changing Face of Labor in the Newspaper Industry." *Newspaper Research Journal* 2, no. 2:49–57.
Beniger, James R. 1986. *The Control Revolution: Technological and Economic Origins of the Information Society.* Cambridge: Harvard University Press.
Blauner, Robert. 1964. *Alienation and Freedom: The Factory Worker and His Industry.* Chicago: University of Chicago Press.
Bocking, Mike (president, CEP 115-M, CEP 2000). 1998a. Interview by author. February.
———. 1998b. Interview by author. May.
Bogart, Leo. 1991. *Preserving the Press: How Daily Newspapers Mobilized to Keep Their Readers.* New York: Columbia University Press.
Bonisteel, Steven. 2000. "BCE, Thomson Combine Canadian Portal, TV, and Paper." 18 September. Online at www.computeruser.com/news. Accessed 10 April 2002.
Boswell, Randy. 1992. "All about Dinosaurs and Newspapers." *Content* (March/April): 8–11.
Brasch, Walter M., ed. 1991. *With Just Cause: Unionization of the American Journalist.* Lanham, Md.: University Press of America.
Braverman, Harry. 1974. *Labor and Monopoly Capital: The Degradation of Work in the Twentieth Century.* New York: Monthly Review Press.
Breed, Warren. 1955. "Social Control in the Newsroom: A Functional Analysis." *Social Forces* 33 (May): 326–35.
Broun, Heywood Hale, comp. 1941. *Collected Edition of Heywood Broun.* New York: Harcourt.
Brown, Duncan (organizing coordinator, GCIU Toronto). 1998. Interview by author. March.
Bruce, Charles. 1968. *News and the Southams.* Toronto: Macmillan of Canada.
Burawoy, Michael. 1979. *Manufacturing Consent: Changes in the Labor Process under Monopoly Capitalism.* Chicago: University of Chicago Press.
———. 1985. *The Politics of Production: Factory Regimes Under Capitalism and Socialism.* London: Verso.
Burr, Christina. 1993. "Defending 'The Art Preservative': Class and Gender Relations in the Printing Trades Unions, 1850–1914." *Labour/Le Travail* 31 (Spring): 47–73.

Buxton, William J. 1998. "Harold Innis' Excavation of Modernity: The Newspaper Industry, Communications, and the Decline of Public Life." *Canadian Journal of Communication* 23, no. 3:321–39.

Buxton, William J., and Catherine McKercher. 1998. "Newspapers, Magazines, and Journalism in Canada: Toward a Critical Historiography." *Acadiensis* 23, no. 1:103–26.

Byerly, Carolyn M., and Catherine A. Warren. 1996. "At the Margins of the Center: Organized Protest in the Newsroom." *Critical Studies in Mass Communication* 13:1–23.

Cagampan-Stoute, Caroline. 1993. "The New CPU: Brawn or Brains?" *Canadian Papermaker* 46, no. 1 (January): 76.

Canada. Industry Canada. 1994. *The Canadian Information Highway: Building Canada's Information and Communications Infrastructure*. Ottawa: Minister of Supply and Services.

Canada. Royal Commission on Newspapers [Kent Commission]. 1981. *Report*. Ottawa: Supply and Services Canada.

Canada. Special Senate Committee on Mass Media [Davey committee]. 1970. *Uncertain Mirror: Report of the Special Senate Committee on Mass Media*. Vol. 1. Ottawa: Queen's Printer.

Carey, James W. 1969. "The Communications Revolution and the Professional Communicator." In *The Sociology of Mass-Media Communicators*, edited by Paul Halmos, 23–38. Sociological Review Monographs, no. 13. Keel: Staffordshire University Press.

———. 1992. "Space, Time, and Communications: A Tribute to Harold Innis." In *Communication as Culture: Essays on Media and Society*, 142–72. New York: Routledge.

Carter, Donald D. 1995. "Collective Bargaining Legislation." In *Union–Management Relations in Canada*, 3d edition, edited by Morley Gunderson and Allen Ponak, 53–72. Don Mills, Ont.: Addison-Wesley.

Case, Tony. 1996. "Guild's New Leader Speaks Out." *Editor and Publisher*, 10 February, 14.

Chaison, Gary N. 1986. *When Unions Merge*. Lexington, Mass.: Lexington Books.

Chaykowski, Richard P. 1995. "The Structure and Process of Collective Bargaining." In *Union–Management Relations in Canada*, 3d edition, edited by Morley Gunderson and Allen Ponak, 229–54. Don Mills, Ont.: Addison-Wesley.

Chitayat, Gideon. 1979. *Trade Union Mergers and Labor Conglomerates*. New York: Praeger.

Coady, Michael A. 1976. "Trade Union Mergers in the Canadian Labour Context: Causes, Effects, Legal Treatment." Master of Law thesis, York University.

Cobb, Chris. 1995. "Is Thomson leaving the Newspaper Business?" *Ottawa Citizen*, 13 May, G1.

Cockburn, Cynthia. 1983. *Brothers: Male Dominance and Technological Change*. London: Pluto.

Cohen, Stanley. 1972. *Folk Devils and Moral Panics*. London: MacGibbon and Key.

Cole, David M. 2000. "Mission: Multimedia." *Presstime*, May. Online at www.naa.org/presstime. Accessed 10 April 2002.

Communications Technology Adjustment Committee (CTAC). 1996. "Strengthening Our Unions: An Action Plan for the GCIU and the CEP." Toronto: Communications Technology Adjustment Committee.

"Competition Bureau and CanWest Resolve Concerns about *ROBTv*." 2000. Competition Bureau news release, 3 November. Ottawa.

Cowan, Jim (international vice-president, GCIU). 1998. Interview by author. March.

Cowan, Ruth Schwartz. 1979. "From Virginia Dare to Virginia Slims: Women and Technology in American Life." In *Dynamos and Virgins Revisited*, edited by Martha Moore Trescott, 30–44. Metuchen, N.J.: Scarecrow Press.

Craig, Alton W. J. 1986. *The System of Industrial Relations in Canada*. 2d edition. Scarborough, Ont.: Prentice Hall Canada.

Craig, Susan. 1987. "Solidarity Is a Sometimes Thing." *Content* (November/December): 2–6.

CWA News. 1994–. Newsletter of Communications Workers of America.

CWA Sector News. 1993–. Newsletter of CWA/ITU Print, Publishing, and Media Workers sector (insert in *CWA News*).

Czitrom, Daniel J. 1982. *Media and the American Mind: From Morse to McLuhan*. Chapel Hill: University of North Carolina Press.

Dalgleish, Brenda. 1999. "Calgary Herald Files Defamation Suit Against Union." *The Globe and Mail*, 27 October, B3.

Dawes, Colin Jonathan. 1987. *The Relative Decline of International Unionism in Canada Since 1970*. School of Industrial Relations Research Essay Series, no. 19. Kingston, Ont.: Queen's University.

de Bonville, Jean. 1988. *La presse Québécoise de 1884 à 1914: Genèse d'un media de masse*. Québec: Presses de l'Université Laval.

Dennis, Everette E., and John V. Pavlik. 1993. "The Coming of Convergence and Its Consequences." In *Demystifying Media Technology*, edited by Pavlik and Dennis. Mountainview, Calif.: Mayfield Publishing.

Derber, Charles. 1983. "Managing Professionals: Ideological Proletarianization and Post-Industrial Labor." *Theory and Society* 12, no. 3:309–41.

De Reimer, Cynthia. 1992. "A Survey of VU/TEXT Use in the Newsroom." *Journalism Quarterly* 69, no. 4:960–70.

Desbarats, Peter. 1995. "The Special Role of Magazines in the History of Canadian Mass Media and National Development." In *Communications in Canadian Society*, 4th edition, edited by Benjamin D. Singer, 72–88. Toronto: Nelson Canada.

———. 1996. *Guide to Canadian News Media*. 2d edition. Toronto: Harcourt Brace.

Dunlop, John Thomas. 1993. *Industrial Relations Systems*. Revised edition. Boston: Harvard Business School Press.

Edwards, Richard. 1979. *Contested Terrain: The Transformation of the Workplace in the Twentieth Century*. New York: Basic Books.

Emery, Edwin, and Michael Emery. 1978. *The Press and America: An Interpretative History of the Mass Media*. 4th edition. Englewood Cliffs, N.J.: Prentice-Hall.

Endres, Frederic F. 1985. "Daily Newspaper Utilization of Computer Data Bases." *Newspaper Research Journal* 7, no. 1:29–35.

Epstein, Edward J. 1973. *News from Nowhere: Television and the News*. New York: Random House.

Fetherling, Douglas. 1993. *A Little Bit of Thunder: The Strange Inner Life of the Kingston Whig-Standard*. Toronto: Stoddart.
Fitzgerald, Mark. 1996. "Don't Count Labor Out." *Editor and Publisher*, 16 November, 18.
Foley, Linda. 1995. "Don't Write off the Guild." *Washington Post*, 30 December, A17.
——— (president, TNG sector, CWA). 1998. Interview by author. February.
———. 2001. Interview by author. May.
Franklin, Steve. 1995. "Which Side Are You On?" *Columbia Journalism Review*, November/December. Online at www.cjr.org. Accessed 21 October 2001.
Fraser, C. R. P., and Sharon Angel. 1981. "Vancouver: A History of Conflict." In *Labour Relations in the Newspaper Industry*, edited by Gérard Hébert et al., 23–49. Royal Commission on Newspapers Research Publications, vol. 5. Ottawa: Minister of Supply and Services.
Friedman, Andrew L. 1977. *Industry and Labour: Class Struggle at Work and Monopoly Capitalism*. London: Macmillan.
———. 1990. "Managerial Activities, Techniques, and Technology: Towards a Complex Theory of the Labour Process." In *Labour Process Theory*, edited by David Knights and Hugh Wilmott, 177–208. London: Macmillan.
Fulford, Robert. 2001. "CRTC Moves into the Newsroom." *National Post*, 4 August. Online at www.friendscb.org. Accessed 10 April 2002.
Fulton, Katherine. 2000. "News Isn't Always Journalism." *Columbia Journalism Review* (July/August): 30, 35.
Funk, Harold (former president, CEP Local 226). 1997. Interview by author. December.
Gans, Herbert J. 1979. *Deciding What's News: A Study of CBS Evening News, NBC Nightly News, "Newsweek," and "Time."* New York: Pantheon Books.
Gildersleeve, Larkie (director of research, information, and technology, CWA/TNG). 1998. Interview by author. February.
Glasgow University Media Group (GUMG). 1976. *Bad News*. London: Routledge.
———. 1982. *Really Bad News*. London: Writers and Readers.
Goldenberg, Susan. 1984. *The Thomson Empire*. Toronto: Methuen.
Goldhaber, Michael. 1986. *Reinventing Technology: Policies for Democratic Values*. New York: Routledge.
Golding, Peter, and Philip Elliott. 1979. *Making the News*. London: Longman.
Goldman, Debbie (research economist, CWA). 1998. Interview by author. February.
Gordon, David M., Richard Edwards, and Michael Reich. 1982. *Segmented Work, Divided Workers: The Historical Transformation of Labor in the United States*. Cambridge: Cambridge University Press.
Grey, Doug (CEP; former Canadian director, CWA Printing, Publishing and Media Workers sector). 1999. Interview by author. May.
Guild Reporter. 1960–. Newsletter of The Newpaper Guild.
Gunderson, Morley, and Allen Ponak. 1995. "Industrial Relations." In *Union–Management Relations in Canada*, 3d edition, edited by Morley Gunderson and Allen Ponak, 1–20. Don Mills, Ont.: Addison-Wesley.
Hackett, Robert A. 1984. "Decline of a Paradigm? Bias and Objectivity in News Media Studies." *Critical Studies in Mass Communication* 1, no. 3:229–59.

Hadley, Karen. 1995a. "Restructuring in the '90s: Fewer People Working Faster." Studies of the Canadian Printing Industry. Toronto: GCIU.

———. 1995b. "Riding the Digital Revolution: Unions Can Survive and Thrive." Studies of the Canadian Printing Industry. Toronto: GCIU.

———. 1995c. "Total Quality Management: The Moore Plant in Fergus." Studies of the Canadian Printing Industry. Toronto: GCIU.

Halberstam, David. 1979. *The Powers That Be*. New York: Knopf.

Hall, Stuart, Chas Critcher, Tony Jefferson, John Clarke, and Brian Roberts. 1978. *Policing the Crisis: Mugging, the State, and Law and Order*. London: Macmillan.

Hamilton, John Maxwell, and George A. Krimsky. 1996. *Hold the Press: The Inside Story on Newspapers*. Baton Rouge: Louisiana State University Press.

Hansen, Kathleen A. 1990. "Information Richness and Pulitzer Prizes." *Journalism Quarterly* 67, no. 4:930–35.

Hansen, Kathleen A., Jean Ward, and Douglas M. McLeod. 1987. "Role of the Newspaper Library in the Production of News." *Journalism Quarterly* 64, no. 4:714–20.

Hardt, Hanno. 1995. "Without the Rank and File: Journalism History, Media Workers, and Problems of Representation." In *Newsworkers: Toward a History of the Rank and File*, edited by Hardt and Bonnie Brennen, 1–29. Minneapolis: University of Minnesota Press.

Hardt, Hanno, and Bonnie Brennen, eds. *Newsworkers: Toward a History of the Rank and File*. Minneapolis: University of Minnesota Press, 1995.

Hayes, David. 1992. *Power and Influence: The Globe and Mail and the News Revolution*. Toronto: Key Porter.

Hébert, Gérard, ed., with C. R. P. Fraser, Sharon Angel, Allan Patterson, John B. Kervin, Donald Swartz, Eugene Swimmer, Pierre-Paul Proulx, and James Thwaites. 1981. *Labour Relations in the Newspaper Industry*. Royal Commission on Newspapers Research Publications, vol. 5. Ottawa: Minister of Supply and Services.

Heilbroner, Robert. 1967. "Do Machines Make History?" *Technology and Culture* 8, no. 3:335–45.

———. 1994. "Technological Determinism Revisited." In *Does Technology Drive History? The Dilemma of Technological Determinism*, edited by Merritt Roe Smith and Leo Marx, 67–78. Cambridge: MIT Press.

Heron, Craig. 1989. *The Canadian Labour Movement: A Short History*. 1st edition. Toronto: Lorimer.

———. 1996. *The Canadian Labour Movement: A Brief History*. 2d edition. Toronto: Lorimer.

Hickey, Neil. 2000. "Converge Me Up, Scottie: Tribune Beams toward a Multimedia Future." *Columbia Journalism Review* (May/June): 18–22.

Hobsbawm, E. J. 1964. *Labouring Men: Studies in the History of Labour*. London: Weidenfeld.

Human Resources Development Canada. 2001. Directory of Labour Organizations in Canada. Online at labour.hrdc-drhc.gc.ca. Accessed 18 June 2001.

Hunter, Scott B. 1985. "Pagination Comes a Long Way." In *Pagination: An Editor's Guide to Understanding New Technology*, report prepared by the Associated Press Managing Editors Telecommunications and Technology Committee, 3.

Im, Yung-Ho. 1997. "Towards a Labor Process History of Newsworkers." *Javnost/The Public Interest* 4, no. 1:31–48.
Innis, Harold A. 1949. *The Press: A Neglected Factor in the Economic History of the Twentieth Century*. London: Oxford University Press.
———. 1951. *The Bias of Communication*. Toronto: University of Toronto Press.
Inside Story. Newsletter of Local 115-M, Communications, Energy and Paperworkers Union of Canada.
Irwin, Manley. 1984. *Telecommunications America: Markets without Boundaries*. Westport, Conn.: Quorum Books.
Jacobson, Sol. 1960. "The Fourth Estate: A Study of the American Newspaper Guild." Ph.D. dissertation, New School for Social Research.
[Jaquet, Janine]. 1998. "The Media Nation; TV Centerfold: Who Controls Television?" *The Nation*, 8 June, n.p.
Jennings, Bob (president, GCIU Local 515-M). 1997. Interview by author. December.
Johnson, Gib. 1990. "The Compleat Reporter." *Washington Journalism Review* (May): 16–19.
Johnson, Tom. 2000. "That's AOL Folks. . . ." 10 January. Online at www.CNNfn.com. Accessed 1 February 2000.
Kalleberg, Arne L., Michael Wallace, Karyn A. Loscocco, Keven T. Leicht, and Hans-Helmut Ehm. 1987. "The Eclipse of Craft: The Changing Face of Labor in the Newspaper Industry." In *Workers, Managers and Technological Change: Emerging Patterns of Labor Relations*, edited by Daniel B. Cornfield, 47–71. New York: Plenum Press.
Kealey, Gregory S. 1986. "Work Control, the Labour Process, and Nineteenth-Century Canadian Printers." In *On the Job: Confronting the Labour Process in Canada*, edited by Craig Heron and Robert Story, 75–101. Kingston: McGill-Queen's University Press.
Kelber, Harry, and Carl Schlesinger. 1967. *Union Printers and Controlled Automation*. Toronto: Free Press.
Kerr, John, and Walter Niebauer Jr. 1987. "Use of Full-text Database Retrieval Systems by Editorial Page Writers." *Newspaper Research Journal* 8, no. 3:21–32.
Kesterton, W. H. 1967. *A History of Journalism in Canada*. Toronto: McClelland and Stewart.
Knight, Graham. 1982. "News and Ideology." *Canadian Journal of Communication* 8, no. 4:14–41.
Koch, Tom. 1990. *The News as Myth: Fact and Context in Journalism*. New York: Greenwood Press.
———. 1991. *Journalism for the Twenty-First Century: Online Information, Electronic Databases, and the News*. New York: Praeger.
Kuczun, Sam. 1970. "History of the American Newspaper Guild." Ph.D. dissertation, University of Minnesota.
Lareau, Lise (president, Canadian Media Guild local, CWA/TNG). 2002. Interview by author. March.
Law, Howard (executive officer, SONG). 1998. Interview by author. December.
Lazarre, Daniel. 1991. "State of the Union: The Newspaper Guild Under the Gun." In *With Just Cause: Unionization of the American Journalist*, edited by Walter M. Brasch, 335–39. Lanham, Md.: University Press of America.

Leab, Daniel B. 1970. *A Union of Individuals: The Formation of the American Newspaper Guild, 1933–1936*. New York: Columbia University Press.
Ledbetter, James. 2000. "When the Infinite Becomes Finite." *Columbia Journalism Review* (July/August): 26–27.
Lem, Gail (vice-president for media, CEP). 1998. Interview by author. February.
———. 1999. Interview by author. May.
Lepper, John (former president, CWA Local 14003). 1997. Interview by author. December.
Linley, William R. 1988. "From Hot Type to Video Screens: Editors Evaluate New Technology." *Journalism Quarterly* 65, no. 2:485–89.
Lipset, Seymour M., Martin A. Trow, and James S. Coleman. 1956. *Union Democracy: The Internal Politics of the International Typographical Union*. Glencoe, Ill.: Free Press.
Lipsig-Mummé, Carla. 1995. "Labour Strategies in the New Social Order: A Political Economy Perspective." In *Union-Management Relations in Canada*, 3d edition, edited by Morley Gunderson and Allen Ponak, 195–225. Don Mills, Ont.: Addison-Wesley.
Loft, Jacob. 1944. *The Printing Trades*. New York: Farrar and Rinehart.
London Free Press. 1966. *Communication in the Community*. London, Ont.: *London Free Press*. (Limited souvenir edition published to mark the opening of the newspaper's new production facility.)
Marvin, Carolyn. 1988. *When Old Technologies Were New*. New York: Oxford University Press.
Matyas, Joe (president, SONG [CEP 87-M]). 1998. Interview by author. March.
Mawhinney, Michele. 1989. *Union Mergers and Small Unions in Canada Since 1967*. Kingston, Ont.: Industrial Relations Centre, Queen's University.
Marx, Leo. 1964. *The Machine in the Garden: Technology and the Pastoral Ideal in America*. New York: Oxford University Press.
McKercher, Catherine. 1991. "Proceeding to Pagination: Ontario Newspaper Editors Assess New Technology." Paper presented to the Association for Education in Journalism and Mass Communication (AEJMC) Newspaper Division, August, in Boston, Mass.
———. 1995. "Computers and Reporters: Newsroom Practices at Two Canadian Daily Newspapers." *Canadian Journal of Communication* 20:213–29.
McKercher, Catherine, and Carman Cumming. 1998. *The Canadian Reporter: News Writing and Reporting*. 2d edition. Toronto: Harcourt Brace.
McLoughlin, Ian, and Jon Clark. 1994. *Technological Change at Work*. 2d edition. Buckingham, U.K.: Open University Press.
McNamara, Tracy. 2000. "Hard Numbers: Now and Then." *Columbia Journalism Review*, (July/August): 25.
Menzies, Heather. 1996. *Whose Brave New World? The Information Highway and the New Economy*. Toronto: Between the Lines.
Mickleburgh, Rod. 1999. "Pacific Press Strike Ends Quickly." *The Globe and Mail*, 8 July, A3.
Miller, Jeffrey M. 1988. *CWA at 50: A Pictorial History of the Communications Workers of America, 1938–1988*. Washington, D.C.: CWA.

Miller, John. 1998. *Yesterday's News: Why Canada's Daily Newspapers Are Failing Us.* Halifax, N.S.: Fernwood.
Mitchell, Bill. 2000. "Crossing Media Lines." 24 April. Online at www.poynter.org. Accessed 30 April 2001.
Morton, Desmond. 1998. *Working People: An Illustrated History of the Canadian Labour Movement.* 4th edition. Montreal: McGill-Queen's University Press.
Morton, John. 2001. "Seattle Strikes Out." *American Journalism Review* (March): 76.
Mosco, Vincent. 1989. *The Pay-Per Society: Computers and Communication in the Information Age: Essays in Critical Theory and Public Policy.* Toronto: Garamond.
———. 1996a. "Myth-ing Links: Power and Community on the Information Highway." Dunton lecture, delivered at Carleton University in Ottawa, November. Online at www.carleton.ca/mosco. Accessed July 2001.
———. 1996b. *The Political Economy of Communication.* London: Sage.
Murdoch, Peter (national representative, SONG [CEP 87-M]). 1998. Interview by author. March.
——— (vice-president for media, CEP). 2001. Interview by author. October.
———. 2002. "CBC Workers Need Canadian Union." *Straight Goods,* 15 January. Online at www.straightgoods.com. Accessed 21 January 2002.
Murray, Gregor. 1995. "Unions: Membership, Structures and Action." In *Union-Management Relations in Canada,* 3d edition, edited by Morley Gunderson and Allen Ponak, 159–94. Don Mills, Ont.: Addison-Wesley.
Needham, Marian V. (director of contract administration, TNG). 2001. Interview by author. May.
Negroponte, Nicholas. 1995. *Being Digital.* New York: Knopf.
Nerone, John C. 1993. "A Local History of the Early U.S. Press: Cincinnati, 1793–1848." In *Ruthless Criticism: New Perspectives in U.S. Communication History,* edited by William S. Solomon and Robert W. McChesney, 38–65. Minneapolis: University of Minnesota Press.
Neuwirth, Kurt, Carol M. Liebler, Sharon Dunwoody, and Jennifer Riddle. 1988. "The Effect of 'Electronic' News Sources on Selection and Editing of News." *Journalism Quarterly* 65, no. 1:85–94.
Noble, David F. 1984. *Forces of Production: A Social History of Industrial Automation.* New York: Knopf.
Nolan, Michael. 1989. *Walter J. Blackburn: A Man for All Media.* Toronto: Macmillan of Canada.
Nord, David Paul. 1984. "The Evangelical Origins of Mass Media in America, 1815–1835." Journalism Monographs. Austin, Tex.: Association for Education in Journalism and Mass Communication.
Nordenstrang, Kaarle, and Herbert I. Schiller. 1993. *Beyond National Sovereignty: International Communication in the 1990s.* Revised edition. Norwood, N.J.: Ablex.
Nye, David E. 1990. *Electrifying America: Social Meanings of a New Technology, 1880–1940.* Cambridge: MIT Press.
O'Brien, Jan (president, CEP 115-M). 1997. Interview by author. December.
O'Connor, Kevin (*Regina Leader-Post* Guild). 1999. Interview by author. April.
Osipa, Robert (former president, GCIU Local 25-C). 1998. Interview by author. February.

Pane, Elissa. 1994. *Machine Bites Bog: A Study of Technology and Work in the Ontario Newspaper Industry*. Tri-union report funded by the Ontario Technological Adjustment Research Program. Toronto: Southern Ontario Newspaper Guild.

Panitch, Leo, and Donald Swartz. 1988. *From Consent to Coercion: The Assault on Trade Union Freedoms*. Toronto: Garamond.

Papp, Leslie. 1992. "Unions Join Forces to Create Loud Voice." *Toronto Star*, 27 November, A21.

Patten, David A. 1985. *Newspapers and New Media*. White Plains, N.Y.: Knowledge Industry Publications.

Pavlik, John Vernon. 1996. *New Media Technology: Cultural and Commercial Perspectives*. Boston: Allyn and Bacon.

Pedersen, Diana and Martha Phemister. 1990. "Women and Photography in Ontario, 1839–1929: A Case Study of the Interaction of Gender and Technology." In *Despite the Odds: Essays on Canadian Women and Science*, edited by Marianne Gosztonyi Ainley, 88–111. Montreal: Vehicule Press.

Phillipson, Donald J. C. 1988. "Georges-Édouard Desbarats." In *The Canadian Encyclopedia*, edited by James H. March, 587. Edmonton: Hurtig Publishers.

Piore, Michael J., and Charles F. Sabel. 1984. *The Second Industrial Divide: Possibilities for Prosperity*. New York: Basic Books.

Pohle, Klaus. 1985. "The *Lethbridge Herald*: A Case Study in 'Thomsonization.'" Master of Journalism thesis, Carleton University.

Postman, Neil. 1992. *Technopoly: The Surrender of Culture to Technology*. New York: Knopf.

Rainwater, Bill (finance administrator, CWA). 1998. Interview by author. February.

Rappleye, Charles. 1998. "Cracking the Church–State Wall." *Columbia Journalism Review* (January/February). Online at www.cjr.com. Accessed 15 November 2001.

Reddick, Randy, and Elliot King. 1995. *The Online Journalist: Using the Internet and Other Electronic Resources*. Fort Worth, Tex.: Harcourt Brace.

Roberts, Eugene, Thomas Kunkel, and Charles Layton, eds. 2001. *Leaving Readers Behind: The Age of Corporate Newspapering*. Fayetteville: University of Arkansas Press.

Robin, Joshua, and Beth Kaiman. 2001. "Vote Ends *Times* Strike." *Seattle Union Record*, 9 January. Online at www.unionrecord.com. Accessed 18 January 2001.

Rosen, Barbara (research librarian, CWA). 1998. Interview by author. February.

Russial, John T. 1989. "Pagination and the Newsroom: Great Expectations." Ph.D. dissertation, Temple University.

Rutherford, Paul. 1982. *A Victorian Authority: The Daily Press in Late Nineteenth-Century Canada*. Toronto: University of Toronto Press.

Salcetti, Marianne. 1995. "The Emergence of the Reporter: Mechanization and the Devaluation of Editorial Workers." In *Newsworkers: Toward a History of the Rank and File*, edited by Hanno Hardt and Bonnie Brennen, 48–74. Minneapolis: University of Minnesota Press.

Schiller, Dan. 1981. *Objectivity and the News: The Public and the Rise of Commercial Journalism*. Philadelphia: University of Pennsylvania Press.

Schiller, Herbert I. 1969. *Mass Communications and American Empire*. New York: Kelley.

———. 1992. *Mass Communications and American Empire*. 2d edition. Boulder, Colo.: Westview Press.
———. 1996. *Invisible Crises: What Conglomerate Control of Media Means for America and the World*. Boulder, Colo.: Westview Press.
Schudson, Michael. 1978. *Discovering the News: A Social History of American Newspapers*. New York: Basic Books.
———. 1989. "The Sociology of News Production." *Media Culture and Society* 11:263–82.
Scoffield, Heather. 2001. "CTV Offers to Draw Up a Code of Ethics." *The Globe and Mail*, 19 April, A8.
Scranton, Philip. 1988. "None-Too-Porous Boundaries: Labor History and the History of Technology." *Technology and Culture* 29, no. 4:722–43.
Shecter, Barbara. 2001. "Canadian View Not Affected by U.S. Deal, CTV Says." *National Post*, 22 August, A9.
Shipley, Linda, and James F. Gentry. 1981. "How Electronic Editing Equipment Affects Editing Performance." *Journalism Quarterly* 58, no. 3:371–74, 387.
Shipman, John M., Jr. 1986. "Computerization and Job Satisfaction in the Newsroom: Four Factors to Consider." *Newspaper Research Journal* 8, no. 1:69–78.
Simurda, Stephen J. 1993. "Sticking with the Union?" *Columbia Journalism Review* (March/April): 25–30.
Slaughter, Jane. 2001. "What Went Wrong in Detroit? Business-as-Usual Unionism Lost the Newspaper Strike." *Labor Notes* (February). Online at www.labornotes.org. Accessed 1 October 2001.
Sleigh, Stephen R. 1998. *On Deadline: Labor Relations in Newspaper Publishing*. New York: Social Change Press.
Smith, Andy (vice-president for human resources, Pacific Press). 1997. Interview by author. December.
Smith, Anthony. 1980. *Goodbye, Gutenberg: The Newspaper Revolution of the 1980s*. New York: Oxford University Press.
Smith, Merritt Roe. 1994. "Technological Determinism and American Culture." In *Does Technology Drive History? The Dilemma of Technological Determinism*, edited by Merritt Roe Smith and Leo Marx, 1–36. Cambridge: MIT Press.
Smythe, Dallas. 1981. *Dependency Road: Communications, Capitalism, Consciousness and Canada*. Norwood, N.J.: Ablex.
Sohn, Ardyth, Chris Ogan, and John Polich. 1986. *Newspaper Leadership*. Englewood Cliffs, N.J.: Prentice-Hall.
Solomon, William S. 1995. "The Site of Newsroom Labor: The Division of Editorial Practices." In *Newsworkers: Toward a History of the Rank and File*, edited by Hanno Hardt and Bonnie Brennen, 110–34. Minneapolis: University of Minnesota Press.
SONGsheet. 1990–. Newsletter of Southern Ontario Newspaper Guild.
Sotiron, Minko. 1997. *From Politics to Profit: The Commercialization of Canadian Daily Newspapers, 1890–1920*. Montreal: McGill-Queen's University Press.
Southern Ontario Newspaper Guild (SONG). 1988. "The Guild and Canadian Autonomy: A Blueprint for Change." Plan submitted to TNG annual convention.
Squires, James D. 1993. *Read All About It! The Corporate Takeover of America's Newspapers*. New York: Times Books.

Staudenmaier, John M. 1984. *Technology's Storytellers: Reweaving the Human Fabric*. Cambridge: MIT Press.
———. 1990. "Comment: Recent Trends in the History of Technology." *American Historical Review* 95 (June): 715–25.
Steward, Gillian. 1999. "Shame on Southam." *The Globe and Mail*, 10 November, A21.
Sussman, Gerald, and John A. Lent. 1998. *Global Production: Labor in the Making of the "Information Society."* Cresskill, N.J.: Hampton.
Sutherland, Fraser. 1989. *The Monthly Epic: A History of Canadian Magazines, 1789–1989*. Markham, Ont.: Fitzhenry and Whiteside.
Swartz, Donald, and Eugene Swimmer. 1981. "Ottawa: A Failure of Management." In *Labour Relations in the Newspaper Industry*, edited by Gérard Hébert, 105–30. Royal Commission on Newspapers Research Publications, vol. 5. Ottawa: Minister of Supply and Services.
Taylor, Frederick Winslow. 1911. *The Principles of Scientific Management*. New York: Harper.
Thompson, Paul. 1989. *The Nature of Work*. 2d edition. London: Macmillan.
"Three-Way Merger Increases Canadian Unions' Power." 1993. *Journal of Commerce*, 28 July, 7A.
Tompkins, Al, and Aly Colón. 2000. "Honeymoon Underway for Tampa's Media Marriage." 24 April. Online at www.poynter.org. Accessed 30 April 2001.
Typographical Journal. Publication of the International Typographical Union.
Underwood, Doug. 1993. *When MBAs Rule the Newsroom: How the Marketers and Managers are Reshaping Today's Media*. New York: Columbia University Press.
———. 1998. "It's Not Just in LA." *Columbia Journalism Review* (January/February). Online at www.cjr.com. Accessed 15 November 2001.
Van Alpen, Tony. 1995. "Fred Pomeroy Elected Head of Giant CEP Union." *Toronto Star*, 27 June, D18.
Vipond, Mary. 1992. *Listening In: The First Decade of Canadian Broadcasting 1922–1932*. Montreal: McGill-Queen's University Press.
Walkom, Thomas. 1983. "The Daily Newspaper Industry in Ontario's Developing Capitalistic Economy: Toronto and Ottawa, 1871–1911." Ph.D. dissertation, University of Toronto.
Walsh, Louise D. 1985. "A Study of the Proposed Merger of the International Typographical Union and The Newspaper Guild: 1974–1983." Master of Science thesis, Cornell University.
Ward, Jean, and Kathleen A. Hansen. 1991. "Journalist and Librarian Roles, Information Technologies, and Newsmaking." *Journalism Quarterly* 68, no. 3:491–98.
Ward, Jean, Kathleen A. Hansen, and Douglas M. McLeod. 1988. "Effects of Electronic Library on News Reporting Protocols." *Journalism Quarterly* 65, no. 4:845–52.
Warnock, Joie (national representative, CEP). 1997. Interview by author. December.
Webster, Frank, and Kevin Robins. 1986. *Information Technology: A Luddite Analysis*. Norwood, N.J.: Ablex.
Wicklein, John. 1981. *Electronic Nightmare: The New Communications and Freedom*. New York: Viking.

Williams, Raymond. 1990. *Television: Technology and Cultural Form.* 2d edition. London: Routledge.
Wilson, Phyllis. 1976. "The Nature of News." In *Journalism, Communication, and the Law*, edited by G. Stuart Adam, 22–33. Scarborough, Ont.: Prentice-Hall.
Winseck, Dwayne. 1998. *Reconvergence: A Political Economy of Telecommunications in Canada.* Cresskill, N.J.: Hampton Press.
Winter, James. 1997. *Democracy's Oxygen: How Corporations Control the News.* Montreal: Black Rose Books.
Woodward, Joan. 1958. *Management and Technology.* Problems of Progress in Industry Report, no. 3, Great Britain, Ministry of Technology. London: HMSO.
———, ed. 1970. *Industrial Organisation: Behaviour and Control.* London: Oxford University Press.
Work Directions Inc. 1993. "Preparing for the Future: A Four-Year Strategic Plan for The Newspaper Guild." Report prepared for presentation at The Newspaper Guild annual convention.
Zerker, Sally F. 1982. *The Rise and Fall of the Toronto Typographical Union, 1832–1972: A Case Study of Foreign Domination.* Toronto: University of Toronto Press.
Zimbalist, Andrew. 1979. "Technology and the Labor Process in the Printing Industry." In *Case Studies on the Labor Process*, edited by Andrew Zimbalist, 103–26. New York: Monthly Review Press.
Zuboff, Shoshana. 1988. *In the Age of the Smart Machine: The Future of Work and Power.* New York: Basic Books.

Index

ABC, 27, 95
ACTRA. *See* Association of Canadian Television and Radio Artists
AFL. *See* American Federation of Labour
AFL-CIO, 58, 78, 89, 90, 110, 142n6
Allied Printing Trades Association, 8, 57, 58
Amalgamated Lithographers of America, 61
Amber, Arnold, 136, 141–42, 174–75, 183n41, 189
American Association of University Professors, 193
American Federation of Labor, 10, 64, 109, 189
American Interactive Media, 25
American Newspaper Guild. *See* The Newspaper Guild
America Online, 4, 28, 200n20
ApexMail, 26
APME. *See* Associated Press Managing Editors
The Associated Press, 68, 95
Associated Press Managing Editors, 53
Association of Canadian Television and Radio Artists, 125, 126, 145n33
AT&T, 98, 99
Austin, Bill J., 79

Bahr, Morton, 80, 86, 95, 98, 100, 102–3, 104–5, 125–26, 128–29, 144n31, 192, 197–98, 199n9
Baltimore Sunpapers, 65
Bank of Montreal, 25
Barrett, Francis G., 58, 59
BCE Inc., 27
Bell, Pat, 133
Bell Atlantic, 99
Bell Globemedia, 4, 27, 198
Bevis, A. Sandy, 72–73
Bingel, Joe, 73, 75, 77–79
Black, Conrad, 22, 25–26, 183n38
Block, Paul, 18
Blockbuster Video, 27
Boarman, Bill, 99–100, 125, 175
Bocking, Mike, 117, 122, 130, 132–33, 136, 143n17, 177, 179
Boots pharmacies, 26
Brabant weeklies, 143n18
British Broadcasting Corporation, 200n20
British Columbia Court of Appeal, 48
British Columbia Labour Relations Board, 147, 150, 172; rulings on Pacific Press consolidation, 165–67, 171
Broun, Heywood, 10, 83n6
Brown, Duncan, 90

215

Brown, Elmer, 11, 59–61, 62, 65, 66, 185–86
Bryant, John, 120
Business Week, 200n20

Calgary Herald, 33, 35n28, 140–41, 200n22
Canada.com, 25–26
Canada Industrial Relations Board, 141–42, 195–96
Canada Labour Relations Board, 130. *See also* Canada Industrial Relations Board
Canadian Auto Workers Union, 109, 131, 135, 136
Canadian Broadcasting Corporation, 4, 96, 130, 139, 141–42, 145n33
Canadian Congress of Labour, 109
Canadian Council of Broadcast Unions, 145n33
Canadian Daily Newspaper Publishers Association, 34n7
Canadian Federation of Labour, 142n7
Canadian Illustrated News, 55n7
Canadian Labour Congress, 110, 121, 142n6; and complaints filed by SONG, 117–19, 132–34, 145n34; standards of self-government, 89, 90, 110–11, 116, 137
Canadian Newspaper Association, 34n13
The Canadian Press, 45
Canadian Radio-television and Telecommunications Commission, 5, 15n5, 194
Canadian Union of Public Employees, 108–9, 131, 141, 145n33
Canoe.ca, 27
CanWest Global Communications, 4, 5, 15n4, 26–27, 33, 181n5, 194, 195–96, 198n2
Carclick.com, 26, 33
Careerclick.com, 26
Carr, Shirley, 117, 119
CAW. *See Canadian Auto Workers Union*
CBC. *See* Canadian Broadcasting Corporation
CBS and Viacom merger, 3–4, 27
CEP. *See* Communications, Energy and Paperworkers Union of Canada
Cesnick, James, 77
Chicago Sun-Times, 26, 68
Chicago Tribune, 5, 17
CIO. *See* Council of Industrial Organizations
Citizens for Independent Public Broadcasting, 193
CLC. *See* Canadian Labour Congress
CMT, 27
CNN, 27
Commission on Freedom of the Press. *See* Hutchins Commission
Communications, Energy and Paperworkers Union of Canada, 1, 106n10, 183n38; creation of, 127; and Canadian nationalism, 136–39, 141–42; and former Guild locals, 131–34, 135, 136; and former ITU locals, 127–30; media workers sector, 140, 191; membership and organizing, 140–41, 187; and public policy, 194–95; and NABET, 128, 141–42, 193, 195–96. *See also* The Newspaper Guild; Pacific Press
Communications Workers of America, 1, 74, 104–5; and Canada, 97, 124–30, 131, 134, 139–40, 175, 194; and ITU merger, 80–82, 87, 97–98, 103, 134, 137; membership and organizing, 95, 98, 99, 102–3, 187, 192–93; and NABET merger, 95, 99–100, 103, 144n25; and Newspaper Guild merger, 87–90, 94–104, 130; and "reverse merger," 134. *See also* Communications Energy and Paperworkers Union of Canada; Pacific Press
Communications Workers of Canada, 106n10, 127. *See also* Communications, Energy and Paperworkers Union of Canada
Compuserve, 28
Condé Nast, 200n20
converged newsrooms, 4

convergence, 2–6, 11–14, 102–3; corporate, 3, 23–28, 32–33, 85, 185–86; labor, 1–2, 37–38, 58–62, 92–93, 96–98, 100–105, 148, 155–57, 187, 191, 192–98; technological, 2–3, 37–38, 51, 101, 147–48, 151–55, 198–87
Council of Industrial Organizations, 10, 58, 64, 109
Conventus Inc., 26
Cromie family, 198n2
CRTC. *See* Canadian Radio-television and Telecommunications Commission
CTV, 4, 5, 27, 194
CUPE. *See* Canadian Union of Public Employees
CWA. *See* Communications Workers of America

Dale, Chuck, 88–89, 93, 98–99, 116–17, 119, 120, 132–34, 143n21
Dallas Morning News, 200n20
Davey committee. *See* Special Senate Committee on Mass Communication
Davies, Michael, 31
DeAndrade, Anthony, 61
Desbarats, Georges-Edouard, 55n7
deskilling, 11–14, 52; uneven effects of, 12, 52–53, 190
Detroit Free Press, 196–97
Detroit News, 196–97
Diebold, John, 68–69, 83n11
Disney, 3, 200n20
divergence: of media, 6; of newspaper unions, 6–11, 37–38
Dow Jones, 15n2, 200n20
Doyle, Dic, 31

Edmonton Journal, 167
Energy and Chemical Workers, 127
ESPN, 27
Esposti, Dave, 130

Farson, William J., 59–60, 61, 62
FLIX, 27
Foley, Linda, 33, 76–77, 97–98, 101, 103–4, 106n11, 186, 191, 192–93, 197, 199n8
FP Publications, 21, 148–49, 198n2
Friends of Canadian Broadcasting, 193
Funk, Harold, 172–73, 178, 179–80, 181n11, 183n44

Gannett Co., 17, 18, 23–24, 26, 31–32, 33, 196
GCIU. *See* Graphic Communications International Union
The Globe and Mail, 4, 17, 26, 27, 30–31, 33n1, 65, 68, 118, 132–33, 198
Gonzalez, Juan, 119
Graphic Arts International Union, 81, 90. *See also* Graphic Communications International Union
Graphic Communications International Union, 76, 78–79, 80, 81, 82, 182n23, 187; and merger possibilities, 87, 88, 90, 94, 95–98, 104–5; and Canadian members, 125, 126–27
Grey, Doug, 124–26, 128–30, 144n22, 144n23, 144n32
Le Groupe Videotron, 27

Halifax Chronicle-Herald, 140
handbag.com, 26
Hansen, Lewis, 173
Harris, Lou, 23
Hearst, 18, 27, 34n4
Heritage, Allan, 75
Hoffa, James, 79
Hollinger International, 4, 17, 25–27, 32, 140, 145n39, 181n5, 198n2
Hudson News, 193
Hutchins Commission, 20, 34n5

InfiNet, 26
Infinity Broadcasting, 27
International Association of Machinists, 80, 150. *See also* Pacific Press
International Brotherhood of Electrical Workers, 150. *See also* Pacific Press
International Brotherhood of Teamsters, 75–80, 87, 89, 94, 105n5

International Federation of Journalists, 118, 193
International Mailers Union, 73
International Photoengravers Union, 61
International Plate Printers, Die Stampers and Engravers, 61
International Printing and Graphic Communications Union, 47, 81, 90. *See also* Graphic Communications International Union
International Printing Pressmen's Union, 8, 15n7. *See also* Graphic Communications International Union
International Typographical Union: and Canadian Labour Congress standards of self-government, 124–25, 128; and Canadian printers, 108, 110, 124–26; and control of craft, 64–66; early years of, 6–9, 15n7, 39; departure of other unions from, 8, 37–38; departure of Canadian locals from, 127–30, 139, 144n27, 175; membership decline, 71, 82n19, 190; merger with Communications Workers of America, 80–82, 95, 99–100, 104; merger with International Mailers Union, 73, 81; organizing editorial workers, 10, 15n9; and relations with Guild, 58–61, 64–77, 71–76, 199n4; "reverse merger" of Canadian locals, 134; and technological change, 8–9, 15n8, 44, 52, 56n21, 67, 70–71, 190. *See also* Communications, Energy and Paperworkers Union of Canada; Communications Workers of America; The Newspaper Guild
International Typographical Union, and failed merger attempts: with Graphic Communications International Union, 76, 78–79, 80, 81, 188; with International Brotherhood of Teamsters, 76–80, 81, 188; with Newspaper Guild, 71–77, 81–82, 87, 188
Inter-Union Newspaper Council, 145n40
Island Medical Laboratories, 150, 151, 167

Jennings, Bob, 181n11

Kheel, Theodore, 71
Kingston Whig-Standard, 31
King World Productions, 27
Kirkland, Lane, 80
Knight-Ridder, 18, 26, 196
Kopek, Thomas, 74–75, 79, 80

Landmark Communications, 26
Lem, Gail, 91, 112, 115, 118, 119, 120, 121, 122–23, 131–33, 200n15; and proposal for Canadian media workers union, 123–24, 125–27, 138
Lepper, Jim, 173, 182n37
Lepper, John, 173, 177–78, 180, 183n37
Lepper, Stan, 183n37
Lethbridge Herald, 32
Lithographers and Photoengravers International Union, 61
London Free Press, 39–43, 47, 51, 53, 55n10, 143n18, 199n6, 200n22
Los Angeles Times, 17, 30, 67
Luce, Henry, 20

MacDonald, Jerry, 116, 143n12
Maclean's, 112–13, 118
Matyas, Joe, 189, 200n13
McCorkindale, Douglas, 24
McInnes, Larry, 117
McLeman, 143n10, 143n14
McMichen, Robert, 75, 77–79, 81
McNeil-Lehrer Productions, 23
Meachum, Bruce, 89, 119, 122
Megarry, Roy, 30
Metro Valley Newspaper Group, 183n44
Moffett, Ken, 99–100
Montreal Gazette, 5
The Movie Channel, 27
Murdoch, Peter, 141–42, 194–96, 198, 200n13, 200n15
MTV, 27

NABET. *See* National Association of Broadcasting Engineers and Technicians

Index 219

National Association of Broadcasting Engineers and Technicians, 95, 99; breakaway Canadian branch, 125, 126, 128. *See also* Communications, Energy and Paperworkers Union of Canada
National Labor Relations Board, 107
National Post, 4, 15n4, 17, 26
National Typographical Union, 7, 108. *See also* International Typographical Union
National Union of Public and General Employees, 109, 142n4
NBC, 95
Neuharth, Al, 23
New Democratic Party, 114
The Newspaper Guild: and Canadian governing structures, 110–12, 114–16, 117–18, 121–23; and Canadian Labour Congress, 90, 110, 118–19, 137; Canadian locals, 91, 105, 108, 111, 115–17, 136; and Communications Workers of America, 87–90, 94–104, 136, 192; and convergence, 101–4, 192–93; and cooperation with other unions, 57–58, 192–94; failed merger with ITU, 71–77, 89; founding of, 10, 18, 55n2; membership, 72, 84n19, 86, 91–92, 105n7; merger possibilities, 87–91, 94, 95–98; and SONG, 112–23, 126–27, 130–34; reform groups within, 119; relations with ITU, 58–61, 63–67, 106n9; "reverse merger" of Canadian ITU locals, 134, 139; strategic planning, 88–89, 91–93, 191; and technological change, 67–70, 85; TNG Canada, 130–31, 134–36, 137–42, 174–75, 194. *See also* Communications Workers of America; Communications, Energy and Paperworkers Union of Canada
newspapers: advertising rates and revenues, 29, 86, 105n3; chain ownership of, 18–21; conglomerate ownership of, 21–28; employment, 92; management practices, 29–32; "paperless" newspapers, 54, 56n23; pressure for profits, 28–32, 86; production process in precomputer, 38–43; production process, impact of computerization on, 43–53; web sites, 4
Newsquest, 23, 24
New York Daily News, 71
New York Times, 17, 31, 71
New York World Telegram and Sun, 58
Nickelodeon, 27
Northern Telecom, 144n31
Norton, Jim, 94

O'Brien, Jan, 136, 151, 168, 174, 176–77, 179, 183n43
Oldfield, Dan, 118
"one big union" drive, 58–62, 104–5, 126
Oregon Journal, 57; and 1959 strike, 57–58
Osipa, Bob, 165, 172, 177, 178, 179, 180, 182n24, 182n36, 183n43
Ottawa Citizen, vii, 17, 44, 167, 174
Ottawa Journal, vii, 44, 55n13

Pacific Newspaper Group. *See* Pacific Press
Pacific Press, 37, 181n5; application for bargaining unit consolidation, 45, 55n1, 147, 150–57, 169–70, 171, 176, 179; bargaining units, 149; campaign for consolidation election, 172–76; CWA Mailers, 150, 163–65, 167–68, 172, 174–75, 181n9; GCIU engravers, 150, 161–62; GCIU pressmen, 150, 163, 164–65, 167–68; Guild/CEP editorial and clerical workers, 150, 160, 172–74, 175–76, 181n8; IAMAW machinists, 150, 162; IBEW electricians, 150, 162; ITU/CEP compositors, 150, 161, 172–73, 180n2, 181n9, 181n16; job guarantees, 71, 161, 181n7; joint council of unions, 52, 149, 157–60, 167, 181n6, 181n13; and jurisdictional disputes, 48, 50, 51–52, 56n16, 170–71; labor relations at, 155,

167, 182n35; and merger of CEP locals, 178; strike history, 47–48, 149–50, 155–57, 178–79; and technological change, 45–53, 151–55; union proposals to revamp bargaining structure, 167–71
Pacific Telesis, 99
Paperworkers Union of Canada, 127
Paramount Pictures, 27
Pattern Makers League v. NLRB, 112, 113
Patterson-McCormick, 18
Payne, Brian, 174
PBS, 200n20
People, 28
Perlik, Charles A., Jr., 72, 73, 82, 85, 112–13, 142n8
Petrie, Bill, 115–16
Polish Alliance, 143n18
Pomeroy, Fred, 128, 144n30, 144n31
Portland Oregonian, 57; and 1959 strike, 57–58
Portland Reporter, 57, 82–83n1
Powers, Bertram, 76, 199n4
President's Commission on Organized Crime, 79
Presser, Jackie, 75–76, 78, 79, 84n22
Public Service Alliance of Canada, 109

Quebecor Inc., 27

Radler, David, 32
Rand formula, 143n13
Ravensbergen, Jan, 116
Reagan, Ronald, 86
Regina Leader-Post, 35n26, 140, 145n39
ROBTv, 26
Rogers Communications Inc., 27
Rosenstock, Arthur, 60
Royal Commission on Newspapers, 21–23, 56n13, 105n1, 186; labor relations research, 148–50, 180n4
Royal Commission on the Press, 34n5
Rupert, Bob, 111, 143n10

San Diego Union Tribune, 199n8
San Francisco Chronicle, 68
San Francisco Examiner, 34n4
Saskatoon StarPhoenix, 35n26, 145n39
Saunders, William, 175, 178
Savage, John, 172
Seattle Post-Intelligencer, 197
Seattle Times, 197
Showtime, 27
Simon and Schuster, 27
Sing Tao Daily, 140
Scripps-Howard, 18, 33n3
Smith, Andy, 176
Smith, Jim, 116
SONG. *See* Southern Ontario Newspaper Guild
Southam newspapers, 20, 22, 33n3, 56n13, 148–49, 150, 181n5, 198n2
Southern Ontario Media Workers' Society, 120
Southern Ontario Newspaper Guild, 91, 112, 143n9, 143n21; blueprint for Canadian autonomy, 113–17, 137; and CEP, 131–34; criticism from other Canadian locals, 117–18; departure from Guild, 130–34, 137–39; establishment of nonprofit corporation, 120–21; and organizing record, 118, 143n18, 143n19. *See also* Communications, Energy and Paperworkers Union of Canada; The Newspaper Guild
Special Senate Committee on Mass Communication, 19–21, 25, 185
Sterling Newspapers, 22
Steward, Gillian, 33, 35n28
StockHouse Media Corp., 26
Sun Publishing. *See* Pacific Press
Sympatico Internet portal, 4, 27

Tampa Tribune, 4
Taylorism, 14
TBO.com, 4
Tedeschi, George, 104–5
Thomson newspapers, 21, 22, 27, 32, 35n27, 56n13, 148–49, 150, 198n2
Time, 28
TimeWarner Inc. *See* America Online

TNG. *See* The Newspaper Guild
TNN, 27
Toronto and District Labour Council, 65
Toronto Star, 65, 67–68, 118, 143n19, 167
Toronto Telegram, 65
trade union membership, United States and Canada, 86, 105n2, 137, 198n1; international unions in Canada, 107–10; rise of Canadian unions, 109
trade union mergers, 61–63, 188–89
Trades and Labour Congress of Canada, 109, 142n3
Trinity Group of Newspapers. *See* Metro Valley Newspaper Group
Trip.com, 25
TVO, 139

UKMax, 25
United Food and Commercial Workers International Union, 109
United Mine Workers, 58
United Papermakers and Paperworkers, 61
United Press International, 68, 95
United Steelworkers of America, 94

United Telegraph Workers, 95
USA Today, 17
USATODAY.com, 24
USA Weekend, 23
U.S. Department of Labor, 78

Vancouver Province. *See* Pacific Press
Vancouver Sun. *See* Pacific Press
VH1, 27
Viacom. *See* CBS and Viacom merger

Wagner Act, 107
Wall Street Journal, 15n2, 17
Warnock, Joie, 183n43
Washington Post, 3, 67, 71, 199n5
Washingtonpost.com, 3
Wartinger, Robert, 75
Watts, Glenn, 74
WFLA-TV, 4
White, Bob, 132
White, James, 69
Windsor Star, 136, 145n35
Winnipeg Tribune, 56n13
Wylie, Andrée, 15n5

Yahoo, 200n20

About the Author

Catherine McKercher is associate professor in the School of Journalism at Carleton University in Ottawa, Canada. She has worked as a newspaper and wire service reporter and copyeditor in Canada and the United States. McKercher is co-author of *The Canadian Reporter,* the leading reporting textbook in Canada, and recently completed a Ph.D. in humanities at Concordia University in Montreal. She lives in Ottawa with her husband and two daughters.